SPSS ESSENTIALS

Managing and Analyzing Social Sciences Data

JOHN T. KULAS

JOSSEY-BASS
A Wiley Imprint
www.josseybass.com

Published by Jossey-Bass
A Wiley Imprint
989 Market Street, San Francisco, CA 94103-1741—www.josseybass.com

Readers should be aware that Internet Web sites offered as citations and/or sources
for further information may have changed or disappeared between the time this
was written and when it is read.

Limit of Liability/Disclaimer of Warranty: While the publisher and author have
used their best efforts in preparing this book, they make no representations
or warranties with respect to the accuracy or completeness of the contents of
this book and specifi cally disclaim any implied warranties of merchantability
or fi tness for a particular purpose. No warranty may be created or extended
by sales representatives or written sales materials. The advice and strategies
contained herein may not be suitable for your situation. You should consult with a
professional where appropriate. Neither the publisher nor author shall be liable for
any loss of profi t or any other commercial damages, including but not limited to
special, incidental, consequential, or other damages.

Jossey-Bass books and products are available through most bookstores. To contact
Jossey-Bass directly call our Customer Care Department within the U.S. at
800-956-7739, outside the U.S. at 317-572-3986, or fax 317-572-4002.

Jossey-Bass also publishes its books in a variety of electronic formats. Some
content that appears in print may not be available in electronic books.

Library of Congress Cataloging-in-Publication Data

Kulas, John T.
    SPSS essentials : managing and analyzing social sciences data / John T. Kulas.
      p. cm.
    Includes bibliographical references and index.
    ISBN 978-0-470-22617-9 (pbk.)
      1. SPSS (Computer file)   2. Social sciences—Computer programs. I. Title.
  HA32.K85 2009
  300.285'555—dc22

                            2008041499

ISBN 13: 978-0-4702-2617-9
ISBN 10: 0-4702-26179-X

Printed in the United States of America
SECOND EDITION

PB Printing   10 9 8 7 6 5 4 3 2 1

CONTENTS

PART ONE: FUNDAMENTALS OF DATA MANAGEMENT

PART TWO: SYNTHESIZING AND ANALYZING DATA

PART THREE: ADVANCED MANIPULATIONS AND PROBLEM SOLVING

PREFACE

SPSS Essentials is intended to help readers learn how to use the software program Statistical Package for the Social Sciences (SPSS). The book is addressed to SPSS users who encounter real-world data and who would benefit from both a user guide and an instructional tool. The primary audience is students (undergraduate and graduate) in the social sciences who are encountering SPSS for the first time, as well as practitioners who are new to it.

The book is based, in large part, on my experience working with students, practitioners, and organizations who all wanted to minimize error and improve their management of their data. You do not need to know anything about SPSS to jump into the book, and by the time you get to the end you will know enough about SPSS to comfortably use the program and its other supplemental guides. The information found in this book will not become outdated with future versions of SPSS—the basic premise will be useful with SPSS version ∞.

This book focuses more attention on data management than it does on statistical analyses (despite the fact that the Statistical Package for the Social Sciences has been designed for the explicit purpose of facilitating statistical analyses). There are plenty of existing references already available for exhaustive statistical concepts, and in my experience typically only 1 to 5 percent of the time spent using SPSS is spent running statistical analyses. *If you use SPSS, you'll spend more time entering, organizing, and manipulating data than you will spend running any actual analyses.* This book's purpose is to teach you how you should use SPSS. The goal throughout is to minimize error. Error can occur in data entry, analysis interpretation, and even the choice of which dataset to use for analysis. This last error, sadly, has increased in probability with the most recently released versions of SPSS as of this writing. If you follow the how-to's of this book, you will greatly decrease the likelihood of introducing error into your research and analyses. Essentially, the book is a template for how you should organize your SPSS life—which you will generally do through keeping diaries of what you plan to do, what you actually do, and what you have done with SPSS.

Students will find this text helpful as a framework for learning—knowing how to properly use the SPSS program will facilitate future knowledge and skill acquisition. Instructors will find this text a useful stepping-off point for instruction (that is, you should be able to focus on SPSS's analytical processing instead of database setup, variable identification, and so on). Practitioners will find this text a useful reference and guide for how the SPSS program should be used (if you *don't* use the recommended syntax-diary method, you *will* make catastrophic mistakes using SPSS—it's only a matter of time).

The book's chapters take a sequential, step-by-step approach, so that initial chapters will prepare you for your understanding of later chapters.

- Part One (eight chapters) is devoted to getting your data ready for analyses.

- Part Two (four chapters) focuses on data synthesis and rudimentary analyses.

- Part Three (two chapters) is a primer on more advanced manipulations and problem solving.

Use this book as a reference guide, working along with SPSS as you read. Those needing the student version of SPSS can obtain it through their college or university or at www.spss.com.

ACKNOWLEDGMENTS

The author would like to thank Andy Pasternack, Merrill Peterson, and Seth Schwartz for their help, support, and guidance in putting this book together. Thanks also go to Zak Kulas for always being a good friend.

THE AUTHOR

John Kulas is assistant professor of industrial and organizational psychology at Saint Cloud State University. His applied background includes current and past appointments as a test publisher, an internal HR practitioner, and an external organizational consultant (focusing primarily on topics of personnel selection and performance assessment). He has authored many conference and journal articles, dealing with issues of measurement in organizational settings. His works can be found in sources such as the *Journal of Psychology*, *Organizational Research Methods*, *Journal of Applied Measurement*, *Journal of Business and Psychology*, *Social Justice Research*, and *Journal of Research in Personality*. He has received research awards from the Society for Industrial and Organizational Psychology and the American Psychological Society.

PART

1

FUNDAMENTALS OF DATA MANAGEMENT

CHAPTER

INTRODUCTION
TO SPSS

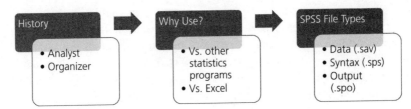

FIGURE 1.1. *History – Why Use? – SPSS File Types.*

Contents

Chapter Learning Objectives

What SPSS Is Used For

    SPSS Versus Excel and Others

How the Program Works

CHAPTER LEARNING OBJECTIVES

1. History of SPSS

2. SPSS advantages (over other programs)

3. Types of files used by SPSS

SPSS is a software program that was created to perform statistical analyses. SPSS is also the name of the company that owns and sells the computer program. The name SPSS is an acronym for Statistical Package for the Social Sciences. Because SPSS is used across many disciplines, the old "social sciences" label is without doubt too narrow for the program's current market.

SPSS has two primary functions: (1) as a data analyst, and (2) as a data organizer and manager. Although we cover both, the primary focus of this book is on the second function, because although the program itself is a powerful data analyst, you will spend most of your time using the program's data organizing and managing functions. You need to organize and manage your data *so that you can eventually do analyses with it*—real world data rarely comes in a form that's immediately ready to analyze.

Like most software programs, SPSS is continually being updated. The current version (15.0 as this book is being written) is quite different from the original and the earlier versions, primarily because those did not have a Microsoft Windows–based interface. The early versions were mainframe and DOS-based programs, which required users to *program* (enter code language) in a less visually appealing and noninteractive computer environment.

In addition to those platform changes, the field of statistics changes over time (improvements and slight alterations are generally made) and new statistics are constantly being discovered. To stay current with statistical advancements and platform limitations and changes (such as changes in Microsoft Windows), the SPSS program is frequently updated. The information in this book is valid for any version of SPSS. It is written from a PC perspective, but the information is applicable to a Mac audience.

WHAT SPSS IS USED FOR

SPSS has the capability to perform a wide variety of statistical analyses, both *descriptive* and *inferential*. It is used by researchers (biologists, psychologists, sociologists, economists) and public and private sector workers (accountants, human resources professionals, actuaries). These individuals use SPSS to test hypotheses in experimental and field settings, summarize information, and create graphs and figures.

The primary power of SPSS lies in its wide variety of statistical options and its ability to perform these analyses quickly. There are other software programs available that do a nice job of, for example, creating graphs and figures, but SPSS creates graphs and figures *in addition to* its primary purpose of processing data using appropriate statistical formulae.

SPSS Versus Excel and Others

SPSS was designed specifically for the purpose of performing statistical analyses. There are other software programs that perform statistics as their primary purpose (such as SAS, Minitab, and BMDP). There are advantages and disadvantages to each software package; the choice of SPSS over the other statistics-oriented programs was likely made by your class instructor or supervisor. If the names of the other titles look a bit more appealing to you than "SPSS," you should drop your statistics class and sell this book now, because once you choose one software package, you will generally stick with it.

In addition to statistical processing competitors, SPSS is somewhat crowded upon by spreadsheet programs that have statistical potential. These programs (such as Microsoft Excel) are generally fine—and usually more flexible—for descriptive statistical analyses (statistics that *describe* a given set of numbers: means, standard deviations, correlations), but they are usually less useful if your goal is to perform inferential statistical analyses, such as t-test, ANOVA, or regression—statistics that make an *inference* about a larger group of numbers, given the associations in your small set of numbers (this will be further discussed in Ch. 10–12). If you are doing inferential statistics, or are very concerned about minimizing error in your processes, you will want to use SPSS instead of Excel or other spreadsheet programs. Spreadsheets are great for organizing data and doing minor computations and manipulations (as well as summarizing information graphically), but if you are doing hypothesis-testing statistics, SPSS is the way to go.

Over the years SPSS has actually slowly grown to look pretty similar (in interface appearance) to Excel. As will be described in Chapter Two, this wasn't always the case. You can think of SPSS as a combination of Word and Excel (to cite the most commonly used word processor and spreadsheet applications). SPSS is conceptually a combination of these two applications, as data is stored in SPSS's Excel-like spreadsheet component and analyses are performed by writing commands in SPSS's Word-similar word processing component.

HOW THE PROGRAM WORKS

When you access the program, by selecting the SPSS icon from your desktop or Start menu, one of two things will happen. First, a Help dialog box may appear that asks "What would you like to do?" There is an option at the bottom of this box: "Don't show this dialog in the future." Go ahead and select that option (you don't want to see this box every time you open SPSS; that would get somewhat annoying). Second, an empty data file may open. This is a good thing—it's what you want to occur.

Important File Types

There are three very important types of files used by SPSS: the afore-mentioned data file type (identified by an .sav file extension), a syntax file type (identified by an .sps file extension), and an output file type (identified by an .spo file extension).

Data Files. *Data (.sav)* files are where you store your numbers and data. Typically you have one *original* data file for each major project that you are working on. Figure 1.2 shows what an empty .sav file (containing no data) looks like.

Notice that the empty data file has (1) a grid of cells (seventy-two cells and part of another twelve are visible in the screen capture), (2) commands and toolbar icons (including the File, Edit, and View commands familiar in Microsoft applications, but also Transform, Analyze, Graphs, and more), and (3) spreadsheet tabs (here labeled Data View and Variable View, which are unique to SPSS and not a shared feature of

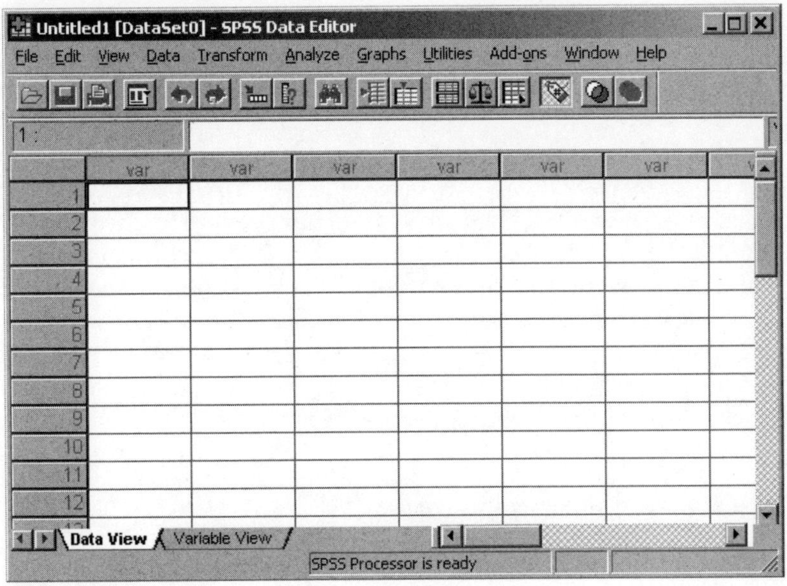

FIGURE **1.2.** *The SPSS Data Editor.*

Excel). [More will be said about data files later; your take-away message here should be "Ah, that's where I put my data; numbers go in there somehow."

Syntax Files. *Syntax (.sps)* files are where you write your syntax diary (of where your data came from, and what analyses you'd like to do, and so on). Conceptualizing your .sps files as a diary constitutes one of the most important elements of this book. Chapter 2 will highlight some lessons for this importance. Figure 1.3 shows an empty syntax file (with no diary entries or statistical commands).

Just as you put your numbers in your data file, you identify what analyses you'd like to do in your syntax file. Notice that: (1) the commands are similar to the commands of the .sav file (with the exception of a Run command included in the .sps file), (2) there is a blank white space instead of a grid (you actually type entries, just as you would in a word processor), and (3) there are no tabs at the bottom of the window (that is, no Data View or Variable View).

These two file types (data [.sav] and syntax [.sps]) are the ones that you as an SPSS user work with. You must enter information into both the .sav file and the .sps file for each project that you do.

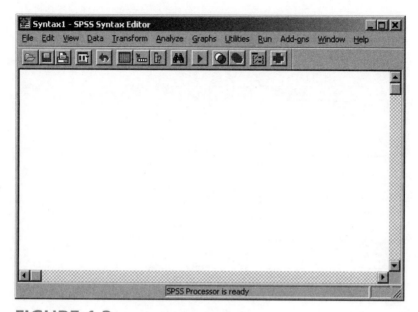

FIGURE 1.3. *The SPSS Syntax Editor.*

Output Files. *Output (.spo)* files are different from data and syntax files. *You* do not create output files—these are created by the SPSS program. If you have a syntax file that is full (with writing in it, instead of a big blank space as in the Figure 1.3 screen capture) and you have a data file that has numbers in it (instead of the blank white cells in Figure 1.2), the result of the interaction of the .sav and the .sps is an output (.spo) file. Figure 1.4 shows a blank output file.

You will rarely see an empty output file like this one, because output files are typically generated, not conjured up as this one has been. When you perform an analysis or a data manipulation—whenever something is done to your data, an output file appears. Output files are also like SPSS security enforcers—any time anything illegal or otherwise noteworthy is done to data, an output file will pop up and report the incident.

Output files have two panes: the narrower left pane and the wider right pane. The right-hand pane presents all of the detailed output you request from your selected analyses. The left pane is merely an outline of the detailed information provided in the right-hand pane. This outline is

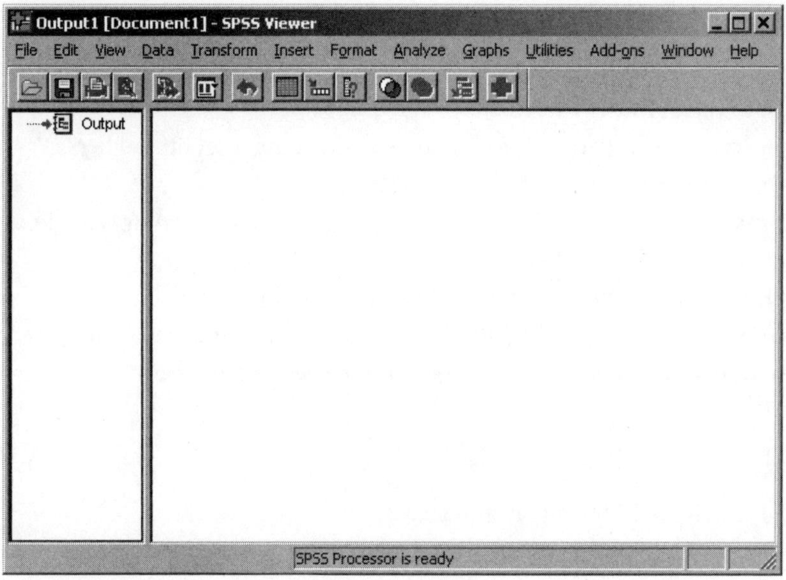

FIGURE 1.4. *The SPSS Output Viewer.*

sometimes useful to help you navigate through the detailed output on the right if you have performed a lot of analyses.

The Other File Types

There are other SPSS file types you will likely encounter, but the big three that you should be concerned with are the data (.sav), syntax (.sps), and output (.spo) files. If after reading this book you decide that you like SPSS enough (or are going to use it enough) to learn more, you can pursue learning about the program's other capabilities.

SUMMARY

SPSS is used not only to perform data analyses but also used to organize and manipulate data. SPSS is considered superior to data spreadsheet programs because with SPSS you can *keep a record* of what you have done. This is done through keeping a *syntax diary*. The program works through the interaction of a data file (.sav) and a syntax file (.sps). When the numbers (data in a .sav file) and instructions (syntax in an .sps file) interact, the result is an output file (.spo).

KEY TERMS

Data Anything informative.

Data (.sav) files Where data is stored in SPSS.

Descriptive statistics Information summarizing a set of numbers.

Excel Computer spreadsheet application.

Inferential statistics Probability-based information relating sample to population characteristics.

Output (.spo) files Where results are reported in SPSS.

SPSS Computer program used to do data manipulations and analyses.

Syntax (.sps) files Where operations are specified in SPSS.

DISCUSSION QUESTIONS

1. Why is SPSS superior to Excel?

2. What are some advantages and disadvantages associated with SPSS's evolution toward an Excel-Word hybrid?

CHAPTER

HOW TO ORGANIZE
YOUR SPSS LIFE

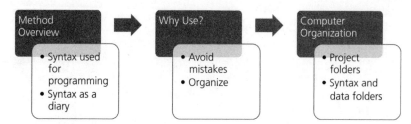

FIGURE 2.1. *Method Overview – Why Use SPSS? – Computer Organization.*

Contents

Chapter Learning Objectives

The Importance of Syntax Files

My Bad – Your Good

CHAPTER LEARNING OBJECTIVES

1. Why using syntax is imperative

2. Computer folder organization

Primitive snakes—like boa constrictors and pythons—have small append-ages in their "torsos" that have no practical purpose but are evolutionary holdovers from the legs of their lizard-like ancestors. Similarly, new versions of SPSS look quite different from their ancestors, but there are a few shared elements and evolutionary holdovers.

THE IMPORTANCE OF SYNTAX FILES

Syntax files (the .sps files) are one of those evolutionary holdovers. In older versions of SPSS, the user had to be part statistician and part computer programmer, feeding code and oddly organized data into the program so it could run the user's analyses. The code that was fed into the program was what is currently known as *syntax language*.

As Windows-based computer environments became popular, SPSS started to develop more user-friendly and interactive user options (this meant getting rid of the requirement that successful users be fairly proficient computer programmers). The main result of this move toward user-friendliness was the introduction of the spreadsheet (.sav file) format, as shown in Figure 2.2. Older versions of SPSS did not have this spreadsheet environment.

The .sav file contains everything the novice SPSS user needs to run analyses—it is a self-contained statistics processor. The syntax files are legacies—they are no longer needed for their original purpose of computer programming. They are lowly remnants of the DOS-based programming days and redundant with the .sav files. You do not need syntax files to run 99 percent of your data analyses.

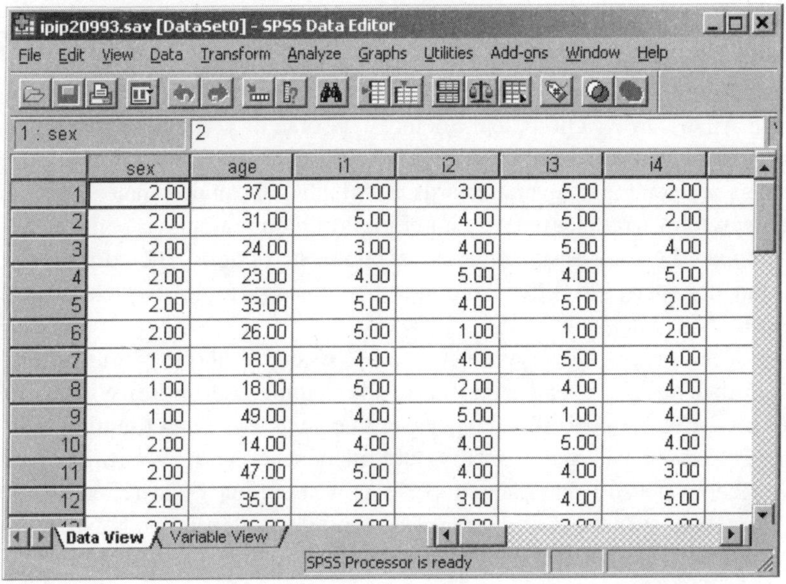

FIGURE 2.2.   *An Example of a "Filled" SPSS Data Editor.*

Although you don't need syntax files to do your analyses, they are important for maintaining a litter-free environment. You absolutely need syntax files to follow the recommendations of this book. For although the Windows-based updates to SPSS have made knowledge of syntax language itself (the code you write) less important, they have concurrently made the *syntax files* themselves extremely important.

Additionally, if you're afraid to press buttons in a statistics processor (as people who first encounter SPSS often are), the syntax diary system overcomes this fear—keeping a document of your analyses enables you to "undo" anything you shouldn't have done. This is the fundamental purpose of this book—getting you into the habit of using syntax files to organize your SPSS life. I cannot overstate how important it is to keep a record of what you've done, and syntax files are the best way to keep such a record. This capability, in fact, is the main reason SPSS is superior to Excel even if you are doing only very basic operations. You will make mistakes while operating in SPSS (or Excel); using syntax means that the mistakes you make are correctable and not a huge problem.

My Bad – Your Good

When I was a graduate student, I conducted a research project, wrote a paper based on the results, and submitted the paper to a conference of the American Psychological Society. As some of you may know, when you submit a paper to a conference to be considered for presentation, there are generally several awards for which you can nominate yourself, if you think you meet minimum eligibility requirements. I, being unencumbered by modesty, selected a bunch of options, including "best student paper" and "ethnic and minority concerns topic" (which seemed to fit).

A few weeks later I was surprised to receive a phone call informing me that my paper had won one of the "ethnic and minority concerns topic" awards. Unfortunately, earlier that *same day* I had found out that everything I had stated in my submitted paper was *backwards*. That probably doesn't make much sense as written, but I had relied a little too much on the new and improved, non-syntax-dependent SPSS, and I had ended up doing a data manipulation twice prior to submitting the paper (effectively undoing the first manipulation; come back and read this after Chapter Six, and it'll make more sense). Everything that I had stated in my paper was 180 degrees wrong. I had said people suffered from decreases of self-esteem—it turns out their self-esteem had actually increased. I had said people were sad—they were actually happy. These mistakes stemmed from my over-reliance on the newer version of SPSS, in which I didn't *have to* use syntax files—and consequently *didn't* use them.

There are several lessons to be learned from my gaffe. Your instructor might point out that one lesson involves the consequences of using *two- versus one-tailed hypotheses* (if this term is new to you, see the Key Terms at the end of the chapter, and rest assured you'll get to it later in the semester; if you're not taking a statistics class, e-mail me and I'll explain the details). The lesson *I* took from this mistake was this: document your steps; keep a diary of what you do.

If I had used the syntax diary system instead of relying on the .sav file to do my analyses, I never would have made that mistake. Don't make the same mistake—which is actually quite easy to do if you don't follow the method in this book! The remainder of this book teaches you to use SPSS in an organized and appropriate manner through the use of the syntax file diary system.

CREATING YOUR PROJECT FILE FOLDERS

Before you start using SPSS, you need to create a place to store your diary (syntax) and data—some place that you can find easily later if you set your project aside for a month or two. It is very important that you have a well-organized folder system within which your analyses reside. I recommend organizing your *file space* as shown in Figure 2.3 (basically organized by project).

The "Kulas" folder represents the root folder for all of your analyses— you can call it "research" or "class" or use your last name. There are specific, project-related folders within your root folder (the figure shows two projects related to my field of I/O psychology: a 360 performance assessment project, and a personality project using an assessment known as the International Personality Item Pool [IPIP]). The folder titles are short but distinctive—this is important. Within each project folder are two folders—one labeled "data" and one labeled "syntax." Each project needs both of these folders.

SUMMARY

With SPSS, you are allowed to work with or without the specification of syntax. However, using syntax diaries is extremely important for mini-mizing mistakes. Mistakes that you make with syntax are correctable, whereas often mistakes that you make without syntax are uncorrectable (or even sometimes undetected). To capitalize on SPSS's ability to

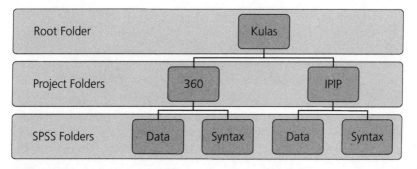

FIGURE 2.3. *File Organization Hierarchy.*

minimize errors, you need to have a syntax diary for every project. Your diaries, as well as your data, should reside in well-organized computer file systems.

KEY TERMS

File space System of folder organization within your computer.

One-tailed hypothesis Prediction that specifies the direction of an effect.

Two-tailed hypothesis Prediction that does not specify the direction of an effect.

DISCUSSION QUESTIONS

1. I have a friend who doesn't use syntax, and she's never made a mistake. Why couldn't I expect to do the same?

2. How common is the mistake that Kulas made?

CHAPTER

TYPES OF DATA

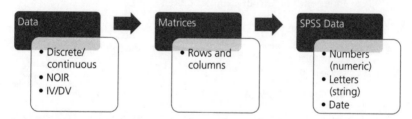

FIGURE 3.1. *SPSS Conceptualization of Data.*

Contents

CHAPTER LEARNING OBJECTIVES

1. Understanding your data types:
   - Nominal, ordinal, interval, ratio
   - Continuous, discrete
   - Independent variable, dependent variable
   - Numeric, string
2. Knowing how SPSS expects data to be organized:
   - People in rows
   - Variables in columns

This chapter prepares you for your first encounter with SPSS. Before you use the program, you have to understand your data and conceptualize how it might look in a matrix format.

UNDERSTANDING YOUR DATA

You have to understand your data before you decide to place it into SPSS cells and do manipulations on it. *Data* is a very broad term that includes anything informative. One way in which data is organized is within *variables*. Variables are things that can take on more than one value. For example, gender is a variable because it can take on a value of either male or female.

Scales of Measurement

An unfortunately popular taxonomy of measurement arose in the mid-1940s. I say unfortunately because it's not really, in my mind, as useful as it ought to be to be as popular as it still is today. To be as useful as it should be, the Stevens (1946) taxonomy of *nominal, ordinal, interval, and ratio scales of measurement* should dovetail nicely with the researcher dichotomy of *discrete* versus *continuous variables*. Unfortunately, it doesn't. For SPSS, I recommend that you consider discrete variables to be measured at the nominal level, whereas continuous variables may be either ordinal, interval, or ratio. You need to know discrete versus continuous for SPSS purposes; you do not need to know Stevens' taxonomy. (Although Stevens would argue with this point—his scales of measurement are based on permissible analyses.) This will facilitate your data management.

Independent Versus Dependent Variables

Data can be grossly classified as representing either independent (IV) or dependent (DV) variables (see Key Terms at the end of this chapter). There are two more possibilities if your data does not fit into either the IV or the DV category: (1) the data represents a *covariate*, or (2) the data exists to organize your information. A covariate is a variable that is measured or recorded but is not of *primary* interest to your research question. Usually these are considered *secondary IVs*. Demographic variables such as age, gender, or race are common covariates used, for example, in psychology. Before you consider how to interface your data with SPSS, you need to make sure you have a clear conceptualization of the following: (1) which are your IVs, which are your DVs, which are covariates, and which are left over (these are commonly used for data organization purposes); and (2) whether the variables you have identified are discrete or continuous.

CONCEPTUALIZING YOUR MATRIX

Data is entered and stored in SPSS as a *matrix* of information. A matrix consists of horizontal rows and vertical columns. Figure 3.2 illustrates a matrix in SPSS.

Variables define columns, and people define rows. (Not every project will collect data from "people"—rows may therefore represent individual rats, pigeons, turkeys, or other members of a research sample.) This is a very important and extremely helpful point in the organization of your data: the number of people you have in your experiment or project equals the number of rows you will have in your SPSS data file. This little tidbit of information will help you immensely as you try to figure out how to organize your data to fit your analyses. Always remember: the number of

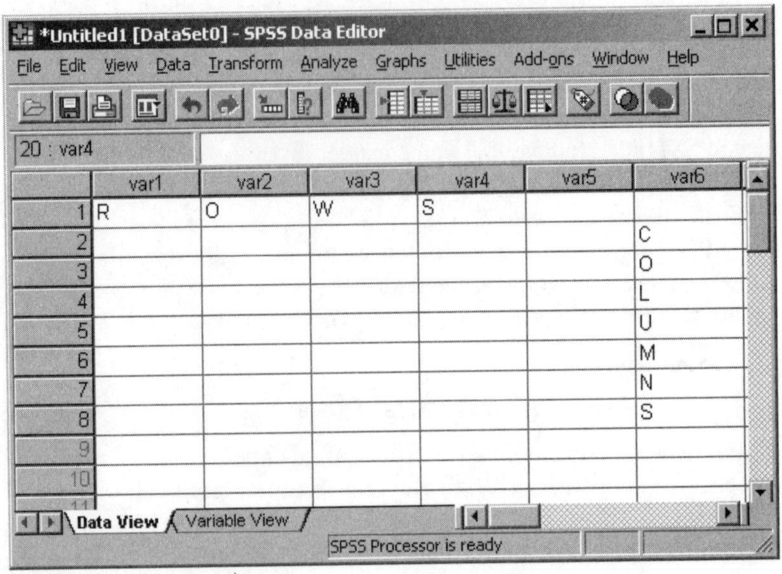

FIGURE 3.2. *The SPSS Data Editor Rows and Columns.*

people or other subjects defines the number of rows you will have in your SPSS data file. (If your unit of analysis is multiple people—that is, groups or teams—then you will have the same number of rows as groups.)

DATA FILES

SPSS is primarily concerned with variables (columns) and the entities (rows) that provide values for those variables. In a typical application, one "entity"—for instance, a person—will provide values to many variables. For instance, I am a male, I do not smoke, and I like SPSS. This information would be entered into one row in SPSS's data file. When more individuals provide information, more rows are added. When more than one individual provides information on more than one variable, you end up with a matrix of information.

If I collected information from myself, Jill, Jan, Juniper, and Jehosaphat regarding gender, smoking preference, and SPSS favorability, I would end up with a 5 × 4 matrix of information (shown in Figure 3.3). Matrix dimensions are always specified by (the number of rows with information) × (the number of columns with information). Your projects will almost always have more rows (people) than columns (variables). The SPSS

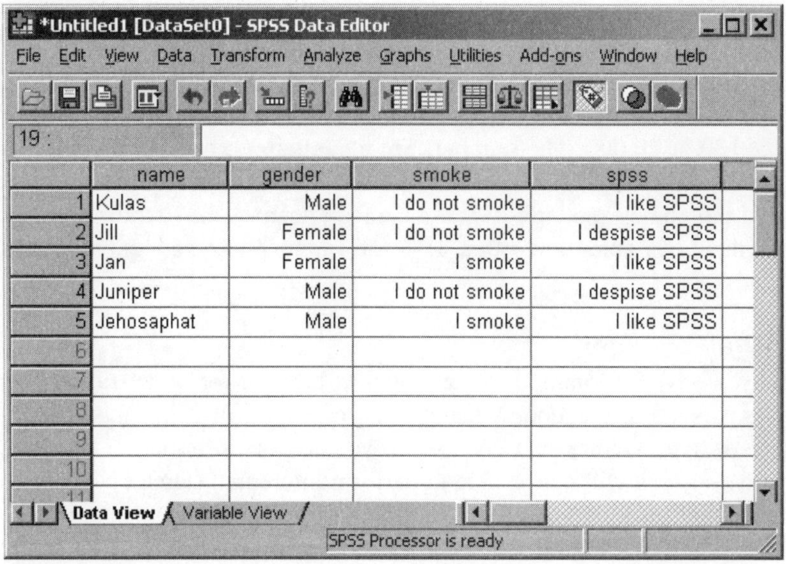

FIGURE 3.3. *Example Data (Gender, Smoking, and SPSS Preference).*

data file can accommodate many, many variables and persons; I have worked with data files that contain information from over a quarter of a million individuals.

KINDS OF DATA: AN SPSS PERSPECTIVE

We've discussed kinds of data from a measurement perspective (nominal, ordinal, interval, ratio, continuous, discrete) and from a methodological perspective (independent, dependent, or covariate), but we've somewhat glossed over data from an SPSS perspective. SPSS allows a great deal of flexibility in what you consider to be data. Basically you can store any little nugget of information you want in SPSS, but for 99 percent of your purposes, there is only one important SPSS distinction to make: is your data best represented by a number or a word?

Numeric

If your data is an IV, DV, or covariate, it should be stored as a number. SPSS refers to all numbers (regardless of whether they represent a nominal, ordinal, interval, or ratio level of measurement) as *numeric* variables.

It is often difficult to think of nominal variables as being represented by a number, but entities that can be sorted into categories—such as (a) male or female, (b) Caucasian, Aleut, or Hispanic, or (c) boxers or briefs— can just as easily have category labels of: (a) 1 or 2, (b) 0, 1, or 3, or (c) 100 or 10,000. The numbers are meaningless, but the information they represent (a *difference*—for instance, boxers *or* briefs) is important and should be stored in SPSS as a number, not a word. Your discrete and nominal variables are often IVs for rudimentary and experimental analyses.

String

If you have information that is going to be used for organization purposes (such as someone's name), you can store that information as a word (*string*) rather than a number. If you do store information as words, however, you will not be able to perform inferential statistical analyses with that information—so if a variable is identified as an IV, DV, or covariate, you should *not* store that variable information as a string variable.

The Other File Types

There are actually quite a few other formats that SPSS uses to store information. In addition to string and numeric, one confusing format that you may occasionally use is *date*. SPSS, of course, conceptualizes dates a little differently than everyone else does. SPSS stores date information as the number of seconds that have elapsed since October 14, 1582 (which apparently is roughly around the time of the acceptance of the Gregorian calendar—an intriguing choice). This actually is not confusing to the SPSS user until the SPSS user attempts to determine the difference between two dates.

If, for example, I want to know how long an employee has worked for an organization, I can compute the difference between the termination date (8/10/2006) and the hiring date (8/9/2006). You'll notice that this particular individual was fired after one day of work. The data file does a very nice job of storing and reporting information in an interpretable manner; however, when I subtract fire date from hire date in SPSS, I get an odd value: 86,400. This number represents the number of seconds in a day. The take-away message here is that SPSS records time and date information in a small metric: seconds. If you want to know the difference between dates in a different metric (days, for example) you have to do further manipulations of the data (more on that in Chapter Six).

SUMMARY

Data can be categorized in a number of different ways. As far as SPSS is concerned, data is most commonly a number (numeric) or a word (string). For your projects, your data should be represented by numbers whenever possible. When trying to figure out what your data will look like in SPSS, remember that the number of people or objects you are dealing with defines the number of rows that your data file will have.

KEY TERMS

Continuous Variables Variables that can assume a large number of possible values.

Covariate Variable not of primary interest, but thought to be related to a DV.

Date SPSS specification of a calendar date.

Dependent Variable (DV) Outcome or criterion variable.

Discrete Variables Variables that have only a limited number of possible values.

Independent Variable (IV) Predictor or manipulated variable.

Matrix A grid formation of two or more rows and columns.

Numeric SPSS specification of a number.

String SPSS specification of a word.

Variable Anything that can possess different values or quantities.

DISCUSSION QUESTIONS

1. What numbers can be used to code the following values?
   a. Gender
   b. Military rank
   c. Height
2. Why would anyone include covariates in a data file?

CHAPTER

4

CREATING AND ACCESSING DATA FILES

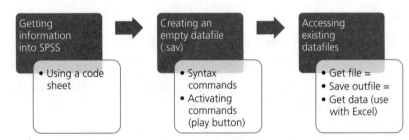

FIGURE 4.1. *Entering and Accessing Data.*

Contents

CHAPTER LEARNING OBJECTIVES

1. The syntax way to create a data file
2. Specifying variables
   - Numbers
   - Words (string)
3. Relying on your syntax files to access data files
   - Controlling the content of your data files

You now know what an empty SPSS data file looks like (see Figure 1.2, p. 7) and what a filled SPSS data file looks like (see Figure 2.2, p. 13), but you don't necessarily know how to get there. This chapter takes you from a blank data file to one that contains information relevant to your project.

Historically, projects accumulate *hardcopies* of data (for instance, paper surveys that individuals have completed). Appendix A contains an example of a completed survey that will be used as one example throughout the remainder of this book—the completed survey is an example of a hardcopy. The first two sections of this chapter deal with circumstances in which you have hardcopies of data and need to transfer information to the computer. Increasingly, data is also *collected* via computer—the last section of this chapter deals with transferring data into SPSS if that data was also collected via computer.

BEFORE YOU OPEN SPSS

Take a look at the sample questionnaire form in Appendix A. (The questionnaire is a version of a personality assessment taken from the international personality item pool (IPIP) [Goldberg, 1999; Johnson, 2005].) It has a number in the upper right-hand corner, asks for the respondent gender, and asks one hundred personality-related questions. Typically, I will have gathered many of these completed questionnaires (say, for example, I administer the questionnaire to one thousand individuals) and will need to transfer the information from each individual form into an SPSS data matrix (respondents [1,000] × variables [102]).

In circumstances in which you have hardcopies of data (like this situation, in which we have a questionnaire), it is a good idea to create a *code sheet*. A code sheet forces you to think in SPSS terms. The general steps for creating a code sheet are as follows:

1. Find a blank questionnaire or administration form.

2. Determine what information should be recorded as numbers and what should be recorded as words.

3. For every piece of information that should or will be recorded as numbers, write those numbers on the code sheet.

4. Give a short name (eight characters or fewer) to each of the variables on your questionnaire. (Current versions of SPSS allow variables to have names longer than eight characters, but just because something is permissible doesn't mean that you should do it. You will make fewer errors in the recollection of syntax specification of variables if you keep the names short. SPSS allows you to add greater description to your variables through other means [see Chapter 5]).

Appendix B shows a code sheet for the questionnaire presented in Appendix A.

In this circumstance, all information can be stored as numbers rather than words, and there are 102 variables to create. The first variable (sometimes called the *case number*—you should always have this variable in your projects) identifies the respondent and questionnaire, the second identifies the respondent's gender, and the remaining one hundred identify responses to one hundred items on the personality questionnaire. The code sheet is the link between our hardcopies and our SPSS data file. We are going to use it to help us create a file that can electronically store our one thousand responses.

SPECIFYING OPERATIONS THROUGH SPSS

Before we venture into the realm of actually using SPSS, there are a few things we need to go over. First, *syntax* is just words, but there are two *types* of words used in syntax: (1) *commands* and (2) your variable names. Commands tell SPSS *what* actions you want to perform; your variable names tell SPSS *where* the actions should be performed. Command language was created by SPSS; your variable names were created by you.

Second, SPSS reads syntax sequentially, from "top" to "bottom." The operations that SPSS performs also occur sequentially (that is, from top to bottom). Third, you do need to know your variable names, but you don't need to be a walking dictionary of SPSS command language. This book does not expect you to remember SPSS code (more on this in Chapter Six). Fourth, for each topic we cover I will present a flow chart detailing the important elements of your syntax as well as screenshots of the actual syntax.

CREATING DATA FILES THE HARD WAY

There are two ways to get from a completely empty, new SPSS data file to one that contains information relevant to your project (what I call a *data shell*). The nonsyntax way to create an empty (but variable-defined) data file will be covered first. Remember those two tabs at the bottom of an empty data file? They are circled in Figure 4.2.

The tabs in SPSS data files facilitate your data file creation—you can define your variables by working in the Variable View tab, and you enter data by working in the Data View tab. Unfortunately, going from Data View to Variable View transposes your matrix (turns columns into rows; see Figure 4.3), which can be a bit confusing.

The file perspective through the Variable View looks similar, but it's actually quite different. Your project data does not go into the cells; rather, information about your definition of the variables goes into each cell. Instead of going through this process of defining your variables one by one (creating your data file "shell"), it is better to just pretend that the Variable View is not even there—there is a shortcut that you should use instead.

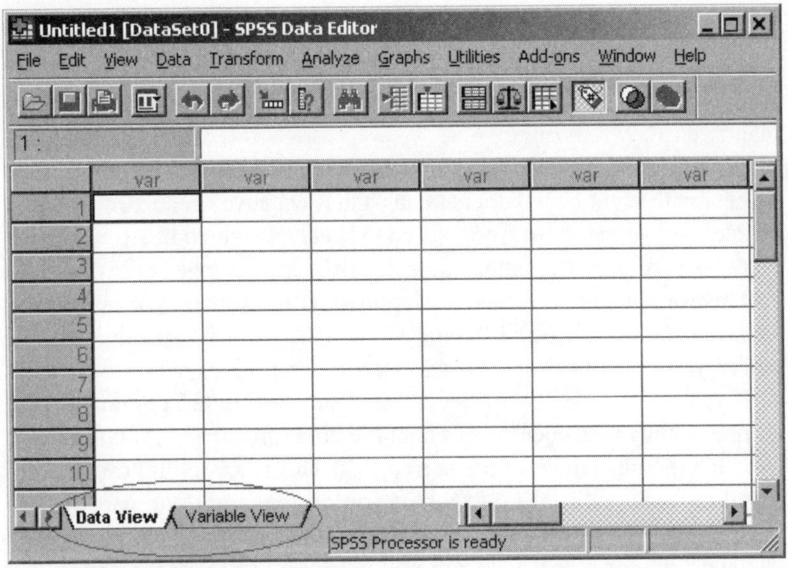

FIGURE 4.2. *The SPSS Data Editor with Data View Circled.*

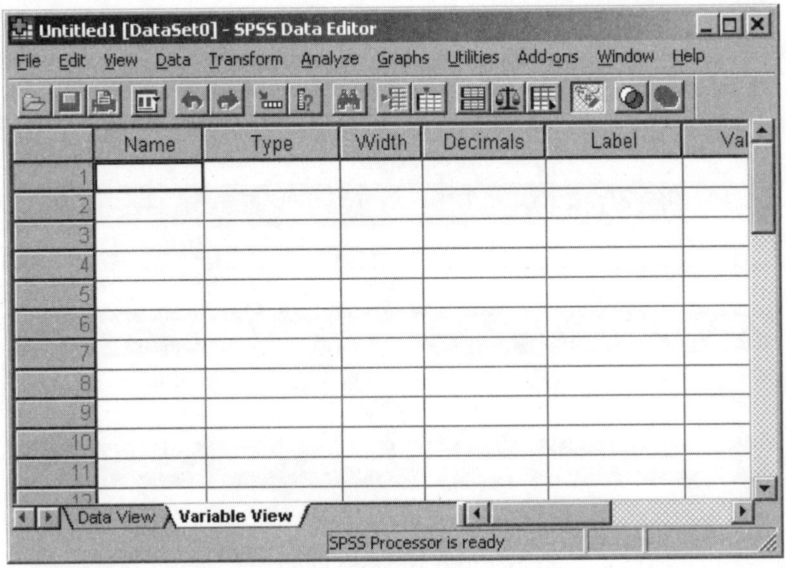

FIGURE 4.3. *The SPSS Data Editor Variable View.*

CREATING DATA FILES THE SYNTAX WAY

When all of your data is represented by numbers (as is the case with Appendixes A and B), you can create a data shell with just four commands, as shown in Figure 4.4.

In addition to these SPSS commands, you need to know the truncated names (with eight or fewer characters) that we gave to the 102 variables of interest (we get these from our code sheet, presented in Appendix B). Figure 4.5 presents the commands and variable names together in one diary.

This format can be copied and applied to any situation, replacing the "casenum," "gender," and "item1 to item100" words with the variable names you give to variables used in your own project.

If you don't include the "begin data" and "end data." commands, the computer may not process your data file creation request. You also need to watch the placement of the period ("."). This is a very important command terminator (it tells SPSS that you're done with one part of your command). The "execute" command is something you'll quickly become familiar with, as we are going to use it to mark the end of just about every manipulation or analysis.

Note that I didn't explicitly specify all one hundred items in this command. SPSS allows you to take a shortcut with numbered variables—if the numbers are located at the end of your variable name. It will automatically

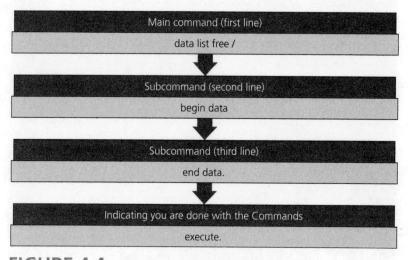

Main command (first line)

data list free /

Subcommand (second line)

begin data

Subcommand (third line)

end data.

Indicating you are done with the Commands

execute.

FIGURE 4.4. *Flow Chart of Data File Creation Process.*

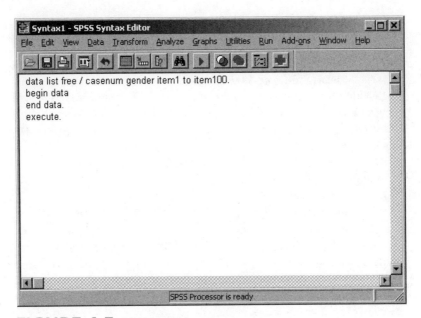

FIGURE 4.5. *Data File Creation Syntax.*

number your variables for you if you tell the program where to start ("item1") and end ("item100").

To initiate the action you've requested in your syntax file, you need to highlight the commands you wish to run (in this and most cases, everything written). You can do this a few different ways; the two most useful are

1. Press **Ctrl+A**; this will select everything in your syntax file.

2. Select all by dragging the cursor to highlight the commands.

I would like you to get in the habit of using the first method, **Ctrl+A**, because we are going to construct our syntax files such that they'll be run in their entirety (top to bottom) every time we use them. After you have highlighted the information in your syntax file (as shown in Figure 4.6), click the Play button on the Syntax Editor toolbar (the right-pointing arrow to the right of the "Find" button—the binoculars), and your diary will be activated.

If you look at your data file now, it will be empty (as shown in Figure 4.7) but will have variables defined. It is now ready for you to enter information—peoples' questionnaire responses.

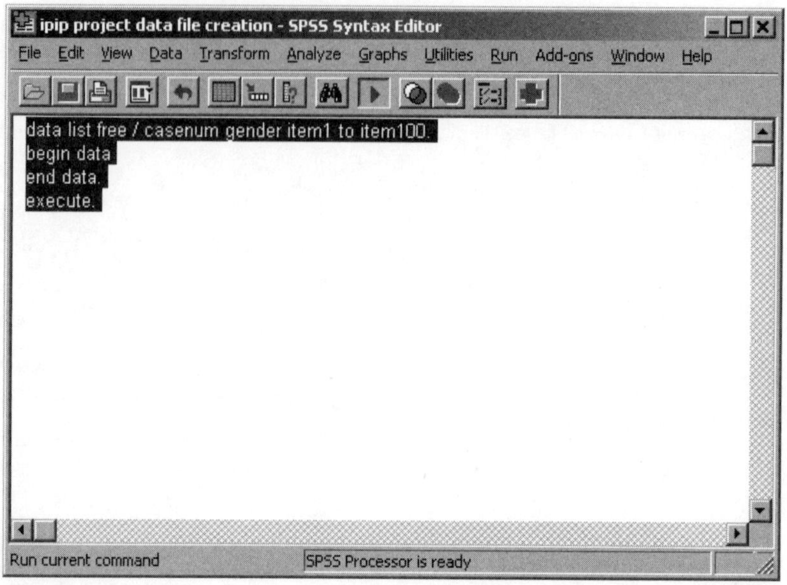

FIGURE 4.6. *Selection and Execution of the Syntax.*

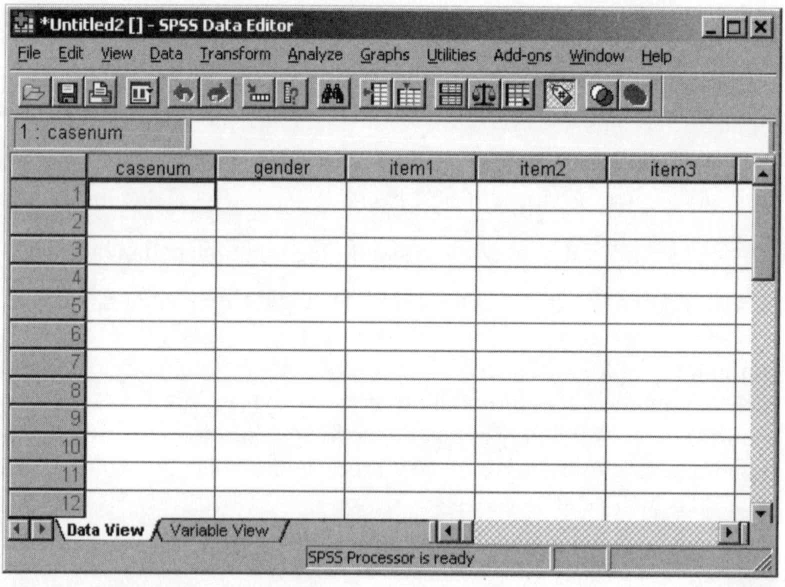

FIGURE 4.7. *The SPSS Data Editor with Variables Defined, Ready for Data Entry.*

NUMERIC VERSUS STRING VARIABLES

If you want to have string variables (words) in your data file, you need to (1) use a different file creation command, and (2) know the SPSS code for words and numbers. The SPSS specification for a string variable is the letter *a*. The specification for a numeric variable is the letter *f*. After each of these letters, you need to specify a number. This number will place boundaries on the number of letters or numbers that are reported by SPSS. The default specification is *f8.2* (an eight-character number with two decimal places [i.e., the *hundredths* spot]), so if all of your variables are represented by numbers, you don't need to worry about using the f or a to differentiate from string variables. If you *do* want string variables in your data file, you need to use the f and a designators, and you'll also need a different initial command: *list* instead of *free*. The process for creating a data file with a mix of number- and letter-variables is shown in Figure 4.8.

Figure 4.9 shows the syntax commands for a data file I created with two strings (sixteen characters each) and two numerics (no decimal places). Note that commas are also used with the data list list—but they're not used with the "data list free" command. It's important that

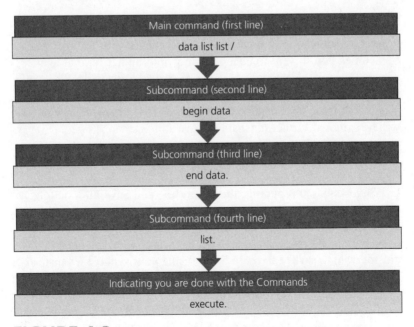

FIGURE 4.8. *Data File Creation Flow Chart when String Variables Are Desired.*

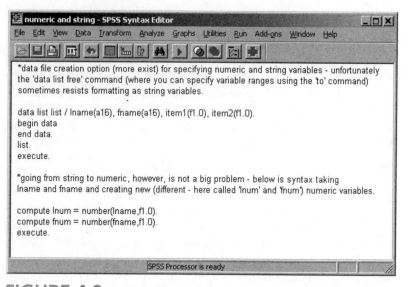

FIGURE 4.9. *Data File Creation with Numeric and String Variables.*

you're able to alter the formatting of variables, because some analytical programs that you may use may have problems with decimal places. Sometimes you'll want to change strings into numerics; that syntax is also included in the example. Note too that in addition to the SPSS commands, I've included comments to myself (indicated by an asterisk). The use of these comment lines (as well as the "compute" statements) will be explored further in Chapters Five and Six.

WORKING WITH YOUR DATA FILES

In Windows-based programs, the Open (file) and Save (file) buttons are generally next to each other (as shown in Figure 4.10). This can be dangerous. Have you ever mistakenly clicked the Save button instead of the Open button and saved changes to the file you already had open that you did not want to save? I have. In SPSS, using your syntax files instead of working directly in data files (as we did in the previous data file creation examples Figures 4.5, 4.6, and 4.9) eliminates that possibility. This is very important because, once you *enter* data into your empty shell, you'll be encouraged to mess around with it, but you never want to permanently alter your *original data file*. It is very important to keep your

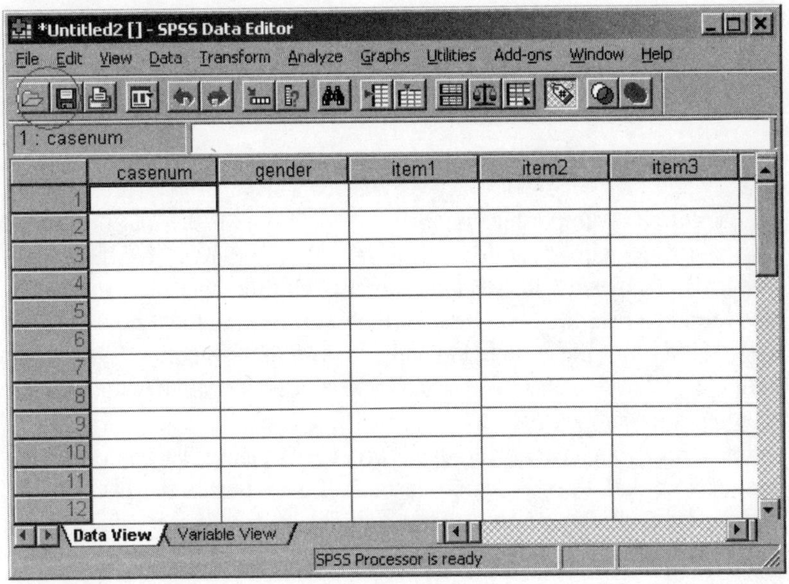

FIGURE 4.10. *Proximity of the Open and Save Buttons.*

original (called *raw*) data untouched. Failing to do so is one of the mistakes I made with the APS award snafu.

The only instances in which you would want to alter and then "save over" your original data file are (1) to enter additional data or (2) to correct misentered data. Other than these two circumstances, you should *never* save over your original raw data file. Learning this basic rule will stand you in good stead.

If there are alterations or changes that need to be made to your original data, you should make sure to document them in your diary (syntax) and also be sure that your original data is kept intact in SPSS, in case you ever need to retrieve it (unfortunately, this need is not uncommon—especially if you're dealing with journal editors or statistics instructors).

To minimize the likelihood that you will save over your raw data file, you will be accessing your data through syntax. *The only time you should ever access a data file directly (open a data file from the Data Editor) is when you are entering data into the file.* You should *never* open a data file directly if your purpose is to do data analyses or manipulations (or anything other than enter data). A further caution: newer versions of SPSS allow the user to have multiple .sav (data) files open simultaneously. Never do this. Only have one data file open—*always*.

Working within the syntax environment and using "get file" and "save outfile" commands will help you achieve this level of data control.

Get File and Save Outfile

For any purpose other than entering data, get into the habit of relying on your syntax files (diaries) to access your data files. In your diaries there are two extremely important commands: "get file" and "save outfile." These two commands allow you to control the data file that is open and avoid problems associated with working directly with the data file. Unless you are *creating* a data file (as we did earlier), your syntax files should always begin with a "get file" command and end with a "save outfile" command. Figure 4.11 presents the basic structure you need to follow when you use "get file" and "save outfile" commands. These two commands are probably the most important syntax commands you need to learn. They allow you to control your data through syntax instead of operating in the Data Editor. "Get file" tells the program which data file you wish to use. After you do manipulations on your data (change it in some fashion), you typically want to use the "save outfile" command to save your new data file.

It's also important that the name of your "save outfile" data file is different from the name of your "get file" data. This ensures that your original, raw data will be left uncompromised (that is, you won't save over it). I suggest that you use one syntax file to create an empty data file (as we did in our first syntax example) and a different syntax file to do analyses, manipulations, and so on. Using the data file creation syntax we looked at earlier, I can save my newly defined data file—I'll name it *ipip raw data .sav*, as shown in Figure 4.12.

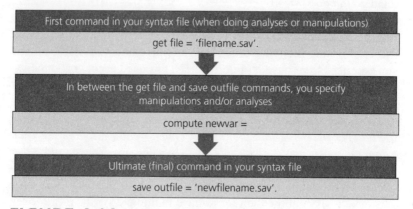

FIGURE 4.11. *Flow Chart of Data Management Process.*

```
ipip project data file creation - SPSS Syntax Editor
File  Edit  View  Data  Transform  Analyze  Graphs  Utilities  Run  Add-ons  Window  Help

data list free / casenum gender item1 to item100.
begin data
end data.
execute.



save outfile='c:\kulas\ipip\data\ipip raw data.sav'.
execute.




SPSS Processor is ready
```

FIGURE 4.12. *IPIP Project Data File Creation with Save Outfile Command.*

It's important that you include the single quotation marks around your file name and location. This is true in both the "get file" and the "save outfile" commands. Typically you'll further define the variables in your newly created data file before saving it (for more on this, see Chapter Five); the brief discussion here simply demonstrates how it's done.

If I later want to access this data file, I simply replace the "save outfile" with "get file" as shown in Figure 4.13.

It's important that you understand these two very basic commands. Religiously using the "get file" and "save outfile" commands will help you keep only one data file open at a time. You cannot overuse these two commands.

You'll have at least two syntax files for every project: one to initially define the data file, and at least one to do manipulations or analyses on your data. The "save outfile" command is useful because it allows you to create new data sets that conform to your needs without altering your original raw data.

Keep/Drop Subcommand

If I decide that I want my new data file to include only questionnaire items 1 and 2, I can specify a useful subcommand of the "save outfile" command—I can do this by specifying either "keep" or "drop" (see Figure 4.14). These commands have the same effect—narrowing down your variables—but you typically use "keep" if you're keeping only a few variables (so you identify only those you are keeping) and "drop" if you're keeping many variables (so you identify only those you are dropping). In this situation, I have chosen to use the "drop" option, and this syntax is shown in Figure 4.15.

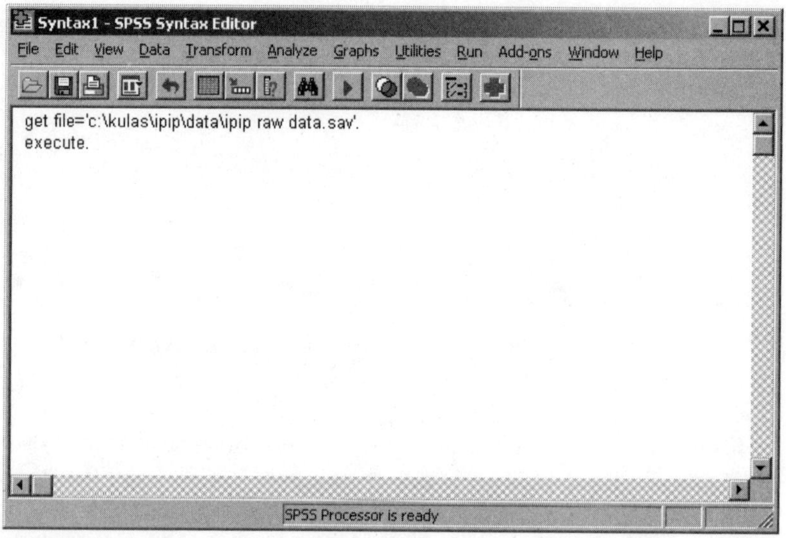

FIGURE 4.13. *Command for Accessing a Data File.*

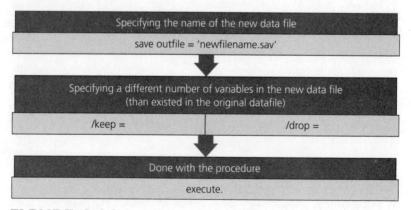

FIGURE 4.14. *Specifying Subcommands to Limit Variables in a Data File.*

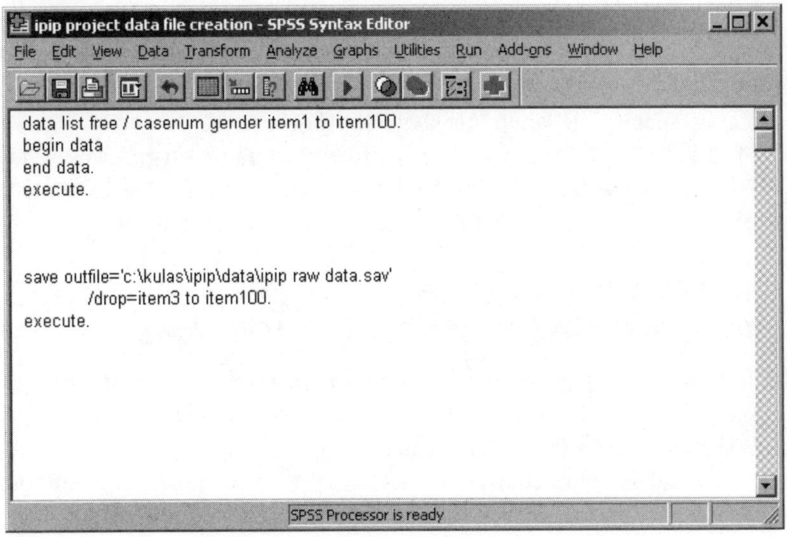

FIGURE 4.15. *IPIP Project Data File Keeping Only Casenum, Gender, item1, and item2.*

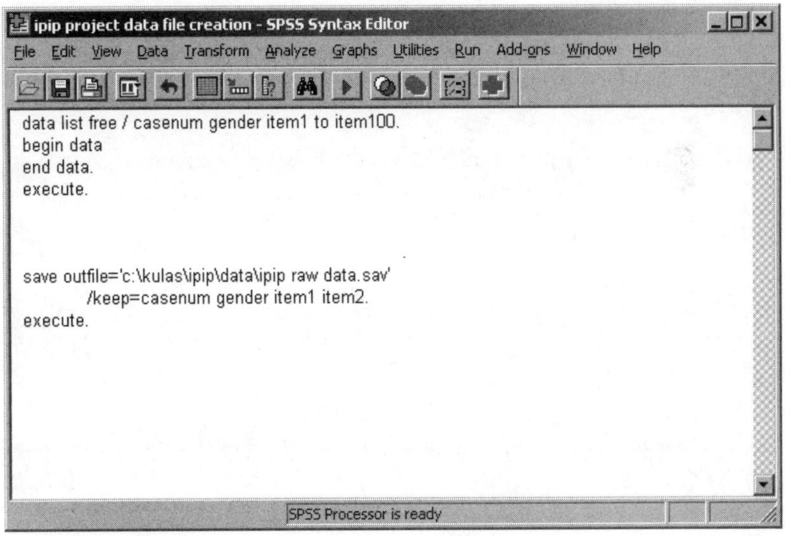

FIGURE 4.16. *Limited Variable IPIP Project Data File Using the Keep Command.*

Notice that when you use subcommands, you include a slash character "/" and you move the command terminator (the period) from the first line down to the last line. Alternatively, you could achieve the same effect by specifying "keep," as shown in Figure 4.16.

You typically would not specify either "drop" or "keep" when you first create your data file, but these two subcommands are extremely useful when you start to do your data analyses and manipulations.

IMPORTING DATA FROM OTHER PROGRAMS

Increasingly, data is collected (or stored) in formats other than hard-copies. Figure 4.17 presents a syntax example of how to "get files" that are originally in an Excel spreadsheet format.

If my data is provided to me in an Excel format as shown, I can import it into an SPSS data file by using the syntax shown in Figure 4.18.

The last subcommand "readnames=on" tells SPSS that the first row in my Excel file contains variable name information. If I highlight and run this syntax, the data file shown in Figure 4.19 will appear.

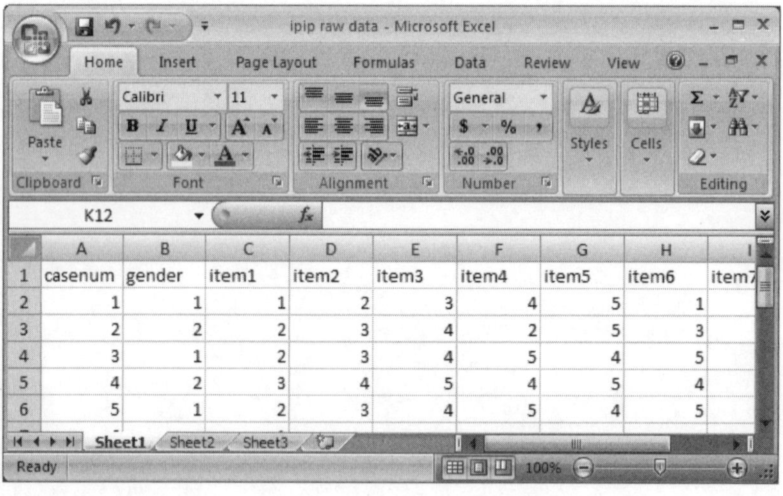

FIGURE 4.17. *IPIP Raw Data (Excel Format).*

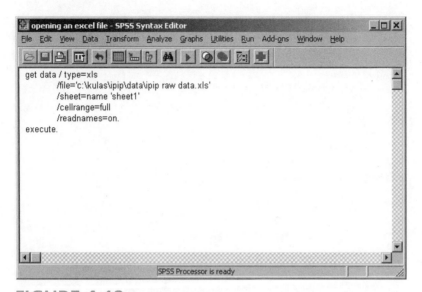

FIGURE 4.18. *Opening an Excel File in SPSS.*

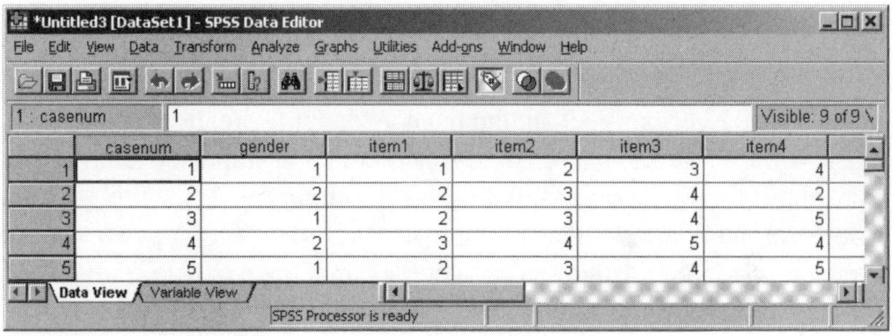

FIGURE 4.19. *Excel Data now in SPSS Format.*

Of course this file is not currently saved as an SPSS file. To do that, I need to add a "save outfile" command to my syntax that retrieves the Excel file, as shown in Figure 4.20.

Now if I highlight and run the entire syntax, I will have my Excel file duplicated in SPSS format and saved in my kulas\ipip\data folder.

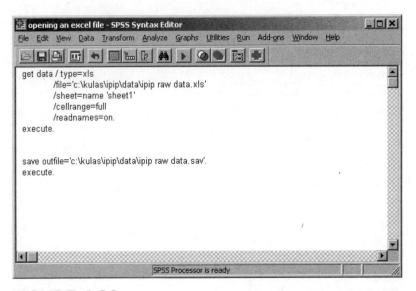

FIGURE 4.20. *Retrieving Excel Data and Saving as SPSS Data.*

SUMMARY

There are syntax shortcuts to creating data files—you will find it helpful to use them. Every project should have a "data file creation" syntax file, whether the SPSS file was created from scratch or imported from Excel. You should always access data files through the "get file" syntax command—this allows you to control which data file is active and to avoid catastrophic mistakes. The "get file" and "save outfile" commands are the two most important syntax commands for you to master.

KEY TERMS

* Indicator that information after the asterisk is an internal comment "for your eyes only"; SPSS won't read this information.

"Begin data" SPSS subcommand used with the "data list free" command.

Case number Confidential person or case identifier.

Code sheet Hardcopy that specifies SPSS variable names and value codes.

Command Wording that tells SPSS what to do.

Ctrl+A Keystroke combination to "select all."

Data list free SPSS command used to create a new data file.

Data "shell" Empty data file, in which variables have been defined but numbers have not been entered.

Data View Traditional view in data (.sav) files—data is stored here.

"Drop" Subcommand used with "save outfile," specifying which variables are to be excluded in the newly saved data file.

"End data" SPSS subcommand to be used with the "data list free" file creation command, along with "begin data."

"Execute" SPSS command that tells the SPSS processor to start working.

F8.2 The default format of SPSS variables.

"Get file" SPSS command used to retrieve a specified data file.

Hardcopy Paper version.

"Keep" Subcommand used with "save outfile," specifying which variables are to be kept in the newly saved data file.

Play button SPSS button, located in syntax files, that activates selected syntax.

Raw data file Electronic storage of variable and person information (a data shell with information in it).

"Readnames=on" Subcommand to be used when retrieving Excel data if the Excel file contains variable names.

"Save outfile" SPSS command used to save the currently open data file.

SPSS code Language used by SPSS.

Variable names Names, of eight characters or fewer, used in the SPSS data file.

Variable View Capability, in newer versions of SPSS, that allows you to define variables from within the data (.sav) file.

DISCUSSION QUESTIONS

1. What is the importance of the case number?

2. Why are the "get file" and "save outfile" commands so important?

CHAPTER

DEFINING YOUR DATA

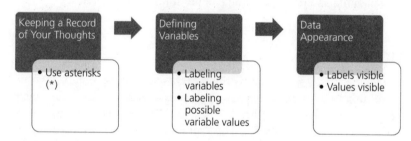

FIGURE 5.1. *Labeling and Record Keeping.*

Contents

Chapter Learning Objectives

Notation

Defining Your Dataset

CHAPTER LEARNING OBJECTIVES

1. Annotating your syntax files (*)
2. Defining your variables
   - Variable labels
   - Value labels
3. How to view your data labels

You should now be familiar with the use of syntax files for the creation of empty (but variable-defined) data files. You'll now want to take your new data file and provide variable definitions and boundaries.

NOTATION

Remember that you will be working exclusively in the syntax environment: this keeps a diary of your steps in case you need to retrace what you did with your data. When you access SPSS, always open up a syntax file rather than a data file. The "get file" command will open up the data file for you—don't go messing around with opening data directly. Before you get too far with this method, however, you'll want to get into the habit of annotating your diary. Figure 5.2 shows my note that the syntax will create a new (empty) data file and that I was working on this project on October 15.

The important elements of a note are at least one asterisk (*) at the beginning and a period (.) indicating the end.

The asterisk tells SPSS to not interpret the information as a command, and the period indicates your note is finished. You should get into the habit of recording the dates you were working within your syntax files.

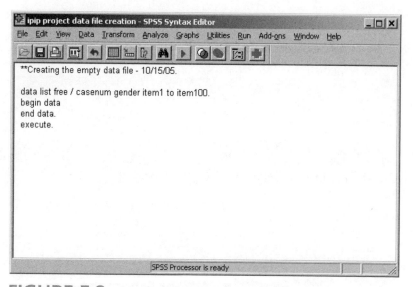

FIGURE 5.2. *Syntax Diary Annotation Example.*

DEFINING YOUR DATASET

There are two main data definition commands that you will frequently use. One provides more descriptive labels to your variables (remember, we use short—eight characters or fewer—variable names in our data files). The other command provides descriptors for possible responses to the variables.

Adding Variable Labels

To provide descriptive information to your data file's variables, the command is simply "var labels". You must use this command individually for every variable in your data file.

Figures 5.3 and 5.4 show examples of giving labels to the variables from the questionnaire in Appendix A; this is actually very useful, because if you do this, SPSS output will report labels instead of variable names.

It's important that you use apostrophes carefully when you define variables like this. If your item has a contraction in it, you need to exclude the apostrophe from your variable label (your fourth-grade grammar teacher might grumble a bit, but SPSS is a bit more mellow, so it won't dock you points). If you include a contraction, you'll get an error message. There are shortcuts to physically typing all of your item

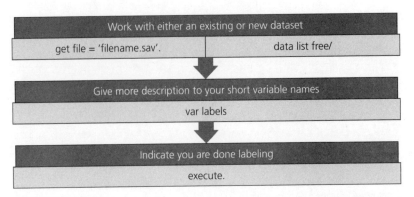

FIGURE 5.3. *Syntax Organization for Labeling Variables.*

```
ipip project data file creation - SPSS Syntax Editor
File  Edit  View  Data  Transform  Analyze  Graphs  Utilities  Run  Add-ons  Window  Help

**Creating the empty data file - 10/15/05.

data list free / casenum gender item1 to item100.
begin data
end data.
execute.

*Giving each variable a more descriptive name - 10/15/05.

var labels casenum 'Case number of participant/questionnaire'.
var labels gender 'Gender of participant'.

var labels item1 'Am the life of the party'.
var labels item2 'Insult people'.
var labels item3 'Am always prepared'.
var labels item4 'Get stressed out easily'.
var labels item5 'Have a rich vocabulary'.

                              SPSS Processor is ready
```

FIGURE 5.4. *Giving Labels to Variables.*

labels into your syntax file (see Chapter Fourteen), and one of the main reasons to use these shortcuts is to get rid of pesky apostrophes.

Adding Value Labels

If you take a look at the example coding sheet in Appendix B, you'll note that we're indicating a response of "male" as a "1" and "female" as a "2." Also, responses to the personality items are recorded as numbers. One through five correspond to responses of "strongly disagree" to "strongly agree." It is useful to have SPSS know this information, in case you forget. After giving all of your variables labels, you should identify responses to the variables as well, as shown in Figure 5.5.

This is actually quite a bit less time-intensive than specifying variable labels, because you can specify ranges of variables instead of listing them all separately. The command for this is: "add value labels".

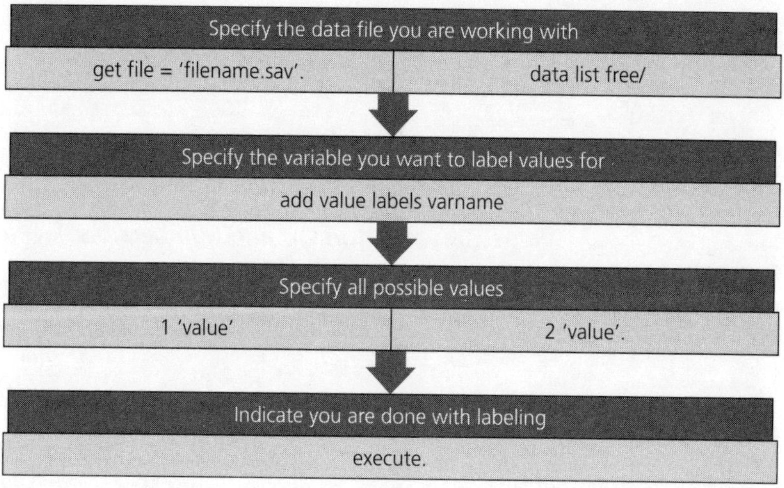

Specify the data file you are working with	
get file = 'filename.sav'.	data list free/

Specify the variable you want to label values for
add value labels varname

Specify all possible values	
1 'value'	2 'value'.

Indicate you are done with labeling
execute.

FIGURE 5.5. *Labeling Responses to Variables.*

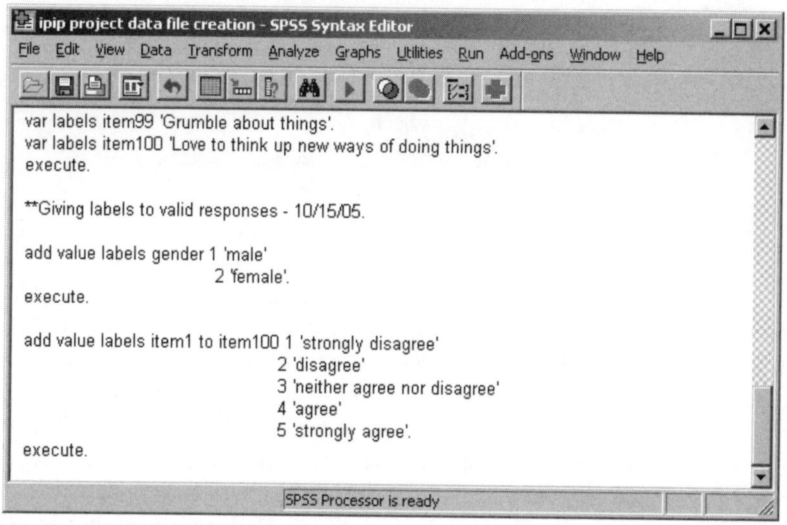

```
ipip project data file creation - SPSS Syntax Editor                    _ □ ×
File  Edit  View  Data  Transform  Analyze  Graphs  Utilities  Run  Add-ons  Window  Help

var labels item99 'Grumble about things'.
var labels item100 'Love to think up new ways of doing things'.
execute.

**Giving labels to valid responses - 10/15/05.

add value labels gender 1 'male'
                        2 'female'.
execute.

add value labels item1 to item100 1 'strongly disagree'
                        2 'disagree'
                        3 'neither agree nor disagree'
                        4 'agree'
                        5 'strongly agree'.
execute.

                        SPSS Processor is ready
```

FIGURE 5.6. *The "Add Value Labels" Command.*

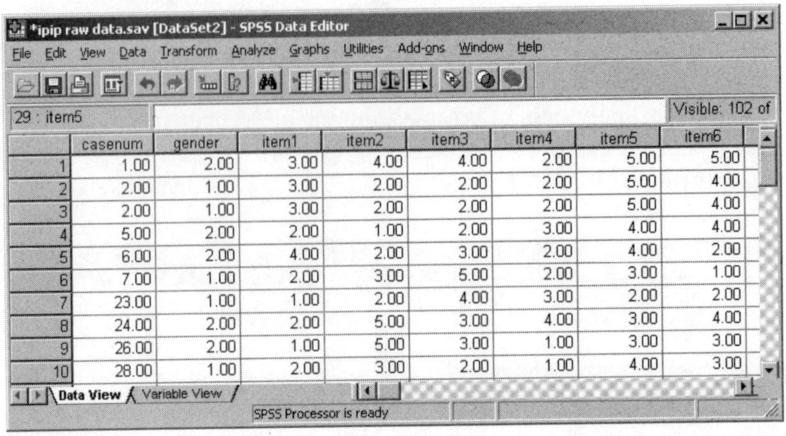

	casenum	gender	item1	item2	item3	item4	item5	item6
1	1.00	2.00	3.00	4.00	4.00	2.00	5.00	5.00
2	2.00	1.00	3.00	2.00	2.00	2.00	5.00	4.00
3	2.00	1.00	3.00	2.00	2.00	2.00	5.00	4.00
4	5.00	2.00	2.00	1.00	2.00	3.00	4.00	4.00
5	6.00	2.00	4.00	2.00	3.00	2.00	4.00	2.00
6	7.00	1.00	2.00	3.00	5.00	2.00	3.00	1.00
7	23.00	1.00	1.00	2.00	4.00	3.00	2.00	2.00
8	24.00	2.00	2.00	5.00	3.00	4.00	3.00	4.00
9	26.00	2.00	1.00	5.00	3.00	1.00	3.00	3.00
10	28.00	1.00	2.00	3.00	2.00	1.00	4.00	3.00

FIGURE 5.7. *Value Labels Button Off and Numbers Displayed.*

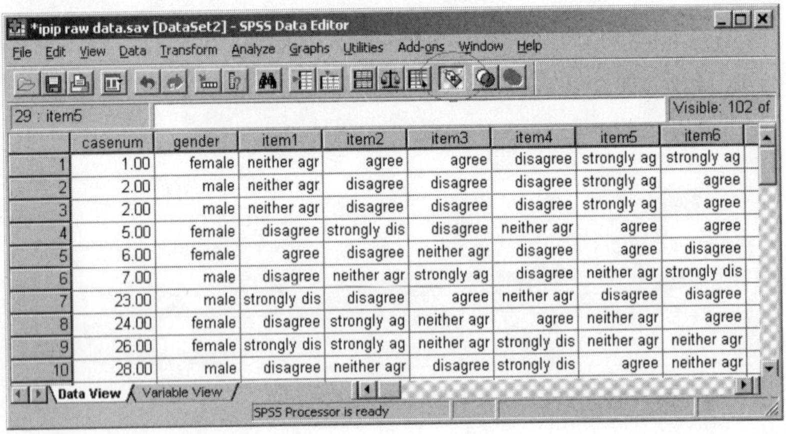

	casenum	gender	item1	item2	item3	item4	item5	item6
1	1.00	female	neither agr	agree	agree	disagree	strongly ag	strongly ag
2	2.00	male	neither agr	disagree	disagree	disagree	strongly ag	agree
3	2.00	male	neither agr	disagree	disagree	disagree	strongly ag	agree
4	5.00	female	disagree	strongly dis	disagree	neither agr	agree	agree
5	6.00	female	agree	disagree	neither agr	disagree	agree	disagree
6	7.00	male	disagree	neither agr	strongly ag	disagree	neither agr	strongly dis
7	23.00	male	strongly dis	disagree	agree	neither agr	disagree	disagree
8	24.00	female	disagree	strongly ag	neither agr	agree	neither agr	agree
9	26.00	female	strongly dis	strongly ag	neither agr	strongly dis	neither agr	neither agr
10	28.00	male	disagree	neither agr	disagree	strongly dis	agree	neither agr

FIGURE 5.8. *Value Labels Button On and Labels Displayed.*

I like to indent with a tab when I add my value labels. This seems to keep my diary a bit more tidy-looking. You don't need to, but I recommend that you do this also. Notice that you don't use a period (.) until you have exhausted all possible responses.

If you run this syntax and decide to take a look at your data file, you'll then have the option of two views—one that displays the numbers you entered and one that displays the labels that you've defined. You can toggle back and forth between these two views by clicking the Value

Labels button (it looks like a price tag) in the SPSS Data Editor—just remember to be careful about altering any of the data in your data file. Figure 5.7 shows the Value Labels button off and numbers displayed.

Figure 5.8 shows the Value Labels button on and labels displayed.

Appendix C presents a step-by-step process for creating an empty data file and defining your variables (giving them descriptive labels). After your data file creation syntax looks like the syntax in Figure 5.6, you can save the outfile (the empty but variable-defined data file) and start entering data (if it's in hardcopy format).

SUMMARY

All variables within your data files should be labeled as specifically as possible. Although we keep SPSS variable names short, we can be more descriptive by using the "var labels" command. When we have categorical (or ordinal) data that is represented by numbers (which is common), it is generally a good idea to use labels for the numbers. If you want to view the labels, you can click the Value Labels button within the data file (although you don't want to spend too much time in the data or .sav file environment).

KEY TERMS

"Add value labels" SPSS command that describes your coding scheme for possible values on categorical variables (for example, does "1" represent male and "2" represent female or vice versa?).

Value Labels button SPSS function allowing you to view category labels within the data file itself.

"Var labels" SPSS command used to give your variables more descriptive definitions (more descriptive than the eight-character variable name).

DISCUSSION QUESTIONS

1. If my variable names are self-explanatory, do I still need to give them labels?

2. Does the coding scheme make a difference if I add value labels?

CHAPTER

6

MANIPULATING
YOUR DATA

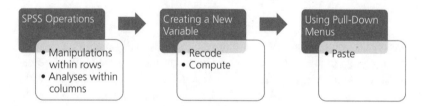

SPSS Operations	Creating a New Variable	Using Pull-Down Menus
• Manipulations within rows • Analyses within columns	• Recode • Compute	• Paste

FIGURE 6.1. *Changing and Manipulating Data.*

Contents

CHAPTER LEARNING OBJECTIVES

1. Recoding variables

2. Creating new variables

3. Using the pull-down menu function with syntax

4. Running the entire syntax file at once with Ctrl+A

5. Peeking at your data file without accessing it

SPSS the *statistical analyst* tends to "prefer" columns to rows. For instance, descriptive statistics (like *means* and *standard deviations*) are reported within columns (collapsing data down rows within the asked-for column). If you request these means and standard deviations for a particular column variable, an output (.spo) file will be created to summarize your request. If you wish to generate means (or standard deviations, or both) *across columns* (for instance, creating a mean score for each individual in your data set), SPSS does this by creating new variables in your data file. The program will not report these means and standard deviations in an output file—it will just place them at the end of your data file.

I don't think SPSS is particularly biased against rows; the program just "thinks" that manipulations done within a column are important enough to report, whereas manipulations done across columns are generally done for further data analysis purposes. It is appropriate for the program to think this way, in part because your data files generally contain many more rows (people) than they do variables (columns). Reporting statistics for each row in an output file would generally overcrowd your output file with needless information.

It will help your understanding of this tendency if you conceptualize SPSS as having two main purposes: (1) as a data analyst—creating summary information (in output files) based on column information—and (2) as a data organizer (creating or changing the data you have in your data file). The main focus of this book, remember, is on the second SPSS purpose—where you will find yourself spending the most time.

Although the data analyst of SPSS thinks within columns, the data organizer of SPSS most commonly thinks within rows.

CREATING SCALE SCORES

One of the most common situations in which you will ask SPSS to think *across* columns is in the creation of a summary score. In psychology, we commonly refer to such a summary score as a *scale score*. For example, psychological constructs (such as the personality trait of *extraversion*) are abstract entities. A common technique of psychological measurement is to consider that extraversion drives responses to many different queries. Personality assessments, therefore, typically ask many extraversion-related questions, even though psychologists are mostly interested in your general standing on the extraversion—introversion continuum.

If you look at the assessment in Appendix A, for example, there are one hundred items, but these measure only five different things of immediate interest to the researcher—extraversion is one of the five. The extraversion scale is an aggregate of twenty individual items.

So if the researcher is interested in an aggregate or summary score instead of twenty or one hundred individual scores, the researcher must create that summary score. To do this in SPSS, you will use two very common commands: "compute" and "recode."

Recoding Your Data

If you look at the twenty items that make up the extraversion scale in Appendix A (items 1, 6, 11, 16, 21, 26, and so on), you will notice that not all twenty measure extraversion—some measure introversion. For example, an extrovert would give a high (Strongly Agree) response to item 1, but an introvert would give a high (Strongly Agree) response to item 6. Before I generate aggregate scores for the extraversion scale (or *any* scale, for that matter), I need to decide whether high scores (higher numbers) should be indicative of introverts or extraverts. The convention in personality assessment is to give the extraverts the higher scores.

Every time an aggregate score is created, you need to first consider whether any scale component (the items themselves) needs "recoding." Because we are starting to fiddle with our data (that is, not just defining the data file), it's time to create a new syntax file, as shown in Figures 6.2 and 6.3.

Specify your data file
get file = 'filename.sav'.
Recode any necessary variables
recode varname (old value x = new value y).
Indicate you are done recoding
execute.

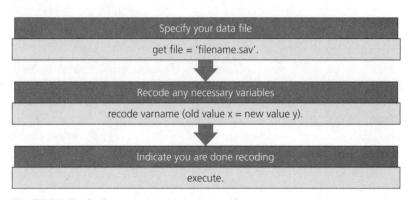

FIGURE 6.2. *Recoding Variables.*

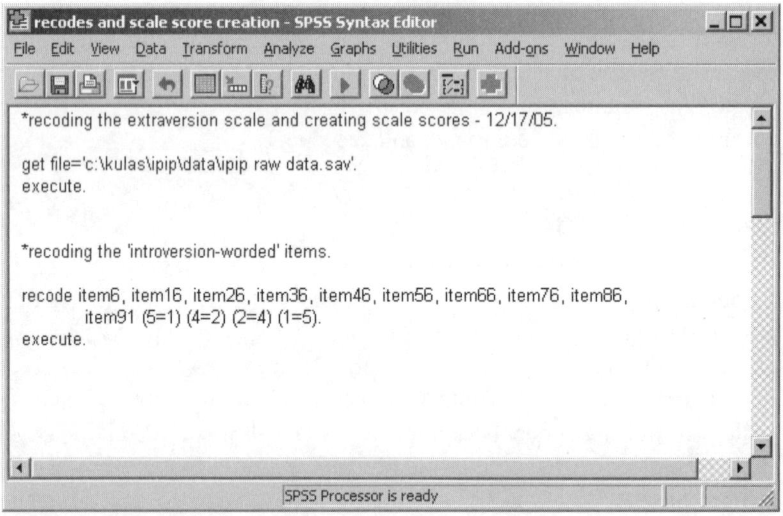

recodes and scale score creation - SPSS Syntax Editor
File Edit View Data Transform Analyze Graphs Utilities Run Add-ons Window Help
*recoding the extraversion scale and creating scale scores - 12/17/05.
get file='c:\kulas\ipip\data\ipip raw data.sav'.
execute.
*recoding the 'introversion-worded' items.
recode item6, item16, item26, item36, item46, item56, item66, item76, item86,
item91 (5=1) (4=2) (2=4) (1=5).
execute.
SPSS Processor is ready

FIGURE 6.3. *Recoding the Introversion Items.*

In the syntax statement shown in Figure 6.3, ten items that were identified as assessing the introversion side of the extraversion continuum
were "reverse scored." For example, a response of "5/Strongly Agree"
to item 6 (Often feel uncomfortable around others) was changed to a
response of 1/Strongly Disagree. A response of 4 (Agree) was changed
to a 2 (Disagree), and disagreement responses (1 and 2) were also
changed for all ten identified items. The original values for these item
responses are identified in the coding sheet (Appendix B).

Creating Your Scales

To create the one summary extraversion score for each respondent,
you'll need to make another decision: what type of summary do you
want? Typically you'll choose from either a sum or a mean. I usually
choose mean scores because: (1) they're not as influenced by missing
data, and (2) they're in the same metric as the scale components
(the items). To *create* a mean score, I'm going to specify the name of the
variable I'm creating (once again, eight characters or fewer, but descriptive as demonstrated in Figure 6.4).

As shown in Figure 6.5, I'll call the new variable "extra." After
choosing a name, I specify which of the 102 variables in my data set
should contribute to the new variable (here every fifth item, starting
with item 1).

The "eq" in "compute extra eq" is a shorthand notation for "="; I
could have written "compute extra = mean.15(item1, item6 . . .)." I use

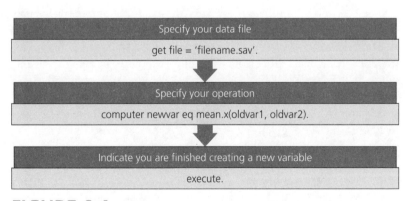

FIGURE 6.4. *Creating New Variables.*

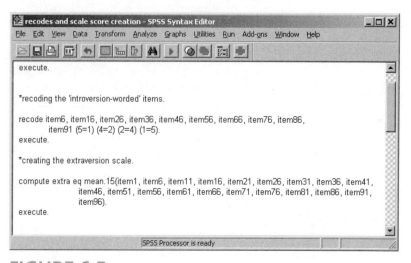

FIGURE 6.5. *Introversion Records and Item Extraversion.*

the "eq" notation because it is consistent with these other data manipulation options:

- "lt" (less than)

- "gt" (greater than)

- "le" (less than or equal to)

- "ge" (greater than or equal to)

These different commands are very useful; for example, in median/ tertile/quartile split applications (a tertile split is done in Chapter Nine).

The ".15" after the mean statement tells SPSS to do the computation if there are at least fifteen non-missing responses across the twenty items. If the ".xx" wasn't specified after the "mean" command, SPSS would compute a mean even if there were only one response across the twenty items. The ".xx" addition allows you to control how many valid responses must be given—I typically require at least 75 percent of item responses, although this convention is rather arbitrary.

Also, it is important to know that parentheses organize your commands for compute statements. The innermost parenthetical command will be initiated first. I could compute the scale score as shown in Figure 6.6. However, typically I do not do this, because if someone has

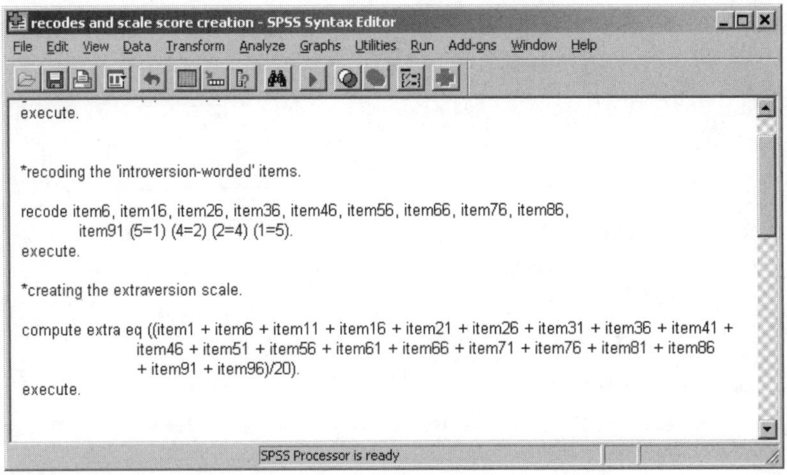

FIGURE 6.6. *Extraversion Scale Score Creation (Formula Method).*

not responded to item26, for example, the respondent's score will still be divided by twenty. Using the "mean" command, SPSS would more appropriately divide that person's total by nineteen.

LEARNING THE COMMAND LANGUAGE

Some commands (such as "compute") are used so frequently that you will soon become skilled at writing the commands directly into your syntax file. There is another option, however: SPSS will generate syntax for you. To do the preceding transformations (recode and compute), I can have SPSS generate the commands by choosing Transform>Recode on the SPSS toolbar available in my syntax file. (Even using this method, I'm still working within the Syntax Editor window, not the Data Editor. Think of the Data Editor as a hot potato: just keep away from it.)

If I choose Transform>Recode, it gives me two options: (1) I can recode my original variable (change my data as circled in Figure 6.7), or (2) I can leave my original variable alone and create a new, recoded variable. More on this later—for now we'll choose the first option (recoding into same variable). Upon choosing this option, you'll get a pop-up like the one in Figure 6.8. You use this by choosing the appropriate variables from the left-hand column and placing them into the right-hand box.

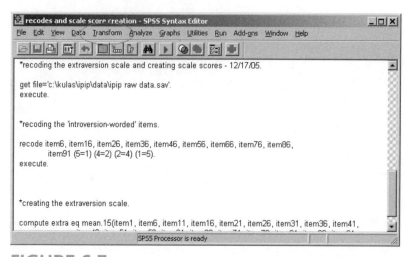

FIGURE 6.7. *Tool for Pull-Down Option for Variable Recodes.*

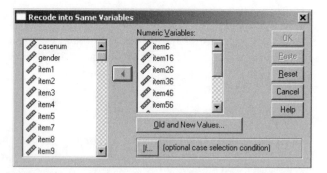

FIGURE 6.8. *Wizard for Recoding Variables.*

You then choose the "Old and New Values . . ." option and specify your old and new values, as shown in Figure 6.9.

Choosing Continue and Paste generates the syntax shown in Figure 6.10.

This is the same syntax we wrote by hand earlier, just organized (and capitalized) a little differently. The reason this looks a little different is because SPSS wrote the syntax, not you. You have the option of having SPSS generate syntax for most transformations you want to do—unfortunately, I think it's more confusing to do this than it is to simply type the syntax directly into your syntax diary. That's why we're spending so

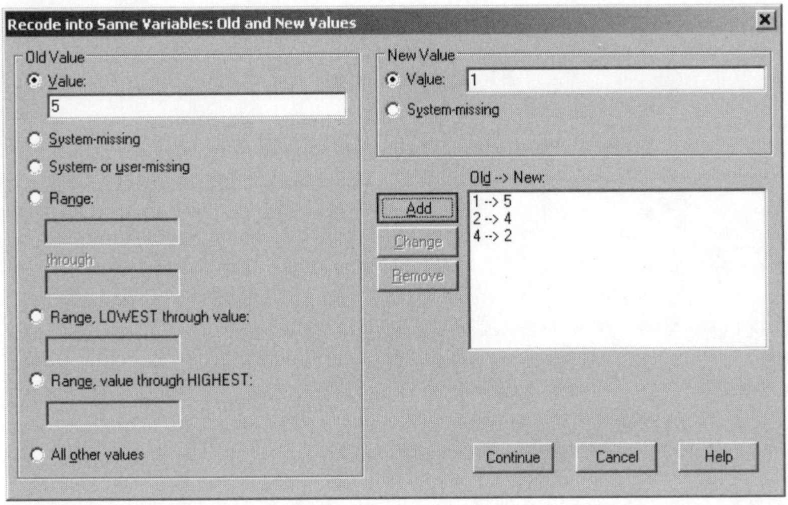

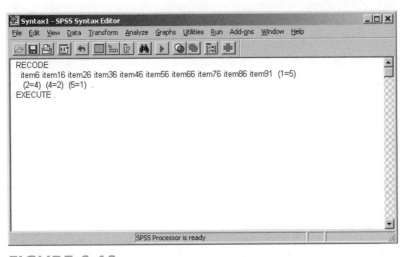

FIGURE 6.9. *Specified Within the Wizard.*

```
RECODE
  item6 item16 item26 item36 item46 item56 item66 item76 item86 item91  (1=5)
  (2=4) (4=2) (5=1) .
EXECUTE .
```

FIGURE 6.10. *Wizard-Generated Recode Syntax.*

much time on common commands in this book. If you follow the rest of this book, you'll be able to generate syntax directly for the majority of your transformations.

The recode and compute commands can be used in many different applications. For instance, if for some reason I wanted to characterize

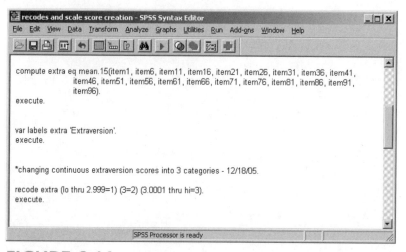

FIGURE 6.11. *Categorizing the Extraversion Scale Score.*

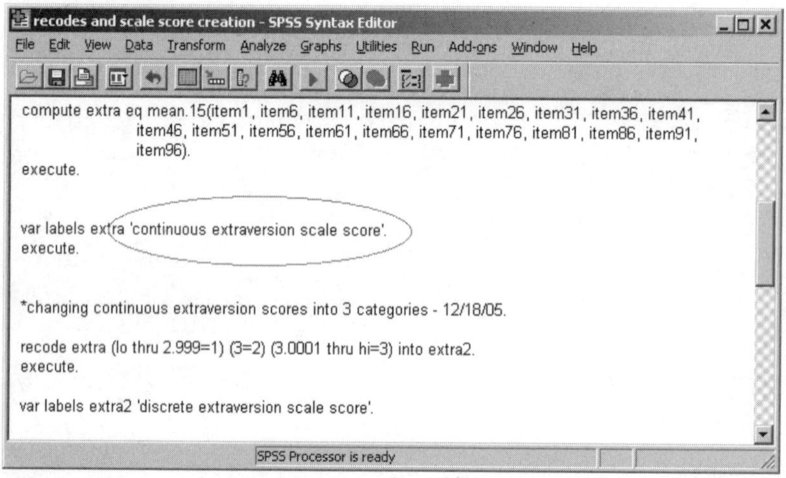

FIGURE 6.12. *Creating a New Variable Using the Recode Command.*

people as either introverted, extraverted, or firmly on the fence, I could first compute a scale score for each person, then use the recode command on the new scale score to put individuals into one of three categories. First I give a variable name to my scale score, as shown in Figure 6.11.

Now my scale score "extra" will possess only three values, unless someone scores a 2.9995 or 3.000001—which is not very likely (actually, it's impossible with only twenty items contributing to the scale score). If I wanted to maintain my original continuous extraversion score as well as having this new way of looking at extraversion, I could compute a new variable by using the "into" command with recode. If I do this, it's necessary to relabel my first extraversion scale score, as shown in Figure 6.12.

THE IMPORTANCE OF SELECTING ALL

Regardless of whether I turn my original scale score into three categories or create a new scale score while maintaining my original continuous scale, it's important that when I activate my syntax, *I do it all at once*. If you get into the habit of using your "get file" and "save outfile" commands, you can run all of your syntax at one time (Ctrl-A and Run) instead of running your commands step by step. Get into the habit of organizing your diaries by "get file" and "save outfile" commands, so you are able to run the entire syntax at one time.

This is important because if you run syntax one command at a time, it is easy to mess up your data. This really isn't a huge deal as long as you do not save what you have done, but it can cause unnecessary head-scratching. Let's take a look at what could have happened to my data if I had run the syntax command-by-command:

First I get my data file, as shown in Figure 6.13.

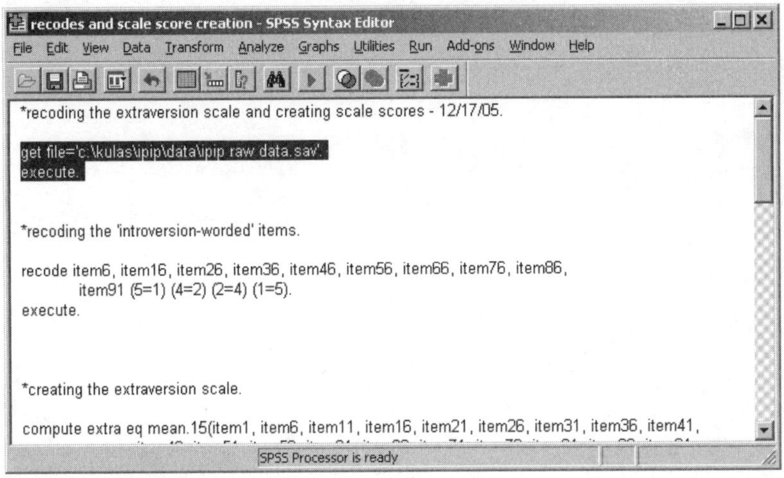

FIGURE 6.13. *One Command at a Time (Get File).*

Next I recode my identified items, as shown in Figure 6.14.

So far, so good; then I create my extraversion scale, as shown in Figure 6.15.

Still good—the problem now arises with the "change" that we made when we decided to keep the first extraversion scale score continuous and to make a second, discrete extraversion scale score. Figure 6.16

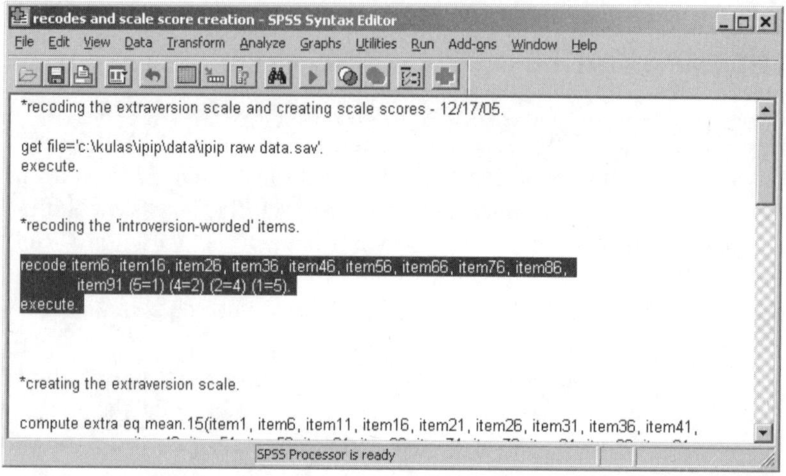

FIGURE 6.14. *One Command at a Time (Recode).*

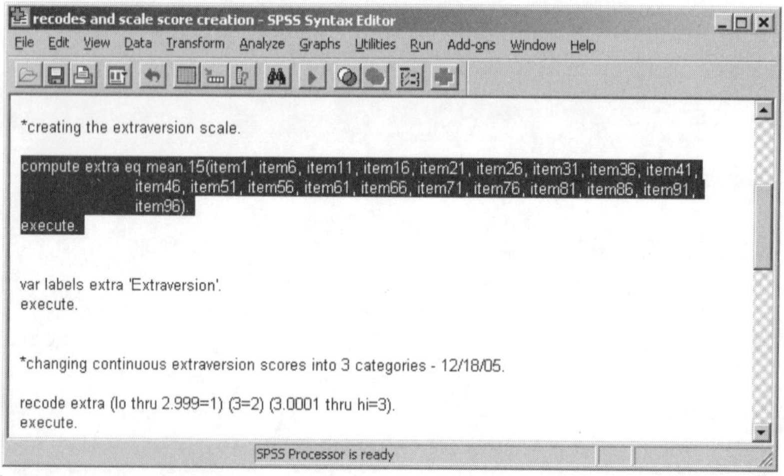

FIGURE 6.15. *One Command at a Time (Scale Score).*

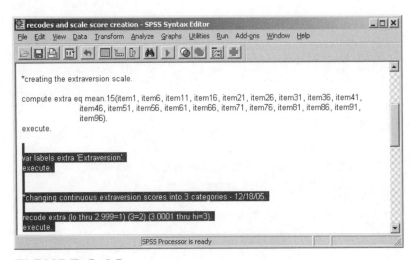

FIGURE 6.16. *One Command at a Time (Categorizing Extraversion).*

shows the next step we would have taken if we were choosing syntax command-by-command.

Now the decision to make a new variable becomes an issue, because we've already changed the "extra" variable. So what if I now change my mind (decide to create two variables) and run the new command, as shown in Figure 6.17?

I've made a huge mistake (once again, not really a problem as long as you don't go into your Data Editor and "save" the new data). Here's what happened in this situation—I recoded an already recoded variable. This wouldn't have been an issue if my initial recodes had been: '(lo thru 2.999 = 1) (3 = 3) (3.0001 thru hi = 4)'. Can you see where the error occurred now? My first recode said, in effect "have fence-sitters be identified by a score of '2.'" My second recode said "someone with a score of '2' must be an introvert."

Here's what the mistake did to my data—first, as shown in Figure 6.18, a screenshot of what the data should look like with two scale scores (when I run all of my syntax at one time).

Now Figure 6.19 shows the data if I ran each command separately. You should note that the "extra" column in the dataset is actually categorized correctly (i.e., it is the same as extra2 in Figure 6.18), but the "extra2" column is now incorrect—this is because, when choosing our transformations command-by-command, we "recoded" a recode. Not good.

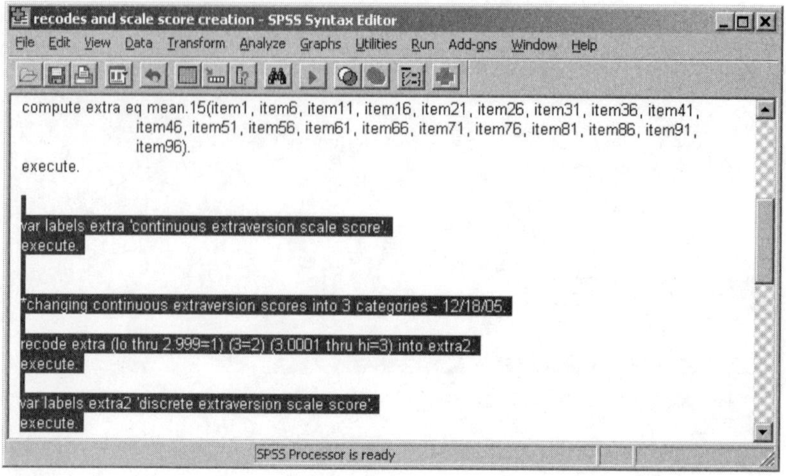

recodes and scale score creation - SPSS Syntax Editor

File Edit View Data Transform Analyze Graphs Utilities Run Add-ons Window Help

```
compute extra eq mean.15(item1, item6, item11, item16, item21, item26, item31, item36, item41,
         item46, item51, item56, item61, item66, item71, item76, item81, item86, item91,
         item96).
execute.


var labels extra 'continuous extraversion scale score'.
execute.


*changing continuous extraversion scores into 3 categories - 12/18/05.

recode extra (lo thru 2.999=1) (3=2) (3.0001 thru hi=3) into extra2.
execute.

var labels extra2 'discrete extraversion scale score'.
execute.
```

SPSS Processor is ready

FIGURE 6.17. *One Command at a Time (New Variable Through Recode Command).*

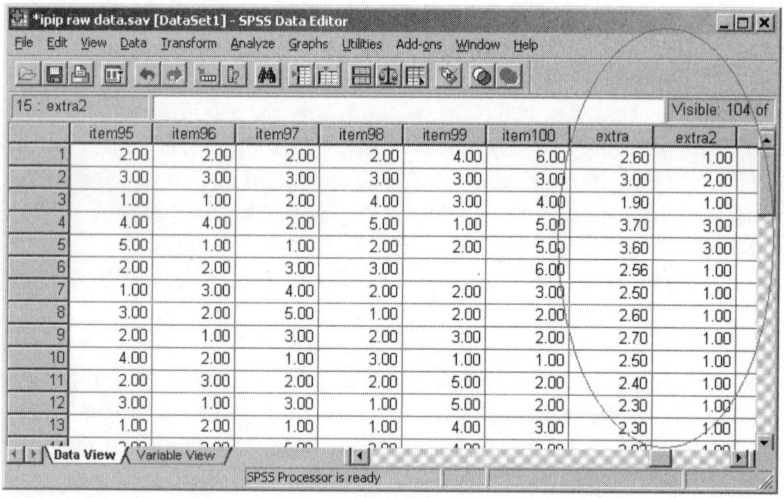

*ipip raw data.sav [DataSet1] - SPSS Data Editor

File Edit View Data Transform Analyze Graphs Utilities Add-ons Window Help

15 : extra2   Visible: 104 of

	item95	item96	item97	item98	item99	item100	extra	extra2
1	2.00	2.00	2.00	2.00	4.00	6.00	2.60	1.00
2	3.00	3.00	3.00	3.00	3.00	3.00	3.00	2.00
3	1.00	1.00	2.00	4.00	3.00	4.00	1.90	1.00
4	4.00	4.00	2.00	5.00	1.00	5.00	3.70	3.00
5	5.00	1.00	1.00	2.00	2.00	5.00	3.60	3.00
6	2.00	2.00	3.00	3.00		6.00	2.56	1.00
7	1.00	3.00	4.00	2.00	2.00	3.00	2.50	1.00
8	3.00	2.00	5.00	1.00	2.00	2.00	2.60	1.00
9	2.00	1.00	3.00	2.00	3.00	2.00	2.70	1.00
10	4.00	2.00	1.00	3.00	1.00	1.00	2.50	1.00
11	2.00	3.00	2.00	2.00	5.00	2.00	2.40	1.00
12	3.00	1.00	3.00	1.00	5.00	2.00	2.30	1.00
13	1.00	2.00	1.00	1.00	4.00	3.00	2.30	1.00

Data View / Variable View

SPSS Processor is ready

FIGURE 6.18. *Correct Data Manipulations.*

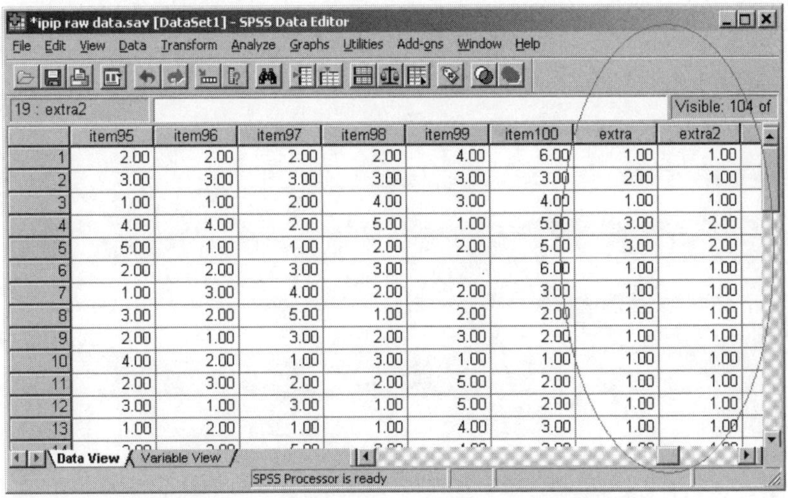

FIGURE 6.19. *Incorrect Data Manipulations.*

Figure 6.20 demonstrates the proper way to construct a syntax file such that the entire file can be selected and run "at once" instead of command-by-command.

Remember that SPSS always does syntax operations in the order that you specify (starts at the top and goes to the bottom). The take-away message from all of this is that you should use "get file" and "save outfile" and get in the habit of running the entire syntax file at once. You should construct your files with this in mind: "I'm going to run everything all at once."

USING THE VARIABLES TOOL

One of the most useful options available to the syntax-user is the Variables tool. The Variables button on the syntax toolbar has a question mark next to a column of data (see Figure 6.21). This feature allows you to keep track of what your data file looks like without actually looking at the data file itself. Think of it as a peephole into forbidden territory.

If you click the Variables button, a pop-up box will open; it lists all of the variables that are in your data file, presented in the order of the variable columns. For example, to ensure that our scale score has been

How all of your syntax files should be structured:
Annotate the top of the file
*outline the plan of analyses.
Specify your data file
getfile = 'filename.sav'.
Specify manipulations/analyses (in proper order)
recode varname
compute newvar
Save new data file
save outfile = 'newfilename.sav'.

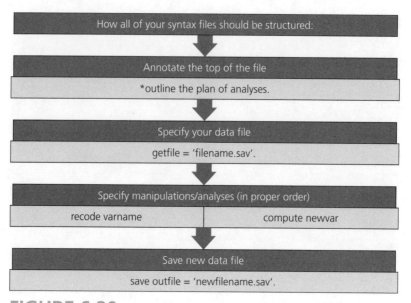

FIGURE 6.20. *Necessary Structure of All Syntax Files.*

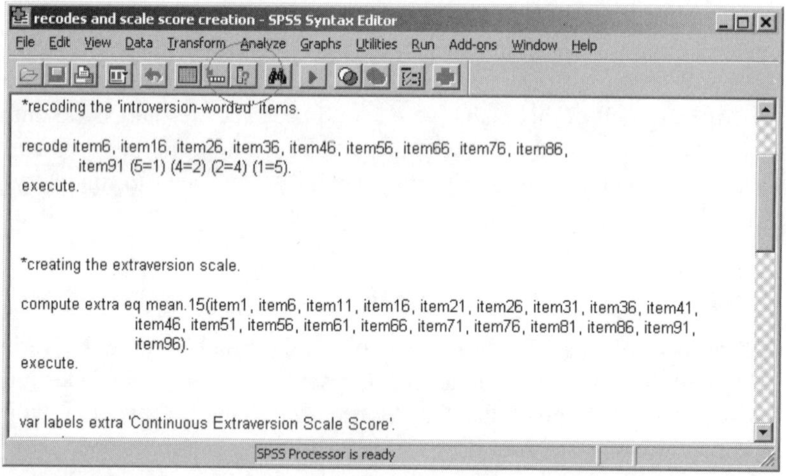

recodes and scale score creation - SPSS Syntax Editor
File Edit View Data Transform Analyze Graphs Utilities Run Add-ons Window Help
*recoding the 'introversion-worded' items.
recode item6, item16, item26, item36, item46, item56, item66, item76, item86,
item91 (5=1) (4=2) (2=4) (1=5).
execute.
*creating the extraversion scale.
compute extra eq mean.15(item1, item6, item11, item16, item21, item26, item31, item36, item41,
item46, item51, item56, item61, item66, item71, item76, item81, item86, item91,
item96).
execute.
var labels extra 'Continuous Extraversion Scale Score'.
SPSS Processor is ready

FIGURE 6.21. *Variables Button Identified Within the Syntax File.*

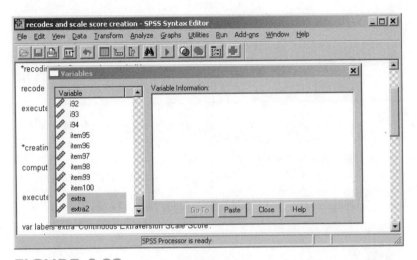

FIGURE 6.22. *Variable View Using the Variables "Question Mark" Button.*

computed successfully, you can click the Variables button and see for yourself. The newly created variables appear at the bottom of the list, because new variables are added at the end—to the far right—of your data file, as shown in Figure 6.22.

You will use the Variables button frequently if you work in the syntax environment.

SUMMARY

The data currently residing in a data file is usually not entirely sufficient for our purposes—we generally need to create new variables. To do this, we sometimes need to first recode the existing data. Both of these basic manipulations can be done directly through syntax or by using the drop-down menus (although we still paste the command into the syntax diary). It is important to construct our syntax files such that they can be run in their entirety. The commands located at the top of the syntax file are activated first. If I want to take a look at my data file, I can do so by using the Variables button on the Syntax Editor toolbar.

KEY TERMS

"Compute" SPSS command used to create a new variable.

Eq SPSS shorthand for "equals."

Ge SPSS shorthand for "greater than or equal to."

Gt SPSS shorthand for "greater than."

Le SPSS shorthand for "less than or equal to."

Lt SPSS shorthand for "less than."

Mean Statistical average.

Paste Option that allows you to activate the operation from syntax when using drop-down menus.

"Recode" SPSS command used to change the entered values of variables.

Scale scores New variables that are defined by two or more existing variables.

Standard deviation Average distance from mean within a set of numbers.

Variables tool Allows you to peek into your data file without directly accessing it.

.xx Specification to be made when computing a new variable; this defines how many original values must be present to create a new summary variable.

DISCUSSION QUESTIONS

1. Is it ever advisable to *not* run the entire syntax at once?

2. If I'm going to use pull-down menus, why don't I just skip the "paste" part?

CHAPTER

COLLAPSING AND MERGING DATA FILES

FIGURE 7.1. *Adding Additional Variables or People to a Data File.*

Contents

CHAPTER LEARNING OBJECTIVES

1.   Combining data files: same people, different variables

2.   Combining data files: different people, same variables

This chapter is something of an advanced course in the use of the "get file" and "save outfile" commands. Here you will learn more about controlling the constituency of your data files. There are two primary reasons you would use the information in this chapter: (1) you have two or more data files with *different information* from the *same individuals*, or (2) you have two or more data files with *similar information* from *different individuals*. In both scenarios you ultimately want to get the files together.

The first situation is exemplified (in my field, for example) by one data file that contains applicant characteristics (typically applicants' scores on selection assessments) and another data file that contains job performance information (collected at a later time from those same applicants, now actual employees). Eventually you'll need to combine these two files if you want to do anything meaningful with the information.

The second situation is exemplified by students whom I recruit to work with me. Any given semester, multiple research assistants provide primarily data entry services. When there are multiple individuals entering data from a stack of, for example, two hundred or more questionnaires (such as the questionnaire in Appendix A), there are several data entry approaches you can take. One is to have students take turns entering information into one master data file. That's not very efficient—so what I typically do is define multiple duplicate empty data files (one for each student), give each student a stack of questionnaires (and an empty but variable-defined data file), and then when they're done with their data entry, I combine all of the files (with *similar information* from *different experimental participants*) into one master data file.

SAME PEOPLE, DIFFERENT INFORMATION

Using our personality questionnaire example, as part of an experiment, I could have my research assistants, while they are administering the questionnaire to participants, guess which of the five measured personality traits is most dominant for each individual who fills out the hundred-item questionnaire.

This scenario would require not only that the study participants complete the questionnaire, but also that my research assistants record two pieces of information: the "casenum" of the individual they are rating, and the trait they believe is most likely to be dominant (Agreeableness, Neuroticism, Extraversion, Openness to Experience, or Conscientiousness). (Appendix D contains another example of a situation in which you would want to combine files with similar people but different variables.)

For these two different sources (research assistants and questionnaire participants) I would construct two different data files. The first data file we've already constructed (one hundred personality items, one casenum, and one gender variable). The second data file contains three pieces of information (casenum, rated dimension, and research assistant who provided the rating). As shown in Figure 7.2, I entered this information as numbers, rather than string variables—the value labels are showing in my data file because I've clicked the Value Labels button (introduced in Chapter Five).

Now, to combine the two data files, I need to know just two things: (1) the names of the data files I want to combine and (2) the variable that identifies individuals in both files (in this situation, casenum).

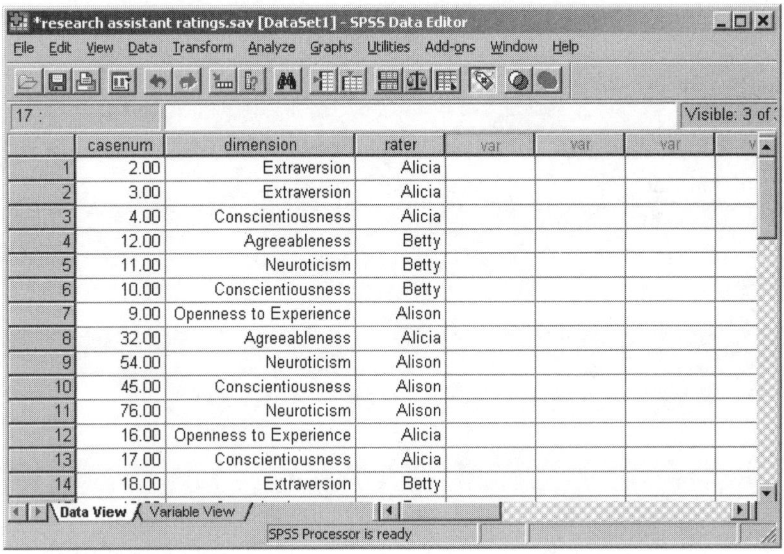

FIGURE 7.2. *Research Assistants' Ratings.*

There is one important requirement when you combine two files with different variables but the same people: you must rearrange your data so the values of your "matching" variables are numbered consecutively in both files. (You can also match files based on shared string variables, but just as with numerics, you must first organize the string variables alphabetically in both files.) This is accomplished quite easily, but it will require a few extra syntax lines, as shown in Figures 7.3 and 7.4.

The example shown accesses my original data file and rearranges the data so the smallest casenum is the first row in the file and the largest casenum is the last row in the file. The other option, with the "sort cases by" command, is to specify a "d" instead of the "a." "D" stands for descending, "a" represents ascending. It doesn't really matter which I choose, as long as I am consistent (if I pick ascending for one data file, I have to do so for the other as well). Next I access the file I want to combine with my original data file, then I combine the two files and save the new data file (this saved file contains unique information from both files), as shown in Figures 7.5, 7.6, and 7.7.

The illustrated command specifications indicate that I want to match a file to the open file (that's what the asterisk represents in the "match files" command line—* here means whichever data file is open). The second line identifies the file I want to combine—this file's variables

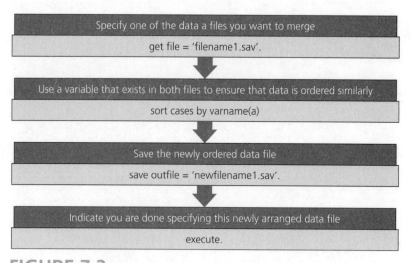

FIGURE 7.3. *Rearranging Data so Matching Variable Values Are Numbered Consecutively.*

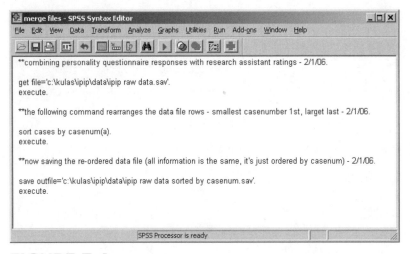

FIGURE 7.4. *Prepping a data File to be matched.*

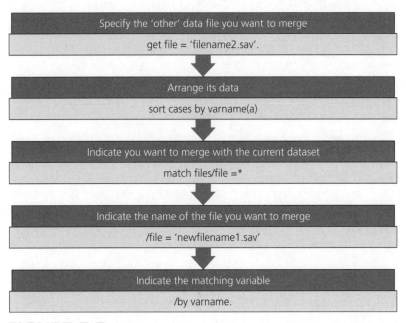

FIGURE 7.5. *Rearranging Data so Values Match the Order of the Matching File.*

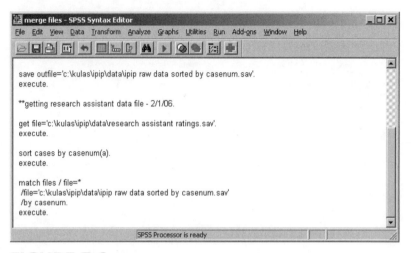

FIGURE 7.6. *Merging the Data Files.*

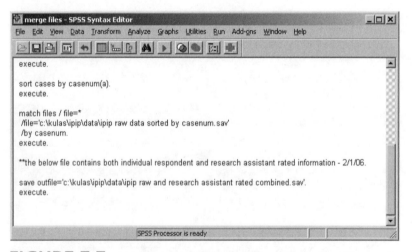

FIGURE 7.7. *Saving the Newly Merged Data File.*

will be added at the end of my open data file (that is, they'll be put to the right of the open file's variables). The third line identifies the variable you want to "match"—this is the person identifier. Notice that no period (.) is used until the third line.

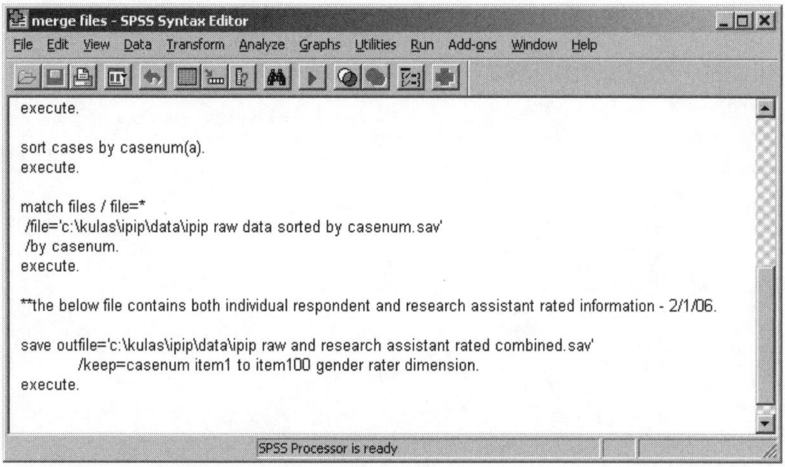

FIGURE 7.8. *Merged Data File with Variable Ordering Rearranged.*

If I wanted my information arranged differently in my new data file, I could either switch the order of specification of the original files (this would put the two rater file variables at the end rather than the beginning of my new file) or use the "keep" subcommand on the "save outfile" statement to rearrange the order of my variables. As shown in Figure 7.8, I've taken the second approach and moved the "gender" variable more toward the end of the data file.

DIFFERENT PEOPLE, SAME INFORMATION

If you have identical data files with different people in them, you can use a similar procedure, although this time you don't have to first do a "sort cases by" command. In the case of multiple research assistants entering data into their own individual data files, I can first use the "save outfile" command at the end of my empty data file creation syntax to create three empty data files (one each for Alison, Alicia, and Betty). First, the data file variables are specified (Figure 7.9), and then the data shells are saved as three separate files (Figure 7.10).

Now I give the three empty (but variable-defined) data files to the three research assistants to work on while I am away for the weekend.

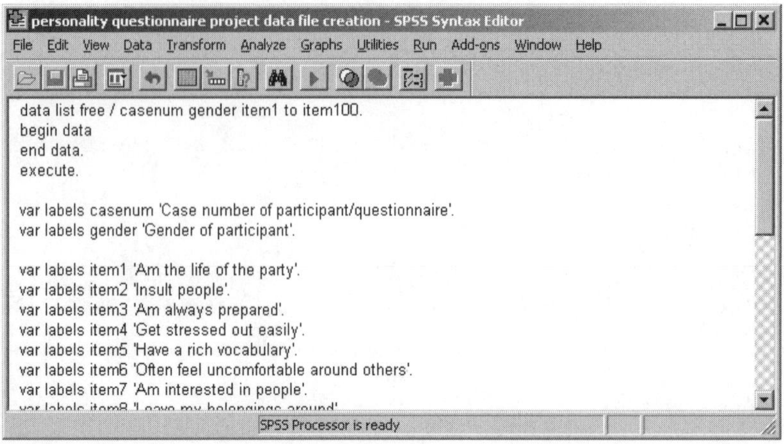

FIGURE 7.9. *Creating an Empty Data Shell.*

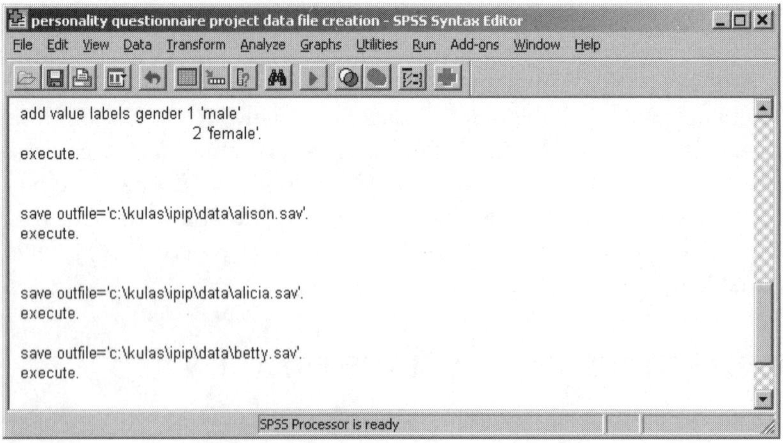

FIGURE 7.10. *Saving the Shell as Three Separate Data Files.*

When I return, I check my e-mail and save the files they've sent me to my "c:\kulas\ipip\data" folder. Then to merge the files together, I use the syntax shown in Figures 7.11 and 7.12.

You can actually specify multiple files to add with one "add files" syntax command, but I recommend doing a separate "add file" command for each file you want to add. At least do this until you're comfortable with

Specify a file you want to add data to

get file = 'filename1.sav'.

Add data to the above file

add files/file =*

Add data from the following file

/file = 'filename2.sav'.

Indicate you are finished adding data

execute.

FIGURE 7.11. *Flowchart to Add Rows to an Existing Data File.*

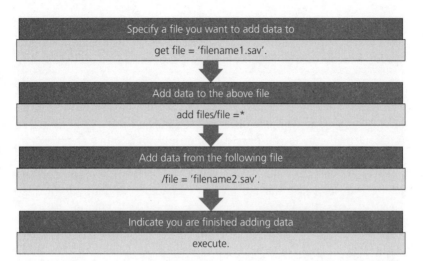

```
*Combining research assistant data files into one master datafile - 2/13/06.

get file='c:\kulas\ipip\data\alison.sav'.
execute.

*First adding Alicia's data to Alison's.

add files / file=*
/file='c:\kulas\ipip\data\alicia.sav'
/in=coder1.
execute.

*Next adding Betty's data to Alison's and Alicia's.

add files / file=*
/file='c:\kulas\ipip\data\betty.sav'
/in=coder2.
execute.
```

FIGURE 7.12. *Adding Cases from Three Research Assistants.*

the use of the command. The "in" variables that I specified (coder1 and coder2) are optional. These are the variables that identify who entered the data—Betty has values in the "coder2" variable column, Alicia has values in the "coder1" variable column, and Alison coded the rest of the rows in my merged data file. SPSS enters this information for you if you specify the "in" subcommand.

SUMMARY

When you need to combine different data files, you can use one of two different methods. If you have different information or variables from the same people, you need to sort both files first, then merge them together. If you have the same information or variables but different people, you can just add the files to each other without sorting first. Generally you'll want to save the new, combined file after the merge or add by using the "save outfile" command.

KEY TERMS

"Add files" SPSS command for combining files containing the same variables but different individuals.

"In" variables Variables created by SPSS to identify which original file is associated with each combined file case/row.

Match files SPSS command for combining files containing the same individuals but different variables.

"Matching" variables Organizing/identifying variables that exist in more than one data file.

"Sort cases by" SPSS command for reorganizing data sequentially.

DISCUSSION QUESTION

1. Why do I need to save a new data file instead of just merging or adding separate files each time I work on a project?

CHAPTER

DIFFERENTIAL TREATMENT OF YOUR DATA

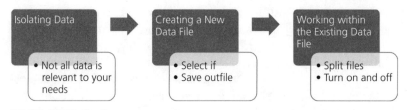

FIGURE 8.1. *Three Ways to Work with Subsets of Data.*

Contents

Summary

Key Terms

Discussion Questions

CHAPTER LEARNING OBJECTIVES

1. Isolating data: Creating new data files

2. Isolating data: Segregating output and analyses

Occasionally you'll want to separate "interesting" data from data that you, for whatever reason, find a bit less interesting. This chapter therefore focuses on manipulation requests that you can use to segregate your data.

ISOLATING INTERESTING CASES

Consider the following imaginary situation: A train leaves San Francisco for Pittsburgh at 8:00, carrying 150 women and 100 men and traveling at 100 miles per hour. Another train leaves Pittsburgh for San Francisco at 9:30 (also going really fast). What's the likelihood of the Pittsburgh conductor getting a date from one of the 150 San Francisco women after the two trains collide?

OK, that's a stupid question—we don't even know if the conductor survived the crash—but it raises a point: to answer the question about the likelihood of a date, we'd have to isolate information about the 150 San Francisco women from information about other passengers. We don't really care about information from other people in this situation.

Taking this scenario as a case study for the chapter, we will demonstrate how to isolate females from a general population. There are a few different options that enable this—I could create a separate data file with only women in it, or I could work within the existing data file but somehow identify that particular pieces of data are associated with men or women. Let's look at the first option.

Creating a New Data File

As shown in Figure 8.1, this option primarily utilizes commands that you're already familiar with—"get file" and "save outfile". Additionally, we need a "select if" command, as shown in Figures 8.2 and 8.3.

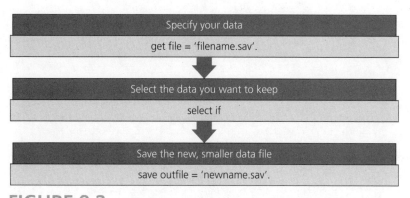

Specify your data
get file = 'filename.sav'.

Select the data you want to keep
select if

Save the new, smaller data file
save outfile = 'newname.sav'.

FIGURE 8.2. *Specifying and Selecting Data and Saving the New Data File.*

```
isolating women - SPSS Syntax Editor                              _ □ ×
File  Edit  View  Data  Transform  Analyze  Graphs  Utilities  Run  Add-ons  Window  Help

*creating a new file with only female respondents - 8/17/06.

get file='c:\kulas\train\data\train raw data.sav'.
execute.

*below I take the variable name and value associated with females from my code sheet (Appendix B).

select if gender eq 2.
execute.

*next I save the file that now only contains women - ooh la la.

save outfile='c:\kulas\train\data\train female passengers.sav'.
execute.

                          SPSS Processor is ready
```

FIGURE 8.3. *Creating a New Data File that Only Contains Information from Women Passengers.*

You can get fairly intricate with the "select if" command, by specifying multiple conditions that must be met for cases to be identified and retained. Figure 8.4 is a screenshot of an example data file I've created to mirror the "two train" scenario (containing information from both male and female passengers).

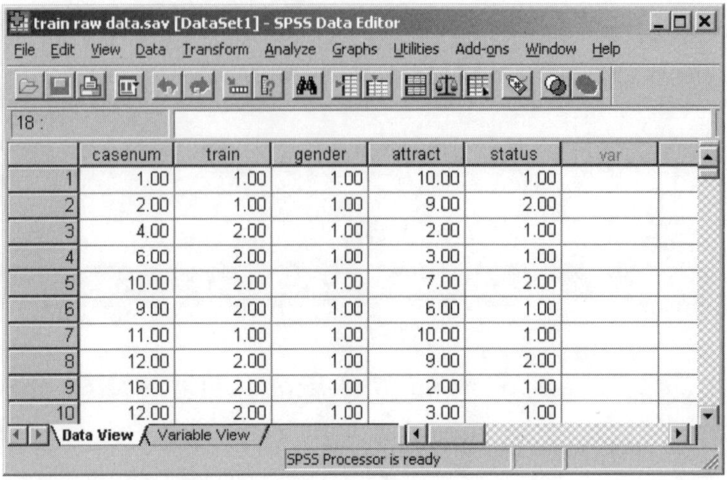

FIGURE 8.4. *Train Raw Data File.*

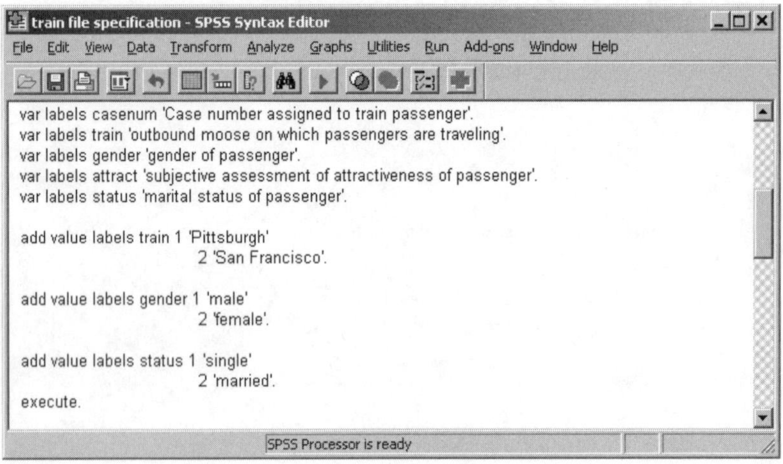

FIGURE 8.5. *Train File Specification.*

Notice that my variables are represented by numbers instead of words (they're numeric variables)—because of this, I would need a code sheet for this example, and I would incorporate that code sheet into my "var labels" and "add value labels" commands, as shown in Figure 8.5.

Usually I place an "execute" after every command (or batches of "var labels" commands). To save space, I've used only one "execute" (you can

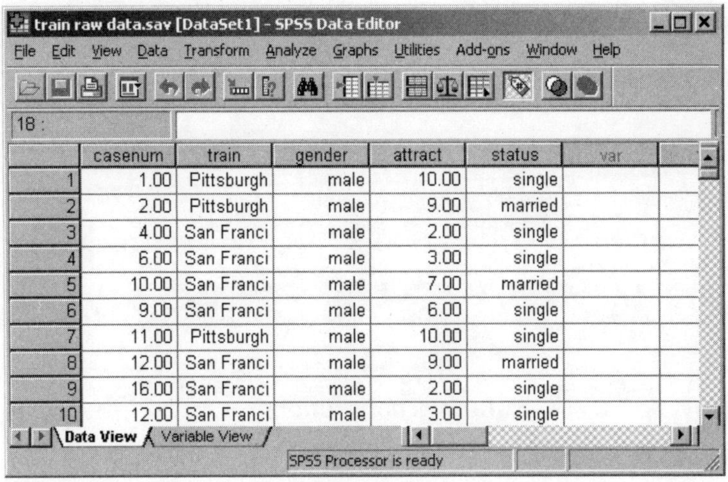

FIGURE 8.6. *Original Train Data File (Containing Both Male and Female Passengers).*

do this too, but it's not a good habit to develop). As shown in Figure 8.6, if I run the same syntax and revisit the original data file (with the Variable Labels button chosen), it looks a little more interpretable.

Now I can get a lot more selective with my data isolation—if I want only women from San Francisco who are single and not too attractive (we don't want the conductor to shoot too high and become discouraged about his dating prospects—especially after he just crashed his choo-choo), I can specify these multiple conditions with *one* select if command. It's important here to note that this command is not constrained just to conditions that are equal (eq) to a particular value (that is, females). Sometimes you'll want to apply the "select if" command to a range of values, which you can do quite easily because the operations you specify with this command can be less than (lt), less than or equal to (le), equal to (eq), greater than or equal to (ge), or greater than (gt) whatever value you desire, as shown in Figures 8.7 and 8.8.

Splitting Files

Creating separate data files as we have just done means that your new files contain only information from whatever data you have decided is important. You therefore do not have *all* of your data contained in the same location. An alternative approach that accomplishes similar goals

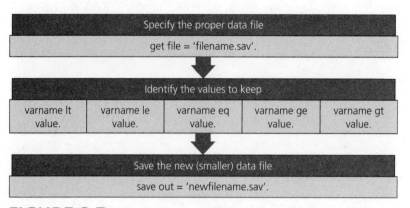

```
┌────────────────────────────────────────────────────────────────┐
│                    Specify the proper data file                  │
├────────────────────────────────────────────────────────────────┤
│                    get file = 'filename.sav'.                    │
└────────────────────────────────────────────────────────────────┘
```

```
┌────────────────────────────────────────────────────────────────┐
│                    Identify the values to keep                   │
├──────────────┬──────────────┬──────────────┬──────────┬─────────┤
│ varname lt   │ varname le   │ varname eq   │ varname  │ varname │
│   value.     │   value.     │   value.     │ ge value.│ gt value│
└──────────────┴──────────────┴──────────────┴──────────┴─────────┘
```

```
┌────────────────────────────────────────────────────────────────┐
│                 Save the new (smaller) data file                │
├────────────────────────────────────────────────────────────────┤
│                save out = 'newfilename.sav'.                     │
└────────────────────────────────────────────────────────────────┘
```

FIGURE 8.7. *Data Selection Options.*

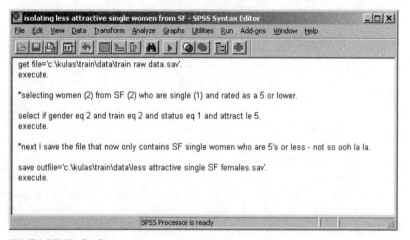

FIGURE 8.8. *Selecting a Specified Subgroup Within the Data File.*

is to simply let SPSS know that you're interested in separating your data. You do this through a "split file" command. I don't frequently use this command because it's what's known as a *light-switch command*— this means you turn it on and off. If you're one of those who forgets to turn off a burner when you're done cooking, don't use this command. If you do decide to use this command, remember to turn it off at the end of your syntax file.

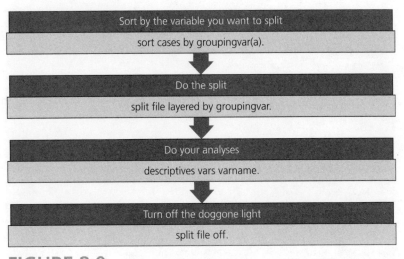

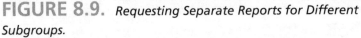

FIGURE 8.9. *Requesting Separate Reports for Different Subgroups.*

Splitting files is considered useful primarily because of what it does to your output (.spo) files. Really, all this command does is organize your analysis and output for you and make it easier to read—it performs analyses and organizes output by your split variable. Using the "two trains" example, if we want to know how attractive our female passengers are, we first need to sort our data (as discussed in Chapter Seven), then we use the "split file" command and request a rudimentary analysis (as we'll cover in Chapter Nine, such analyses are called *descriptives*— they give means, standard deviations, and so on). Examples of this general procedure are highlighted in Figures 8.9 and 8.10.

The output we receive (from the descriptives command) is computed separately for males and females, as shown in Figure 8.11.

Similarly to using the "select if" command, we can get fairly intricate with "split file" commands—it's important, however, that for every variable you want to split, you also first sort by that variable. If we want to isolate single women from San Francisco, we can do that, but if we do that through the "split file" command, we are also simultaneously isolating married women from San Francisco, single women from Pittsburgh, single men from Pittsburgh, married men from Pittsburgh—the point is, with "split file" you don't truly isolate, you just categorize (while retaining all possible categories). To get attractiveness ratings for

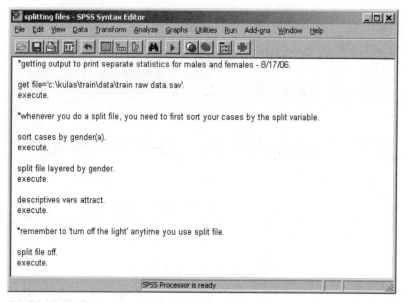

FIGURE 8.10. *Requesting Attractiveness Data Separated by Gender.*

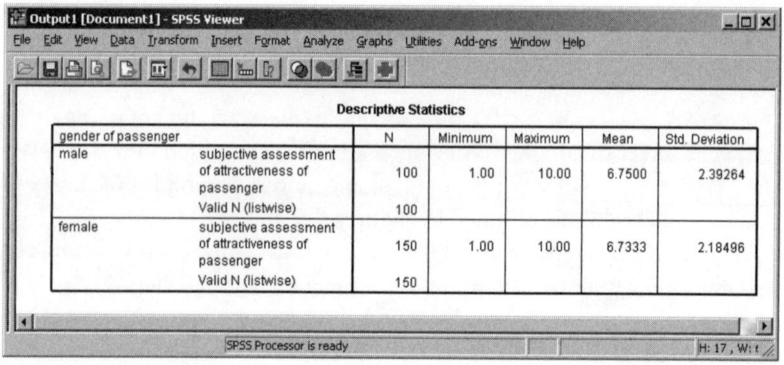

Descriptive Statistics

gender of passenger		N	Minimum	Maximum	Mean	Std. Deviation
male	subjective assessment of attractiveness of passenger	100	1.00	10.00	6.7500	2.39264
	Valid N (listwise)	100				
female	subjective assessment of attractiveness of passenger	150	1.00	10.00	6.7333	2.18496
	Valid N (listwise)	150				

FIGURE 8.11. *Descriptive Attractiveness Statistics for Males and Females.*

single women from Pittsburgh, I can use the following split file syntax shown in Figure 8.12 (which will also give me attractiveness ratings for all other possible combinations of Pittsburgh/San Francisco, married/ single, and male/female). Regardless of how many categories you use to split a file, you need only one "split file off" command. The "split file off" command is your "off" position for the light-switch.

Figure 8.13 shows what your output request (frequencies) looks like for this particular split file.

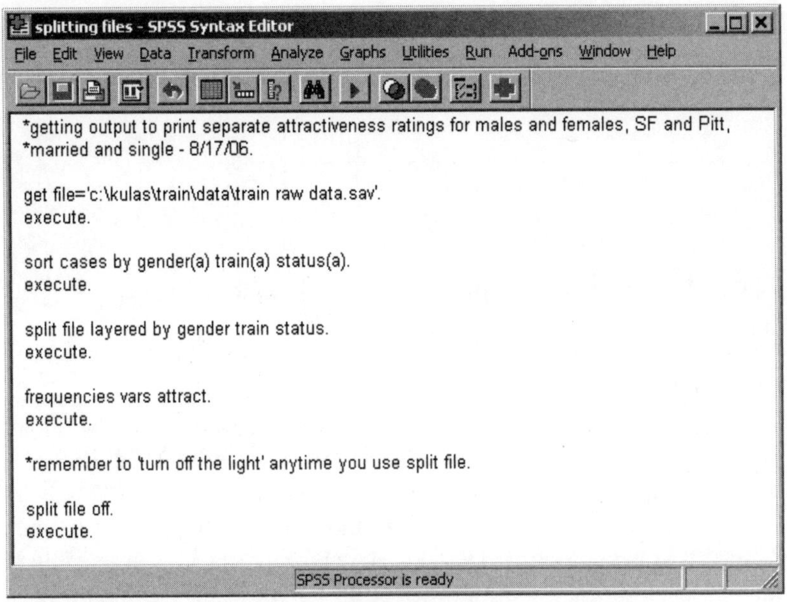

FIGURE 8.12. *Turning the Split File On and Off.*

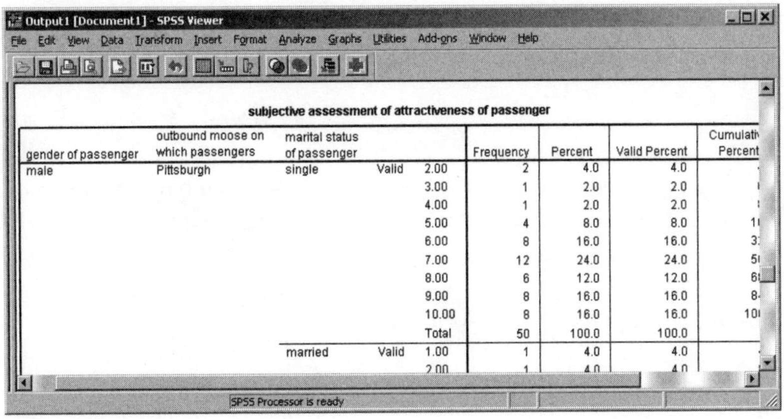

FIGURE 8.13. *Output for the Split-File Request (Single Men from Pittsburgh Visible).*

			7.00	21	31.3	31.3	74.6
			8.00	6	9.0	9.0	83.6
			9.00	5	7.5	7.5	91.0
			10.00	6	9.0	9.0	100.0
			Total	67	100.0	100.0	
San Francisco	single	Valid	2.00	2	2.9	2.9	2.9
			5.00	16	22.9	22.9	25.7
			6.00	6	8.6	8.6	34.3
			7.00	16	22.9	22.9	57.1
			8.00	22	31.4	31.4	88.6
			9.00	4	5.7	5.7	94.3
			10.00	4	5.7	5.7	100.0
			Total	70	100.0	100.0	
	married	Valid	1.00	6	4.4	4.4	4.4
			2.00	6	4.4	4.4	8.8
			3.00	4	2.9	2.9	11.8

FIGURE 8.14. *Output for the Split-File Request (Single Women from San Francisco Visible).*

To get to the data I'm interested in, I have to scroll through the output until I get to the point where it's organized by females from San Francisco who are single. Data from these individuals is shown in Figure 8.14.

Looking at this output, I see that there are seventy single women from San Francisco in my data file. The "Women" label is not visible in this screenshot because of the way SPSS output labels multi-split files. The "attractiveness" label is also not visible (but is present at the top of the output file). The column to the right of the word "valid", however, lists attractiveness ratings (i.e., 2.00, 5.00, 6.00, etc.). They range in attractiveness from a couple of 2's to four who are 10's.

SUMMARY

If you are interested in only a subset of your data, you have two different options. You can exclude unwanted cases from your existing dataset ("select if") or you can request that SPSS analyzes and reports information for separate groups ("split file"). The "split file" command is a light-switch command—if you turn it on, you have to remember to also turn it off.

KEY TERMS

"Descriptives" SPSS command requesting summary sample characteristics (such as mean, standard deviation).

Light-switch command Command that must be turned off after it's activated.

"Select if" SPSS command used to identify and retain only certain rows (people) within your data file.

"Split file" SPSS command to perform analyses and manipulations separately (within groups).

"Split file off" The "other half" of the "split file" command, it tells SPSS to "stop organizing what you do by group and consider all my data at once."

DISCUSSION QUESTIONS

1. "Select if" and "split file" do essentially the same thing; why do I need to learn both?

2. What happens if I forget to turn the "split file" command off?

PART

2

SYNTHESIZING AND ANALYZING DATA

CHAPTER

REQUESTING OUTPUT

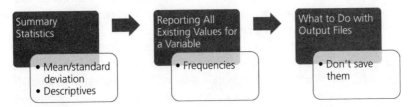

FIGURE 9.1. *Common Output Requests (Descriptive Statistics).*

Contents

Summary

Key Terms

Discussion Questions

CHAPTER LEARNING OBJECTIVES

1. Requesting descriptive statistics

2. Requesting frequency distributions

3. Using frequency information to create new variables

This chapter covers syntax commands that will meaningfully activate output files (that is, we'll actually be *requesting* output).

After you manipulate data, it's often useful to take a look at what you've done. Remember, as long as you operate within the syntax environment and control your data files with the "get file" and "save outfile" commands, there's no need to fear that you've horribly disfigured your sole copy of your data, but it is generally a good idea to take a look at your potentially Frankensteinian creation.

There are two very useful commands that allow you to look at your data: "descriptives" and "frequencies". These are the two most basic and common "analysis" commands you will use, and you've already gotten a brief preview of what output from these commands looks like in Chapter Eight.

THE "DESCRIPTIVES" COMMAND

Commonly (for example, after a scale score has been created) you'll want to look at the distributional properties of that new variable (we'll use the example of the extraversion variable from Chapter Six). If I want to know the descriptive statistics associated with the variable, the command is simply "descriptives". This command is requesting summary information in the form of descriptive statistics. Therefore we expect information to be reported in an output file rather than putting the information in the data file. The command for this request is shown in Figure 9.2.

If I highlight and run my file, I'll get a brief summary of the "extra" scale in an *output* window as shown in Figure 9.3—nothing in my data file has been altered by this analytical request.

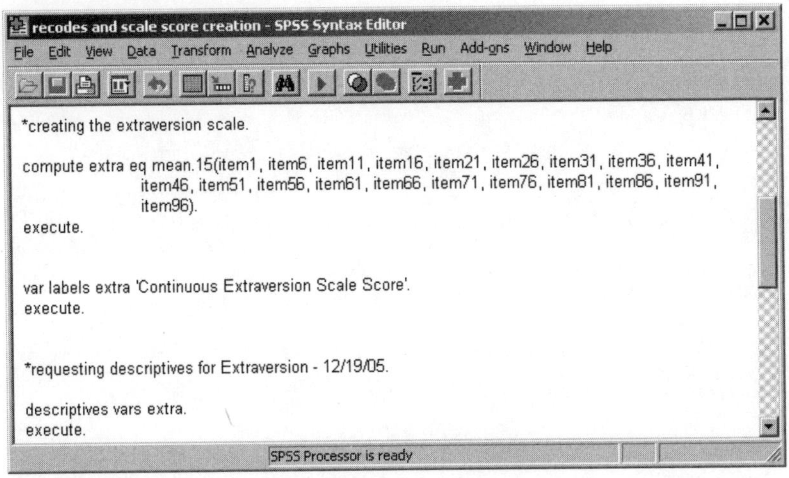

FIGURE 9.2. *Asking for Extraversion Descriptive Statistics.*

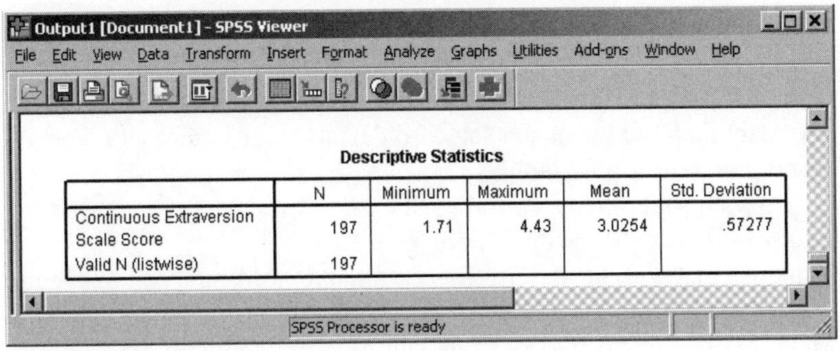

Descriptive Statistics

	N	Minimum	Maximum	Mean	Std. Deviation
Continuous Extraversion Scale Score	197	1.71	4.43	3.0254	.57277
Valid N (listwise)	197				

FIGURE 9.3. *Output Window of Descriptive Statistics for the Extraversion Variable.*

This table gives me some very important (and basic) pieces of information. First, I can see that the scale score variable label (continuous extraversion scale score) is reported instead of the smaller variable name (extra). A score for this variable was computed for 197 participants. If I know that my data file contains two hundred people, this means that three people did not have responses to at least fifteen items (remember the "compute extra eq mean.15(item . . .)" command). Next, looking at my *minimum* and *maximum* scores, it seems that these are possible (within the range of possible scores). Scores outside of the possible range

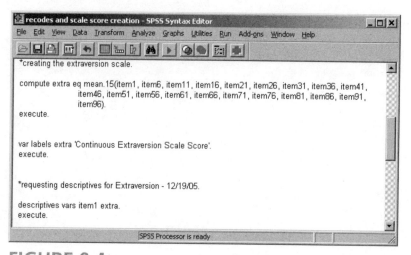

FIGURE 9.4. *Asking for Descriptive Statistics for item1 and the Extraversion Variables.*

of scores can help you identify data entry or other errors that exist in your data file. The mean and standard deviation are commonly reported descriptive statistics—you likely need these for some purpose.

If I want descriptives for more than one variable, I just expand my syntax request, as shown in Figure 9.4.

Notice that with the descriptives command (unlike the compute command), you do not need to separate the variable names with commas. There are additional statistics that can be generated with the "descriptives" command, but range, mean, and standard deviation should be sufficient for most of your applications.

THE "FREQUENCIES" COMMAND

If you want to look at individual, rather than summary responses to your variables, you can request a frequency distribution. This chapter demonstrates how to request this information in table form (using the "frequencies" command).

As shown in Figure 9.5, the simple command for a tabular frequency distribution is "frequencies".

Looking first at my output for responses to item1 (in Figure 9.6), I see that all two hundred people gave a response of either strongly disagree (fifteen people), disagree (thirty-three people), neither agree or

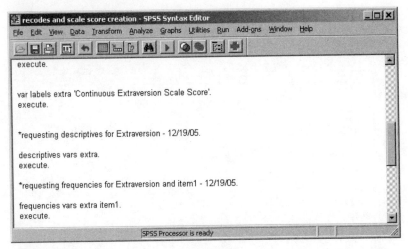

FIGURE 9.5. *Asking for Individual Values of the item1 and Extraversion Variables.*

Am the life of the party

		Frequency	Percent	Valid Percent	Cumulative Percent
Valid	strongly disagree	15	7.5	7.5	7.5
	disagree	33	16.5	16.5	24.0
	neither agree nor disagree	59	29.5	29.5	53.5
	agree	51	25.5	25.5	79.0
	strongly agree	42	21.0	21.0	100.0
	Total	200	100.0	100.0	

FIGURE 9.6. *Frequency Information for item1.*

disagree, agree, or strongly agree (these responses were coded as numbers 1 through 5 but reported as labels here because of our previous "add value labels" command). The last three percentage columns are standard and may be useful for further analyses.

The frequency table for the "extraversion" scale score, as shown in Figure 9.7, is going to contain more rows than the table for item1. This is

		Frequency	Percent	Valid Percent	Percent	
Valid	1.71	1	.5	.5	.5	
	1.86	2	1.0	1.0	1.5	
	2.00	5	2.5	2.5	4.1	
	2.14	4	2.0	2.0	6.1	
	2.29	13	6.5	6.6	12.7	
	2.43	13	6.5	6.6	19.3	
	2.57	19	9.5	9.6	28.9	
	2.71	17	8.5	8.6	37.6	
	2.86	16	8.0	8.1	45.7	
	3.00	14	7.0	7.1	52.8	
	3.14	25	12.5	12.7	65.5	
	3.29	9	4.5	4.6	70.1	
	3.43	12	6.0	6.1	76.1	
	3.57	15	7.5	7.6	83.8	
	3.71	10	5.0	5.1	88.8	
	3.86	10	5.0	5.1	93.9	
	4.00	7	3.5	3.6	97.5	
	4.14	2	1.0	1.0	98.5	
	4.29	1	.5	.5	99.0	
	4.43	2	1.0	1.0	100.0	
	Total	197	98.5	100.0		
Missing	System	3	1.5			
Total		200	100.0			

FIGURE 9.7. *Frequency Information for Extraversion.*

because there are only five valid responses to item1 (strongly disagree through strongly agree), whereas there are a bunch of possible responses for an average score created across twenty different items.

Labels are not reported for values here (for example, 4.43) because we did not enter an "add value labels" command for the scale score. Typically you do not add value labels to scale scores. Because three individuals did not have scores computed (because they did not respond to at least fifteen items), the "Percent" and "Valid Percent" columns are slightly different. Both of these columns represent the percent of respondents who gave a particular response. The difference between the two columns is the "Percent" column divided by the total number of rows in your data file (200); the "Valid Percent" column is divided by the total number of responses to the variable (197). The cumulative percent column is always based on the total number of responses to the variable (in this case, 197).

What to Do with This Information

Although this part of the book deals primarily with analyses, there are common manipulative purposes for using "descriptives" and "frequencies". In Chapter Six we categorized people as either introverted, extraverted, or on the fence. If I, for example, administered my questionnaire to two hundred members of the university chess club (instead of randomly sampling people off of the street), I might expect scores to range from "extremely introverted" to "fairly introverted." Similarly, if I administer my questionnaire to two hundred members of the university glee club, I might expect scores to range from "fairly extroverted" to "extremely extroverted." *Categorization* in these extreme cases will sometimes be more usefully based on distributions, rather than absolute (that is, greater or less than 3) scores. If I wanted to create three roughly equal-sized categories, I could use the frequency information to group people into roughly lower third, middle third, and upper third categories (called *tertiles*). To do this, you need to know real score equivalents (left-hand Frequency column) for percentile data (right-hand Frequency column). Also, when you do this, you should take relevant frequency information from your output file and put it in your syntax annotation (the numbers you use will likely change if you add data to or delete data from your data file). The process and syntax for this type of manipulation is shown in Figures 9.8 and 9.9.

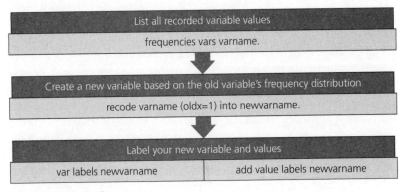

FIGURE 9.8. *Using Information Taken from a Frequency Table.*

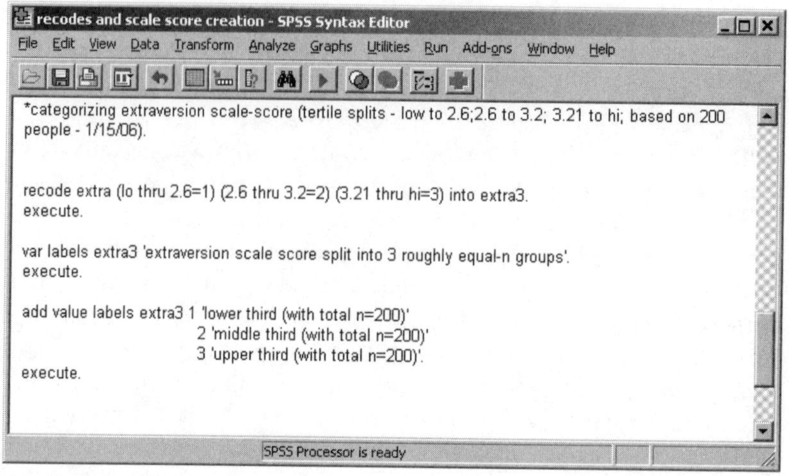

FIGURE 9.9. *Syntax for Categorizing Extraversion.*

A GENERAL NOTE ON ANALYSES

Organizing data into categories like the ones just described is sometimes done to facilitate later data analyses. (I am not advocating that anyone actually do this; it seems to be frequently done to force a continuous IV into an ANOVA model. For individuals unfamiliar or uncomfortable with regression analyses—both ANOVA and regression are covered in Chapters 11 & 12, respectively). It was stated earlier that you do not need to know SPSS syntax code to use the syntax file organizing system, yet I have given examples of simple code commands that are useful for your SPSS life (such as "add value labels", "compute", "descriptives", and "frequencies"). These commands are so common that they are useful for you to remember, but it is not *necessary* that you remember them. Remember that SPSS will find the command language for you and write your syntax files for you through the use of the Paste function. Although you will soon become familiar with basic syntax *manipulation* commands, it's less likely that you will become as proficient at remembering *analysis* commands. Therefore it's OK to use the drop-down menus for analyses; just make sure that you use these only to generate commands that you then paste into your syntax diary.

When you use the drop-down menus to find and run analyses, it's useful to know that SPSS organizes the available menu options from the simple to the complex. Analytical options toward the top of the page (or menu) are more common and simple. Analytical options toward the bottom of the menu are more complex and generally less common. If you aren't sure which analysis you should be running (and are afraid to call your professor in the middle of the night), choose the "higher" (simpler) alternative—it's most likely to be correct.

To demonstrate this procedure, consider the following research question: are there mean "conscientiousness" score differences for my three newly created extraversion groups? To answer this question, I need to take the following steps, as shown in Figure 9.10:

1. Recode appropriate conscientiousness items.

2. Create the conscientiousness scale score.

3. Select the appropriate ANOVA analysis from the drop-down menu (this will be covered in greater detail in Chapter Eleven).

4. Paste the command syntax from the drop-down menu.

5. Cut and paste the generated command to the appropriate location in my syntax diary.

This last step is important, because SPSS will always paste the menu-generated command at the bottom of your syntax file. Usually that's not where you want the command to be located (remember, syntax runs sequentially from top to bottom).

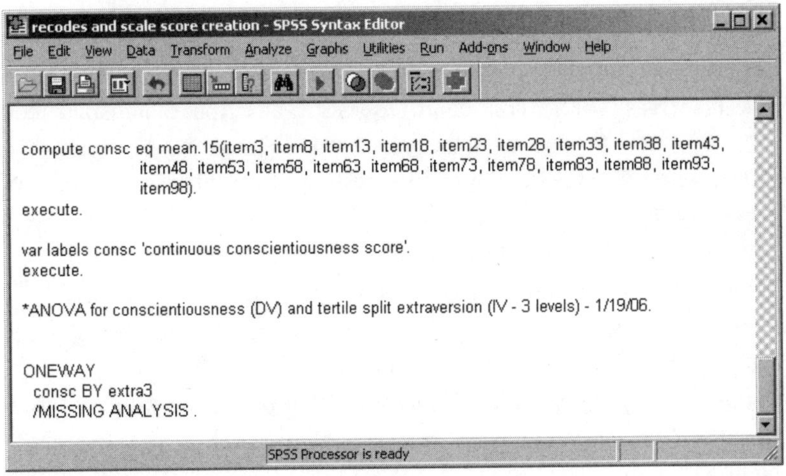

FIGURE 9.10. *Looking for Mean Conscientiousness Differences Across 3 Extraversion Categories.*

A GENERAL NOTE ABOUT OUTPUT FILES

This chapter dealt with commands that generate output files. I very rarely save output files. If you save your syntax files, you will receive output whenever you activate your syntax. There's typically no need to directly save output. Treat it like a newspaper—read it over, take note of the important information, then use it to line the bottom of a birdcage or to wrap a nice cut of halibut—just like a newspaper, you can get a new one tomorrow.

SUMMARY

You will eventually need to request output when working with SPSS—almost every project will require you to look at either descriptive information or frequency distributions (or both). The descriptive and frequency information that you request can be used for other data manipulative purposes, such as categorizing people. When you receive an output file, take note of the important information, but do not save the output file.

KEY TERMS

Categorization Process of forcing continuous data into a limited number of categories.

Cumulative percent Frequencies output column presenting percentile information (cumulative valid percent).

"Descriptives" SPSS command requesting descriptive statistics such as variables means and standard deviations.

"Frequencies" SPSS command requesting the number and percent of cases within each observed variable value.

Maximum score Largest data value within a column or variable.

Minimum score Smallest data value within a column or variable.

Percent Frequencies output column summarizing the number of cases for a given value divided by the total number of data file cases.

Percentile Percentage of individuals at or below a given value or score.

Tertiles One common form of categorization, based on three percentile breaks.

Valid percent Frequencies output column summarizing the number of cases for a given value divided by the total number of responses to the variable of interest.

DISCUSSION QUESTIONS

1. What are some applications of the descriptives information?
2. What are some applications of the frequencies information?

CHAPTER

INFERENTIAL ANALYSES (T-TESTS)

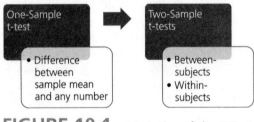

FIGURE 10.1. *Varieties of the T-Test.*

Contents

CHAPTER LEARNING OBJECTIVES

1. Selecting the appropriate analysis for your data
   - One-sample t-test
   - Two independent-samples t-test
   - Two correlated-samples t-test
2. Identifying important and unimportant output
   - Mean difference
   - Standard error
   - t
   - p

Welcome to the wonderful world of inferential analyses. In the next three chapters, you will be regaled with everything you need to know about common *inferential statistics*. These chapters are *not* "best practice" recommendations on performing statistics—you need to get that information from your statistics instructor (*alphas* and hypotheses and all the rest of it). I'm just trying to show you how to run some common analyses and navigate the output.

You will be best served if you have already had an undergraduate class on statistics. If the terms "alpha" and "hypotheses" from the above sentence leaves you addle-brained, you should probably hold off on reading Chapters Ten through Twelve until you refresh your memory a bit. If you are undaunted by these statistical terms, these three chapters should come to you easily. All analyzed data is presented, so you can enter data and follow along if you are so inclined.

THE T-TEST

The most basic analytical procedure you'll want to perform involves a determination of whether or not two numbers differ from each other. The appropriate analysis for this situation is the t-test. We will learn about three different types of t-tests. One is intended to be used when you want to compare your set of numbers against a known number—this is called the *one-sample t-test.* The other two are more practical and compare a mean calculated from one set of numbers against a mean calculated from another set of numbers—these are both called *two-sample t-tests.*

One-Sample T-Test

If you want to know whether a mean calculated from your set of numbers is different from a *known mean*, you'll want to perform a one-sample t-test. You won't encounter our example situation very often outside of a statistics classroom (unless you're a sasquatch hunter). Imagine you are walking through the woods in the Pacific Northwest and you come across multiple sets of footprints. You record all of these sizes and then want to compare your estimate against the average human shoe size (which you look up on the Internet).

I have the record of the found footprints in an SPSS file that I access through the syntax shown in Figure 10.2.

The data file that I've retrieved is shown in Figure 10.3.

To see how likely it would be to find these eleven footprints from the normal *population* of people, I look up the average shoe size: 9.5. Next, I perform the one-sample t-test by choosing from my SPSS Data Editor Analyze>Compare Means>One-Sample t-test, which opens the dialog box shown in Figure 10.4.

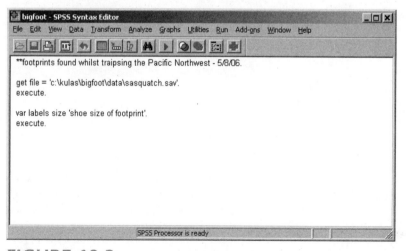

FIGURE 10.2. *Accessing the Bigfoot Data File.*

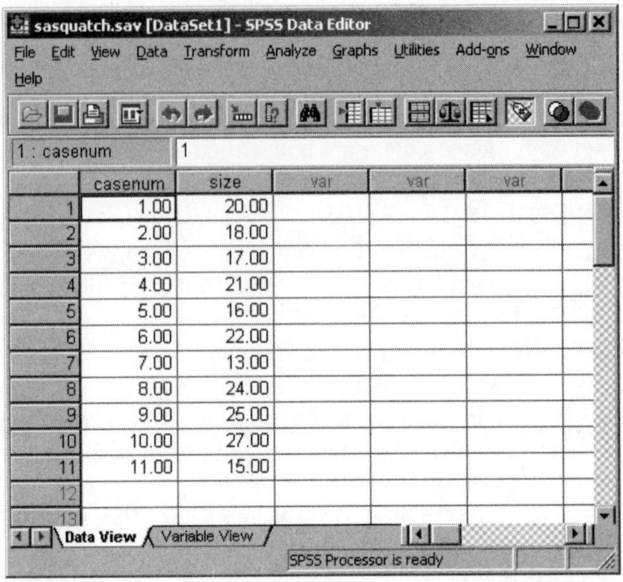

FIGURE 10.3. *Bigfoot Footprint Data.*

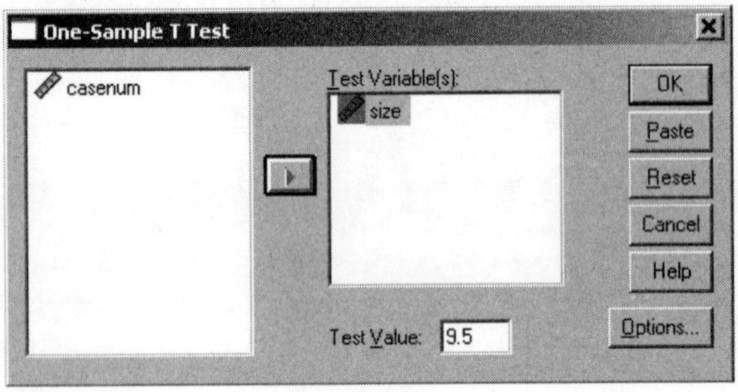

FIGURE 10.4. *One-Sample T-Test Dialog Box.*

The information I enter into this dialogue box is the *dependent variable* (also called *test variable*) and the number I'm using as a comparison (in this case, the average person's shoe size). Pasting this information to my syntax gives me everything I need to run this t-test, as shown in Figure 10.5.

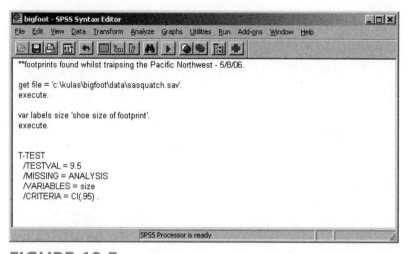

FIGURE 10.5. *Pasted Syntax for the Bigfoot T-Test.*

Selecting all (Ctrl+A) and running results in the following output (I've minimized the outline to the left of the main output window for space-saving purposes) produces the output shown in Figure 10.6.

The first reported table contains descriptive information (the "Std. Error Mean" is the standard deviation of your *sampling* distribution). The second table presents my t-test results. To make a determination whether my mean (19.8) differs from the expected population mean (9.5), the "df " (degrees of freedom) of 10 can be used to select a *critical t-value* from a statistics book appendix, and you can compare the tabled value against your obtained (7.698) value. Alternatively, a specific *significance estimate* is also provided. You "want" this significance estimate to be small (less than your alpha), although you should note that the reported significance estimate is "conservative." If you had specified a directional hypothesis (sometimes called a *one-tailed hypothesis*), the significance estimate would be even smaller (that is, even less than your alpha).

In this case, it is quite obvious that there is a difference between our eleven Pacific Northwest footprints and the average shoe size—the implication is that these eleven footprints were not sampled from the human population. The formula used to calculate the obtained t-value is the mean difference (10.3) divided by the standard error (1.34), and this information is also provided in the tables. The 95-percent confidence interval is redundant with the significance information. If the significance

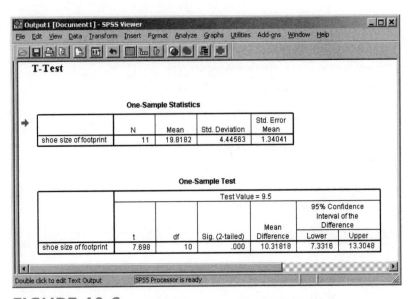

FIGURE 10.6. *Bigfoot One-Sample T-Test Output.*

estimate is less than .05 (as it is in this case), the 95-percent confidence interval will exclude 0; if the significance estimate is greater than .05, the confidence interval will include 0. You can change this confidence interval if you want to use a different alpha (look at the last line of the syntax specification in Figure 10.5).

Two Independent-Samples T-Test

For our two independent-samples t-test example, I'm using information regarding intelligence scores from twenty-five men and twenty-five women. These fifty people have no relationship to each other. If there's no reason to link people, I perform an independent-samples t-test. Loaded with the knowledge of the appropriate analytical procedure, I first access and run my existing syntax, as shown in Figure 10.7.

The syntax retrieves data and defined variables in the data file shown in Figure 10.8.

To perform the t-test, I choose Analyze>Compare Means>Independent-Samples t-test. In the dialog box shown in Figure 10.9, I put my IV/Grouping Variable (gender) and DV/Test Variable (intel) in the appropriate SPSS windows.

Because your grouping variable/IV may have more than two levels, you need to "define your groups," which is SPSS's way of asking *What*

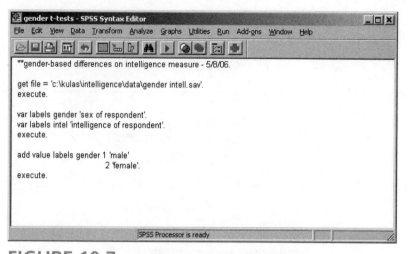

FIGURE 10.7. *Retrieving the Intelligence Data File.*

	casenum	gender	intel
1	1.00	2.00	116.00
2	2.00	1.00	90.00
3	3.00	1.00	95.00
4	4.00	2.00	102.00
5	5.00	1.00	103.00
6	6.00	1.00	100.00
7	7.00	2.00	95.00
8	8.00	1.00	110.00
9	9.00	2.00	95.00
10	10.00	1.00	105.00
11	11.00	2.00	95.00
12	12.00	2.00	105.00
13			

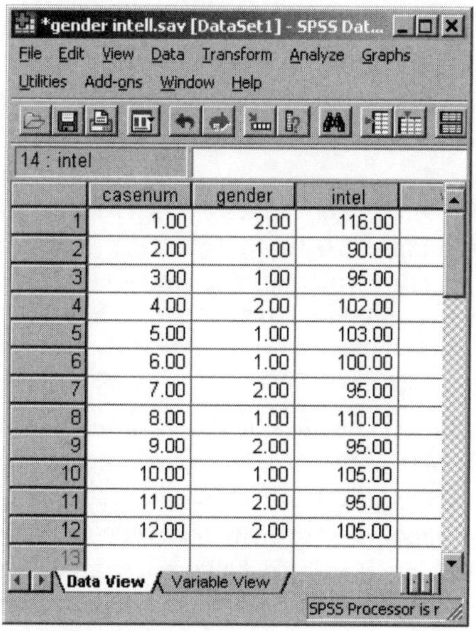

FIGURE 10.8. *Intelligence Data File.*

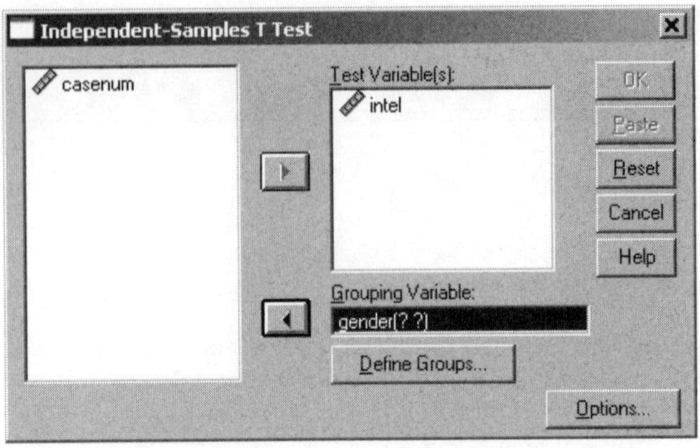

FIGURE 10.9. *Independent-Samples T-Test Dialog Box.*

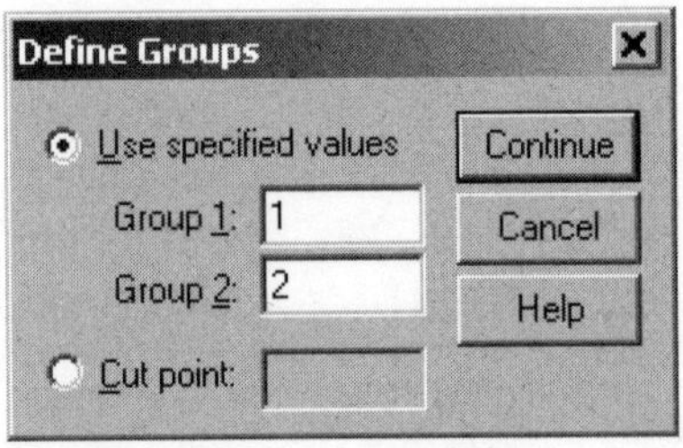

FIGURE 10.10.
Define Groups Dialog Box.

are the levels of your IV? The numeric codes for our gender levels are 1 and 2, as shown in Figure 10.10.

If I continue past this window, I can now paste the command into my syntax file, as shown in Figure 10.11.

Running the entire syntax file at once (Ctrl+A) gives me the output file shown in Figure 10.12.

I can see that there is only a small mean difference in the samples—not likely to achieve significance, but we did the analysis, so we should check our t anyway. Figure 10.13 shows the results.

Good thing we looked—who's this Levene person and why has he hijacked my analysis? It turns out that one of the assumptions of the t-test is that your two samples have similar distributional shapes. SPSS checks this assumption for you through computing a "Levene's test." It's a bit disconcerting, because not only does SPSS run this check for you, but it also gives you an alternative set of numbers to report if the

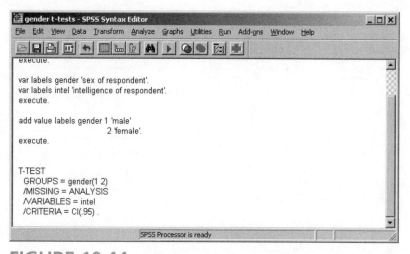

FIGURE 10.11. *Pasted Syntax for Independent-Samples T-Test.*

Group Statistics

	sex of respondent	N	Mean	Std. Deviation	Std. Error Mean
intelligence of respondent	male	6	100.5000	7.17635	2.92973
	female	6	101.3333	8.35863	3.41240

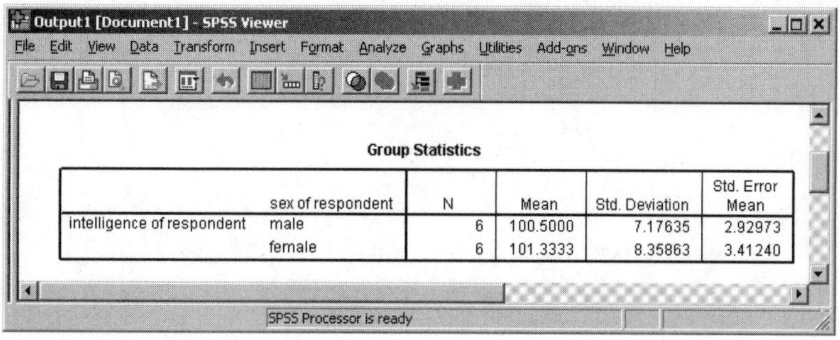

FIGURE 10.12. *Descriptive Statistics Given by T-Test Output.*

Levene's test is significant (for example, if you have a big F). This is why there are two rows of information reported in your t-test table. Our F is small, so we don't have to worry about Levene; we can focus only on the top row of the table. Figure 10.14 shows the output of relevance (scrolling to the right of the table).

Our obtained t is –.185. Because we specified "males" before "females" in our syntax, the female mean was subtracted from the male mean. If I change the order of my groups in my syntax, I'll change the valence of

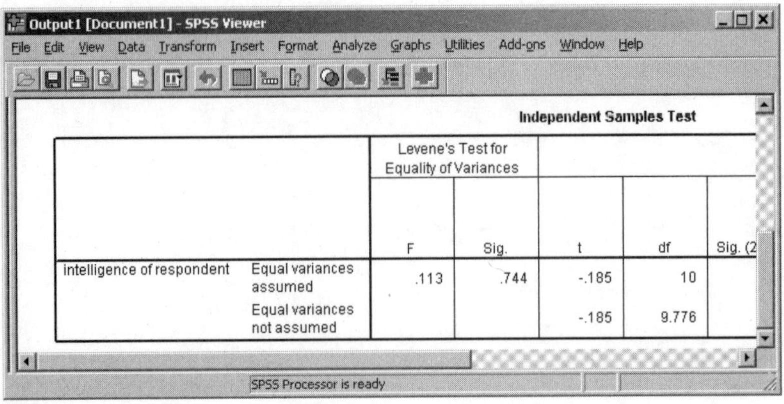

Independent Samples Test

		Levene's Test for Equality of Variances				
		F	Sig.	t	df	Sig. (2
intelligence of respondent	Equal variances assumed	.113	.744	-.185	10	
	Equal variances not assumed			-.185	9.776	

FIGURE 10.13. *T-Test Output of Direct Relevance for Our Analysis (Partial Table Shown).*

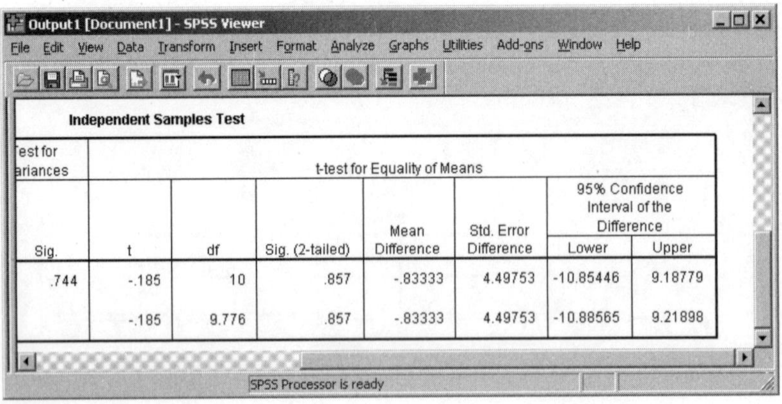

Independent Samples Test

est for ariances	t-test for Equality of Means						
						95% Confidence Interval of the Difference	
Sig.	t	df	Sig. (2-tailed)	Mean Difference	Std. Error Difference	Lower	Upper
.744	-.185	10	.857	-.83333	4.49753	-10.85446	9.18779
	-.185	9.776	.857	-.83333	4.49753	-10.88565	9.21898

FIGURE 10.14. *T-Test Output of Direct Relevance for Our Analysis (Continuation of Figure 10.13).*

my obtained statistic, but nothing else. Swapping the order of entry of the two groups (in syntax) is shown in Figure 10.15.

Running the same syntax (once again in its entirety—there's no waste associated with doing this) results in the t-test summary table shown in Figure 10.16.

This table is identical to the previous summary except that the *valence* of your obtained statistic has flip-flopped. Regardless of whether the obtained t is positive or negative, it's small. Too small for us to say that

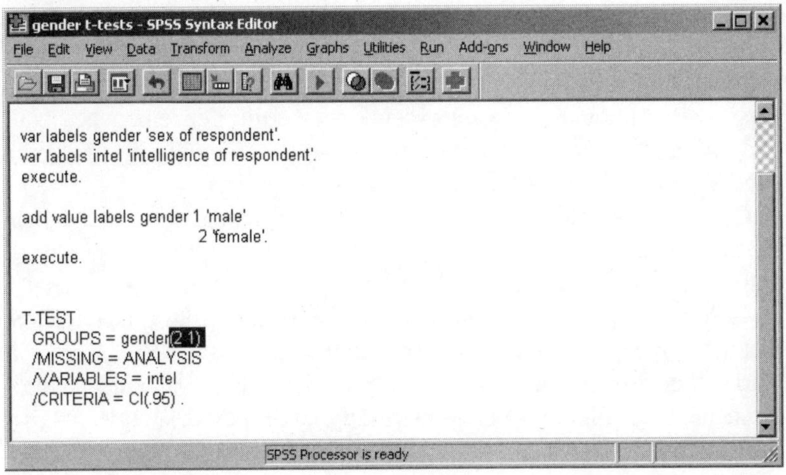

FIGURE 10.15. *Changing the Order of Entry (Female then Male) in the T-Test Analysis.*

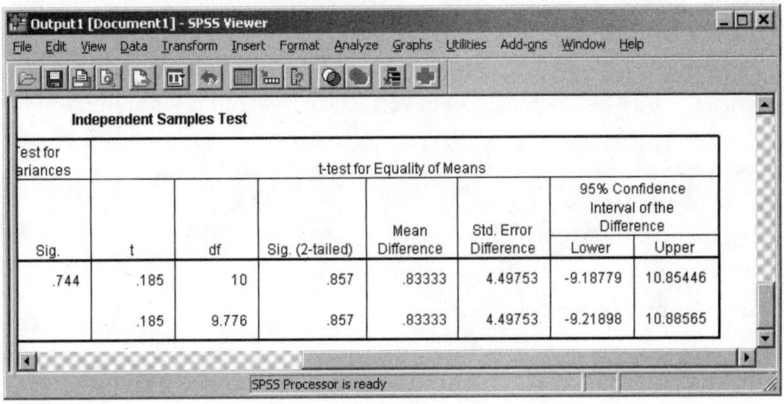

Independent Samples Test

'est for ariances	t-test for Equality of Means						
						95% Confidence Interval of the Difference	
Sig.	t	df	Sig. (2-tailed)	Mean Difference	Std. Error Difference	Lower	Upper
.744	.185	10	.857	.83333	4.49753	-9.18779	10.85446
	.185	9.776	.857	.83333	4.49753	-9.21898	10.88565

FIGURE 10.16. *T-Test Output Table with Females Specified Before Males.*

there's a difference in intelligence between men and women. To conclude the analysis, we close out of the output (don't save) and save the syntax.

Two Correlated- or Paired-Samples T-Test

In social sciences, variable values taken from two groups can be grossly categorized as being best represented by either randomized groups or repeated measures. These terms are statistical, but they have method-ological correlates. Methodologically, experiments are classified as between-subjects (randomized groups) or within-subjects (repeated measures). Although there are exceptions, the difference between your two options for the two-sample t-test is most commonly decided by a consideration of design (between or within-subjects).

Our paired-samples example compares employees' productivity on the third shift with their productivity on the first shift. In this sample, all employees have tried working both shifts. The most appropriate analysis is therefore the paired-samples t-test. Remember from Chapter Three that the number of people equals the number of rows in SPSS. This will help you determine both how to enter your data and also the most appropriate analysis. Figure 10.17 shows the syntax for this example.

Running this syntax brings up the data file shown in Figure 10.18—note that although there is one IV (shift) and one DV (productivity), these variables are presented a little differently because all people experienced both the first and the third shift.

Going through the same steps as the one-sample and independent-sample t-tests, I choose Analyze>Compare Means>Paired-Samples t-test to reach the dialog box shown in Figure 10.19.

This paired-samples t-test window is a bit different from the others because you're not expected to have separate IV and DV columns. With

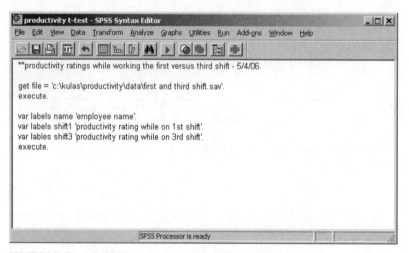

FIGURE 10.17. *Syntax for Productivity Paired-Samples T-Test.*

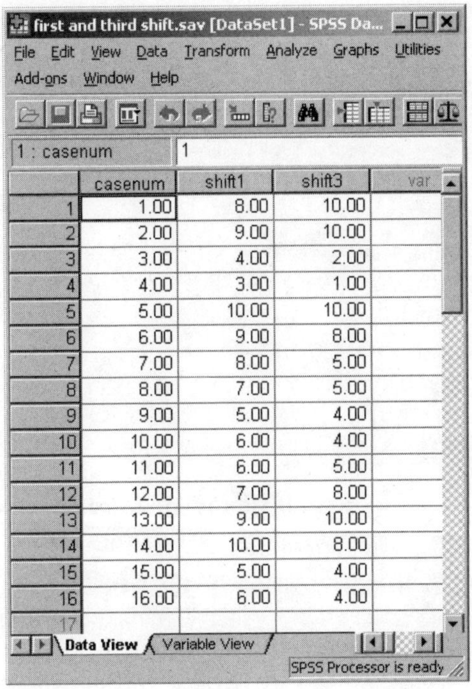

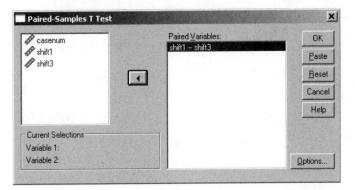

FIGURE 10.18. *First and Third Shift Data File.*

FIGURE 10.19. *Paired-Samples T-Test Dialog Box.*

a paired-samples situation, you have to store your data by "combining" your IV and DV information. If I paste the paired variables, I get my syntax command, as shown in Figure 10.20.

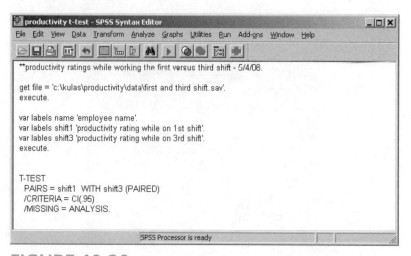

FIGURE 10.20. *Pasted Syntax for Paired-Samples.*

```
productivity t-test - SPSS Syntax Editor                          _□×
File  Edit  View  Data  Transform  Analyze  Graphs  Utilities  Run  Add-ons  Window  Help

**productivity ratings while working the first versus third shift - 5/4/06.

get file = 'c:\kulas\productivity\data\first and third shift.sav'.
execute.

var labels name 'employee name'.
var labels shift1 'productivity rating while on 1st shift'.
var lables shift3 'productivity rating while on 3rd shift'.
execute.


T-TEST
  PAIRS = shift1  WITH shift3 (PAIRED)
  /CRITERIA = CI(.95)
  /MISSING = ANALYSIS.

                          SPSS Processor is ready
```

```
Output1 [Document1] - SPSS Viewer                                 _□×
File  Edit  View  Data  Transform  Insert  Format  Analyze  Graphs  Utilities  Add-ons  Window  Help

   T-Test
```

Paired Samples Statistics

		Mean	N	Std. Deviation	Std. Error Mean
Pair 1	productivity rating while on 1st shift	7.0000	16	2.12916	.53229
	productivity rating while on 3rd shift	6.1250	16	3.00832	.75208

Paired Samples Correlations

```
Double click to edit Text Output          SPSS Processor is ready
```

FIGURE 10.21. *Paired-Sample T-Test Output (Descriptive Statistics).*

Selecting "ctrl'-'a" gives me the output shown in Figure 10.21.

This first table is the same as the first table in the independent-samples t-test (Figure 10.12), the only difference being that the sixteen first-shift workers are the same people as the sixteen third-shift workers. Here there is a larger mean difference—it will be interesting to see what our t-test will yield. Figure 10.22 shows the correlations and differences.

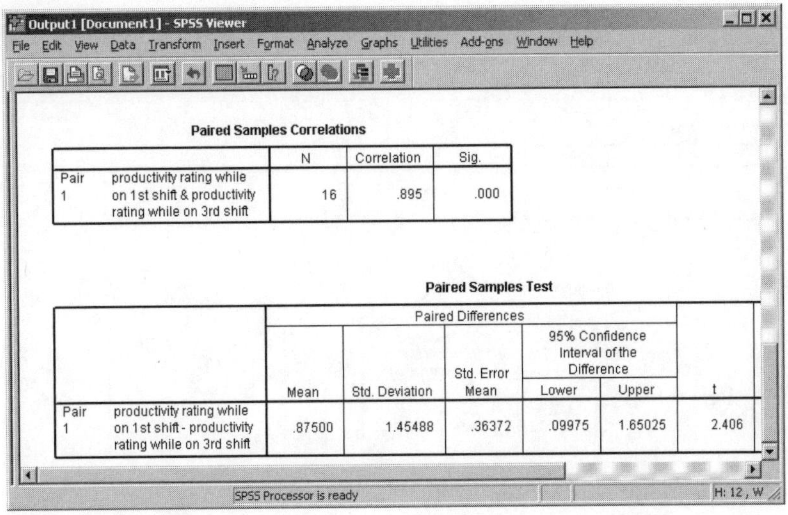

FIGURE 10.22. *Paired-Samples T-Test Output (Correlation and T-Value).*

Because the DV information is stored in separate columns, SPSS is able to calculate a correlation between first-shift productivity and third-shift productivity. (Correlations will be covered in more detail in Chapter Twelve.) From this correlation, you get a sense that workers who were productive in the first shift were also generally productive in the third shift—however, it does not tell us anything about whether there are *mean* differences between shifts.

The third table ("Paired-Samples Test" in Figure 10.22 and 10.23) contains our desired output. Once again, the formula for the t-test (mean difference divided by standard error) is fully represented in the table. Workers were, on average, rated as being .875 more productive when working the first as opposed to third shift. Dividing this average difference by the standard error gives a t estimate of 2.406.

I can use the df information to look up a tabled critical value, or I can simply take the conservative significance estimate as evidence for the effect (if I had thought that first-shift workers would be more productive and specified a directional hypothesis, the reported significance estimate would be too high). Regardless of which approach I take to using this information, it is clear that workers are more productive on the first shift than the third (at an alpha of .05)—the boss had better invest in some 24-hour coffee makers.

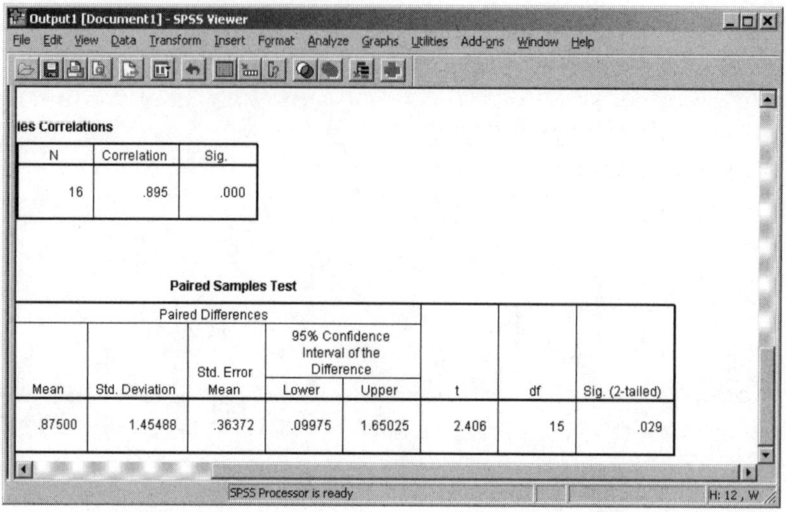

les Correlations

N	Correlation	Sig.
16	.895	.000

Paired Samples Test

Paired Differences					t	df	Sig. (2-tailed)
Mean	Std. Deviation	Std. Error Mean	95% Confidence Interval of the Difference Lower	Upper			
.87500	1.45488	.36372	.09975	1.65025	2.406	15	.029

FIGURE 10.23. *Paired-Samples T-Test Output (Significance Value Shown).*

SUMMARY

T-tests are fairly simple inferential analyses. If you have information from only one group of individuals, you can perform only a one-sample t-test. To do this, you need to provide a comparison mean. If you have information from two groups, you can perform a two-sample t-test, but you need to determine whether those numbers come from the same people (paired-samples) or different people (independent-samples).

KEY TERMS

Alpha criterion Percentage of the time you're willing to incorrectly state that an effect exists when in fact it does not. This is set by the researcher, but the common social sciences convention is to set alpha at 5 percent.

Critical value Tabled value of a test statistic (for example, t, F, r) associated with a particular α and df; the threshold that the obtained statistic has to breech to be considered significant.

Degrees of freedom (df) A mutual consideration of the number of statistical parameters estimated and the number of numbers used to estimate the parameters.

F Ratio of treatment to error variance.

Groups SPSS label for "levels" of an IV within the t-test analysis.

Independent-samples t-test The two-sample t-test to be used with between-subjects situations.

Inferential statistics Procedures estimating the probability that a given sample effect would occur if there were no effect present in the population.

Known mean A value that is given instead of being computed.

Levene's test Estimate of the t-test assumption of equal group variances.

Obtained value The computed value of a test statistic (such as t, F, r). To be compared against a tabled or critical value.

One-sample t-test Difference between a sample mean and a given mean.

Paired-samples t-test Two two-sample t-tests to be used with within-subjects situations.

Population The larger group of interest from which the sample was drawn.

Significance estimate Alternative to comparing obtained and tabled or critical test statistics—SPSS reports specific probabilities associated with each estimated obtained test statistic.

Standard error Standard deviation of a sampling distribution, commonly the denominator in inferential analyses.

T-test Analysis used to determine whether or not sample mean differences indicate population differences.

Two-sample t-test Difference between two estimated sample means.

Valence "Sign" (+/–) of a statistic value.

DISCUSSION QUESTIONS AND PROBLEMS

1. What would happen to my obtained t if I ran a paired-samples t-test situation as an independent-samples t-test?

2. How practical is the one-sample t-test?

3. Your parents claim college students sleep too much. They claim the average amount of sleep "normal" people get is eight hours. You survey seven of your classmates, who sleep nine, eleven, seven, eight, thirteen, twelve, and ten hours per night. Do college students sleep more than what your parents claim is "average"?

4. You believe men at your college are more attractive than the men at the neighboring rival college. You spend one half hour at each

campus, rating the men who walk by. Your school: 10, 9, 10, 7, 5, 6, 8, 9, 10, 10. Neighbor U: 4, 6, 2, 7, 8, 3, 10, 6, 8, 4, 8. Are the guys at your school more attractive (on average)?

5. You want to know the effect of caffeine on reaction time. You recruit your friends on two different occasions. Once you have them drink five cups of coffee before you throw foam-tipped darts at them; on the second occasion you have them drink five cups of water before trying to hit them with darts. You record the following number of hits (out of twenty throws):

	CAFFEINE	WATER
Bob	5	10
Sally	15	16
Persephone	12	15
June	4	6
Eunice	8	12

Does caffeine affect reaction time?

CHAPTER

INFERENTIAL ANALYSES (ANOVAS)

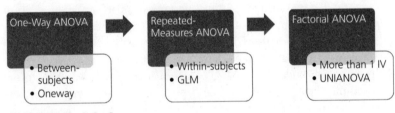

FIGURE 11.1. *Varieties of ANOVA Analysis.*

Contents

Summary

Key Terms

Discussion Questions

CHAPTER LEARNING OBJECTIVES

1. Select the appropriate analysis for your data
   - One-way
   - Repeated measures
   - Factorial

2. Identify important and unimportant output
   - Mean Square (between groups) [aka $MS_{treatment}$]
   - Mean Square (within groups) [aka MS_{error}]
   - F
   - p

When you are still interested in mean differences but find yourself dealing with more than two means at a time, you need to perform an *analysis of variance (ANOVA)* instead of a t-test. As in Chapter Ten, there are three different ANOVAs that we're going to cover (although there are more types of ANOVA that could be specified).

You should think of the ANOVA as a superordinate analysis to the two-sample t-test. ANOVA *can* be applied to the two-sample t-test situation (except it reports an F instead of a t), but ANOVA has the flexibility of also being able to accommodate more than two means at one time. The one-way ANOVA is used in an independent-samples t-test situation, the repeated-measures ANOVA is used in a correlated-samples t-test situation, and the third ANOVA (factorial) doesn't really have a straight t-test analogy—it is used when we have more than one predictor or IV.

ONE-WAY ANOVA ("ONE-WAY" COMMAND)

We'll use a prototypical drug and placebo example for the one-way ANOVA; Figure 11.2. shows my "get file" syntax.

Running this syntax calls up the data file shown in Figure 11.3.

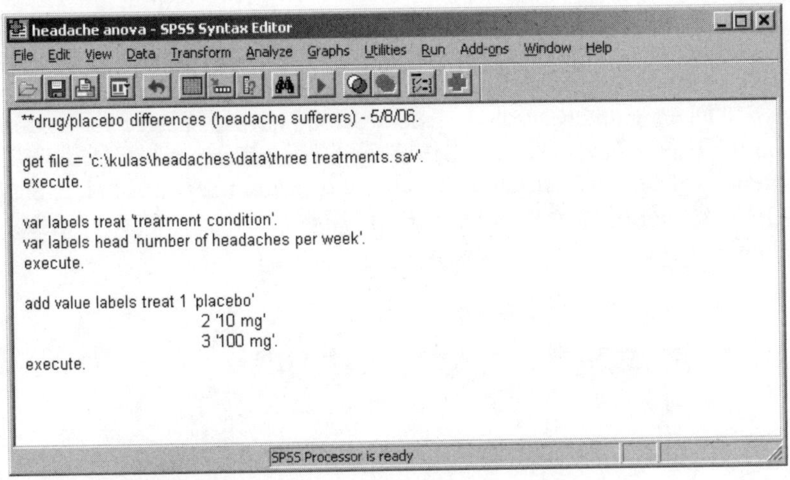

FIGURE 11.2. *Retrieving Headache Data File.*

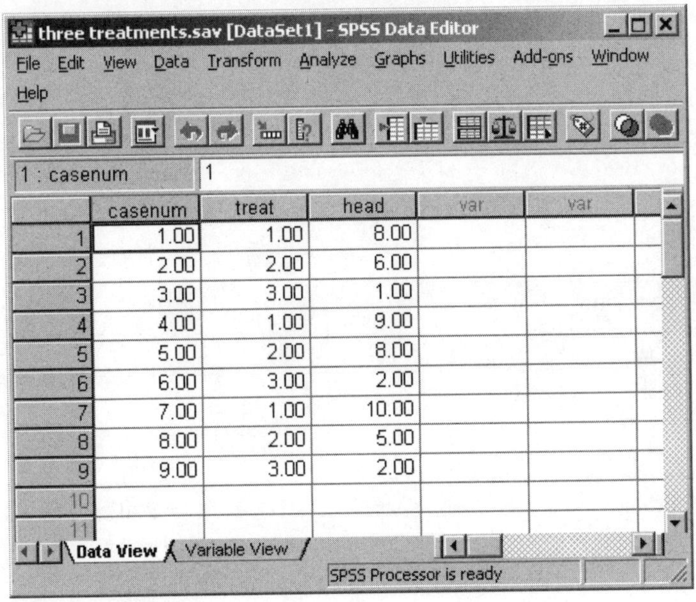

FIGURE 11.3. *Headache Data File.*

For the actual ANOVA analysis, I have two options. I can run a straightforward one-way ANOVA and receive a simple summary table, or I can run a *general linear model* (GLM) and get a bunch of supplementary information. We'll be forced to run the general linear model with different

ANOVA designs, so whenever possible, run the easier one-way ANOVA (Analyze>Compare Means>One-Way ANOVA), as shown in Figure11.4.

This should look very similar to the independent-samples t-test dialog box. The main difference here is that we don't have to specify our groups (in the Factor field) because the ANOVA can accommodate an infinite number of levels. Pasting this (and ignoring Contrasts, Post Hoc, and Options) yields the ANOVA command shown in Figure 11.5. Running the syntax generates the output shown in Figure 11.6.

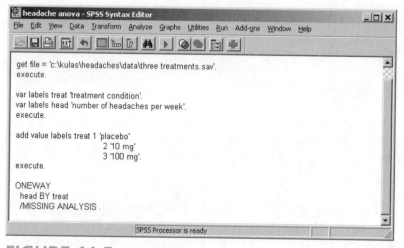

FIGURE 11.4. *One-Way ANOVA Dialog Box.*

```
get file = 'c:\kulas\headaches\data\three treatments.sav'.
execute.

var labels treat 'treatment condition'.
var labels head 'number of headaches per week'.
execute.

add value labels treat 1 'placebo'
                        2 '10 mg'
                        3 '100 mg'.
execute.

ONEWAY
 head BY treat
 /MISSING ANALYSIS .
```

FIGURE 11.5. *Headache ANOVA Syntax.*

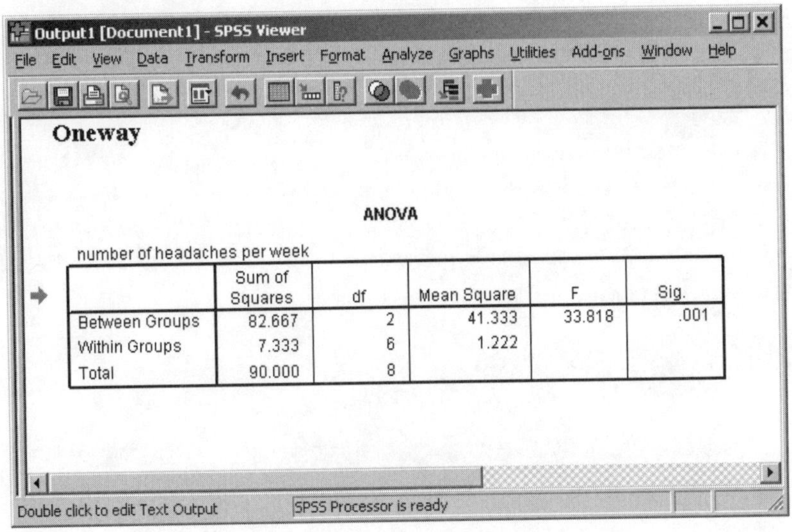

ANOVA

number of headaches per week

	Sum of Squares	df	Mean Square	F	Sig.
Between Groups	82.667	2	41.333	33.818	.001
Within Groups	7.333	6	1.222		
Total	90.000	8			

FIGURE 11.6. *One-Way ANOVA Results.*

The table in Figure 11.6. contains all the information you need to know for the *omnibus* (overall) ANOVA, and is one of the simplest pieces of output you will ever see from SPSS—I think it's very pretty. Similar to the t-test, you could find a statistics table and look up the critical value of F at 2 and 6 degrees of freedom, then compare that tabled value against your obtained value of 33.82. Alternatively, you could simply use the specific significance information provided for your obtained F (that is, .001 is less than $\alpha = .05$). It all boils down to your level of comfort in using the test statistic to make a decision (the F, as you are taught in statistics), or using the significance estimate (the Sig., as SPSS wants you to do). Both paths lead to the same conclusion (rejection of the null), but you may feel a little uncomfortable at first when you rely on the SPSS significance number.

REPEATED-MEASURES ANOVA ("GLM" COMMAND)

For the *repeated measures* situation, I'm going to use GPA information across years in college as the example. First, let's look at the syntax calling up the data file, as shown in Figure 11.7.

Running this syntax accesses the data file shown in Figure 11.8.

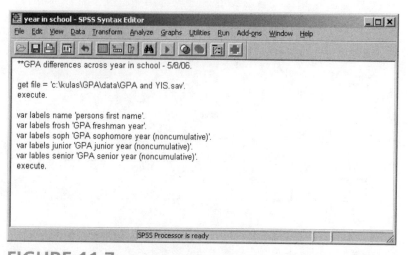

FIGURE 11.7. *Retrieving the GPA Data File.*

	casenum	name	frosh	soph	junior	senior
1	1.00	Bobby	2.30	4.00	3.00	3.50
2	2.00	Jane	2.40	2.50	3.20	3.30
3	3.00	Sue	3.00	3.30	3.30	3.40
4	4.00	Martinique	3.90	3.80	3.90	4.00
5	5.00	Sally	1.50	1.60	2.80	4.00
6	6.00	Sobriquet	2.00	2.50	2.90	3.90
7	7.00	Persephone	2.30	2.20	2.80	3.10
8	8.00	Snoopy	2.00	1.50	3.00	3.20
9	9.00	Woodstock	1.90	1.50	2.50	3.10
10						
11						

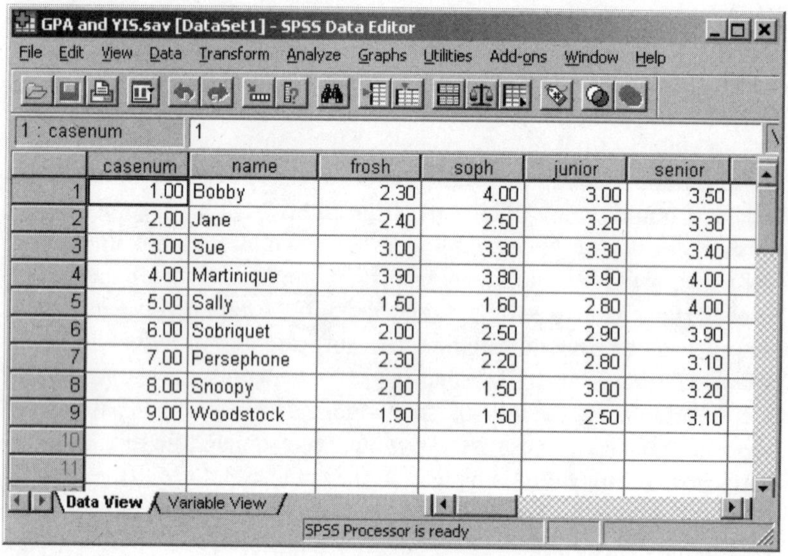

FIGURE 11.8. *GPA and YIS Data File.*

You'll note in Figure 11.8. that there is no IV identifying column—this is because we are in a repeated-measures, within-subjects situation. In these cases you'll always have a different organization of your data (because the number of rows in SPSS has to equal the number of people). To select the repeated measures ANOVA, we have to use the general

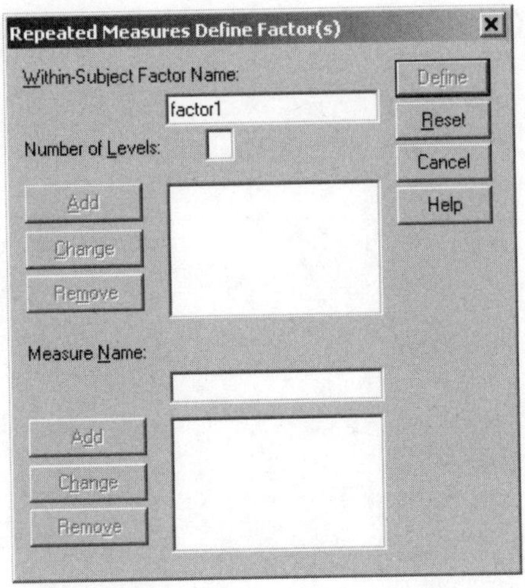

FIGURE 11.9. *Repeated Measures Define Factor(s) Dialog Box.*

linear model option from the SPSS drop-down menu (Analyze>General Linear Model>Repeated Measures). Choosing this menu opens the dialog box shown in Figure 11.9.

Because you do not have an IV or predictor column for your within-subjects variable, you need to specify which of your columns contain IV level information in this window. For our analysis, there are four IV levels—freshman, sophomore, junior, and senior—so I name my IV, specify four levels, and add to the analysis, as shown in Figure 11.10.

Choosing the Define option, I'm able to specify which of my columns are associated with the different levels of my within-subjects IV, as shown in Figure 11.11.

The Between-Subjects and Covariates dialog boxes are letting you know that if you want to complicate your design beyond a simple repeated measures ANOVA, SPSS is OK with that. We don't need to complicate things any further, so we'll paste the syntax shown in Figure 11.12 into our diary.

Running the full syntax file (Ctrl+A) gives me a complete mess of an output file (you can do basically anything with this command—except simplify your output). We'll take the output one table at a time, starting with Figure 11.13.

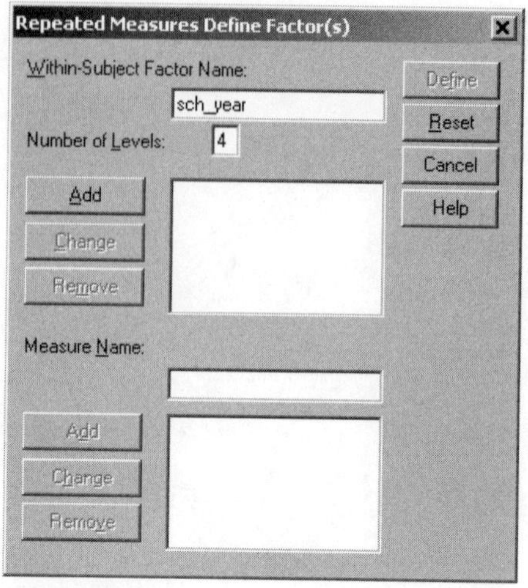

FIGURE 11.10. *Repeated Measures Define Factor(s) Dialog Box with Within-Subject Factor (sch_year) and Number of Levels (4) Specified.*

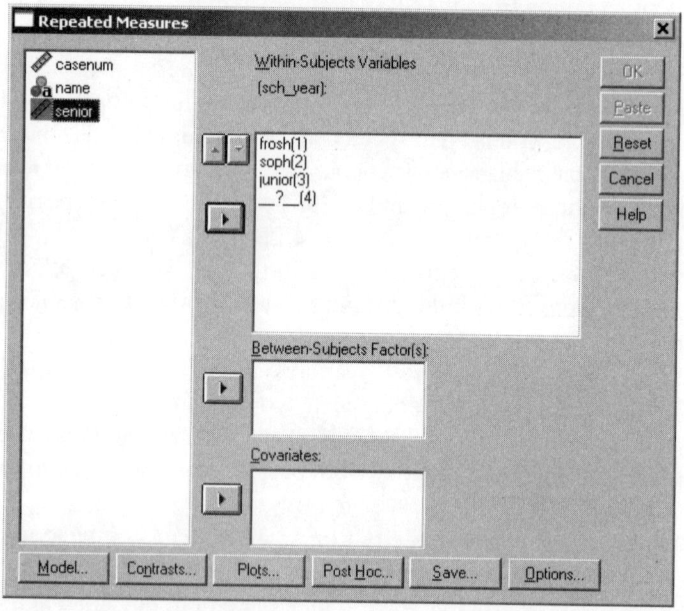

FIGURE 11.11. *Selecting Variables (Columns) that Identify IV Levels (The Senior Year Level Will Occupy the 4th Slot).*

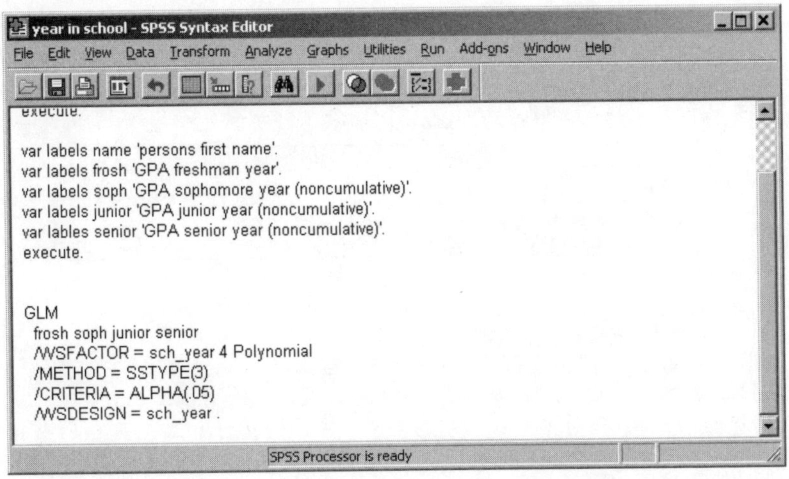

FIGURE 11.12. *Pasted Repeated-Measures ANOVA Syntax.*

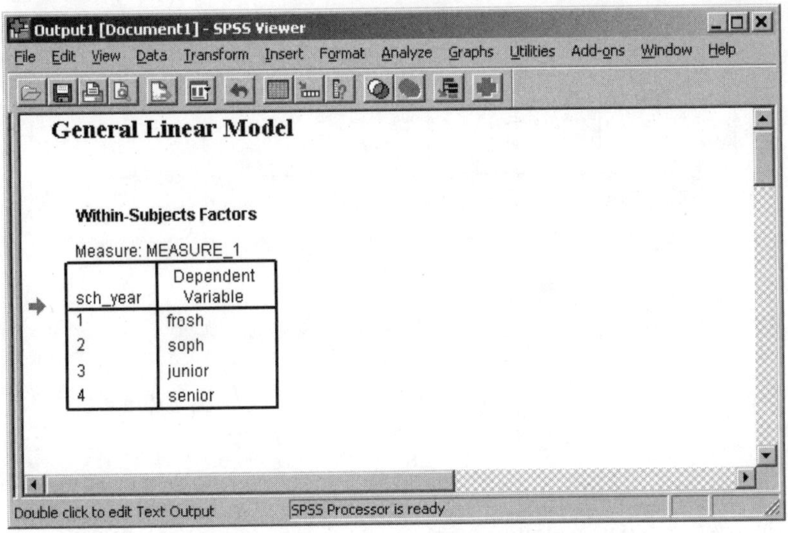

FIGURE 11.13. *Table #1 (GLM) Repeated-Measures ANOVA.*

Not much there: this first table, the General Linear Model (GLM) simply identifies our IV. On to the next table, shown in Figure 11.14.

This table is more interesting, but a little scary. Because the GLM is a very flexible command, you're given all kinds of output. This table

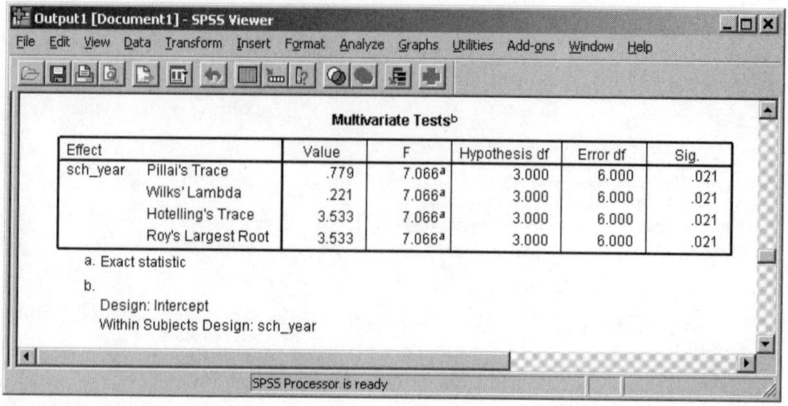

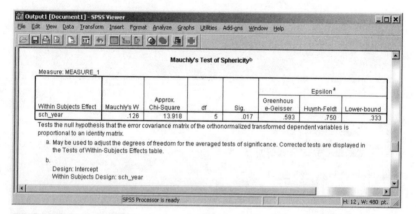

FIGURE 11.14. *Repeated Measures ANOVA Table #2 (Multivariate Tests).*

FIGURE 11.15. *Repeated Measures ANOVA Table #3.*

actually contains four different multivariate options that you may choose to report as your overall effect, but you don't have to. If you do report these, you report the values under the Value column, not the associated F. On to the next table, shown in Figure 11.15.

Sphericity is an overarching assumption of repeated-measures ANOVA (it essentially combines all of the repeated measures assumptions into one). If sphericity is *violated*, as it is here (significance is less than our $\alpha = .05$), it is recommended that you go back to the multivariate table and report *Wilks' Lambda*. If the significance estimate had been greater than $\alpha = .05$, you could go on to the tests of within-subjects effects, as shown in Figure 11.16.

The *Sphericity Assumed* row contains your traditional F—this is what you generally want to report from this analysis (for example, $F_{(3,24)} = 10.62$, $p < .05$). This is the F that you would obtain if you had done the analysis by hand, and is therefore the primary statistic you are looking for in this entire output. However, because of the violation of Sphericity (Figure 11.15), you may want to ignore Sphericity Assumed and consider the *Huynh-Feldt* results (which is less significant than the traditional F due to the adjusted df results).

Your choice of reporting the traditional F or the Huynh-Feldt value needs to be made under advisement of a statistical guide. A good source for helping with this decision is Tabachnick & Fidell (2007). After deciding which value to report, you'll want to continue through your output. The next table of which (Figure 11.17) is only informative under very specific circumstances (i.e., not usually).

The F column results in Figure 11.17 are useful only if your *IV is quantitative* (that is, the values given to your IV levels have sequential meaning). Our situation with progressive years in school probably qualifies to make this table relevant, although more commonly it won't apply to your situation. Our linear trend is significant, meaning that GPA is linearly related to progressive year in school; that is, it tends to get better as

Tests of Within-Subjects Effects

Measure: MEASURE_1

Source		Type III Sum of Squares	df	Mean Square	F	Sig.
sch_year	Sphericity Assumed	7.079	3	2.360	10.617	.000
	Greenhouse-Geisser	7.079	1.778	3.981	10.617	.002
	Huynh-Feldt	7.079	2.250	3.145	10.617	.001
	Lower-bound	7.079	1.000	7.079	10.617	.012
Error(sch_year)	Sphericity Assumed	5.334	24	.222		
	Greenhouse-Geisser	5.334	14.224	.375		
	Huynh-Feldt	5.334	18.004	.296		
	Lower-bound	5.334	8.000	.667		

FIGURE 11.16. *Repeated Measures ANOVA Table #4 (What You Typically Want).*

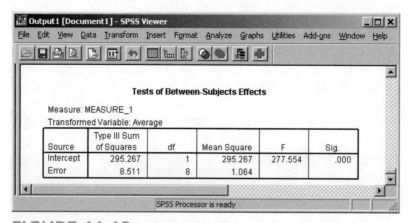

FIGURE 11.17. *Repeated-Measures ANOVA Table #5.*

Tests of Between-Subjects Effects

Measure: MEASURE_1
Transformed Variable: Average

Source	Type III Sum of Squares	df	Mean Square	F	Sig.
Intercept	295.267	1	295.267	277.554	.000
Error	8.511	8	1.064		

FIGURE 11.18. *Tests of Between-Subjects Effects.*

you approach your senior year). We don't really care, as this isn't typically the focus of an ANOVA—let's move on to the final table, shown in Figure 11.18.

Figure 11.18 contains important information, but it's labeled a bit peculiarly. The Error row actually contains your repeated measures' *subjects effect.* If SPSS were capable of producing a nice and simple summary table as it did for the one-way ANOVA (instead of the reams of output that it provides), it would look like the table in Figure 11.19.

GPA (DV)	SS	df	MS	F
Between Groups/Treatment	7.079	3	2.36	10.617
Subjects	8.511	8	1.064	
Within Groups/Error	5.334	24	.222	
Total*	20.924	35		

*SPSS does not report totals – you need to calculate these yourself if you want them

FIGURE 11.19. *GPS (DV) Standard Repeated-Measures ANOVA Table Produced from Information Contained in GLM Output.*

You should be able to construct one of these simple tables for every repeated-measures ANOVA that you conduct, if you follow the progression of tables that we have just visited. Out of all that output, we needed only these few pieces of information, but we had to pull them from different locations—quite confusing. Additionally, there was a lot of information in the output that we did not need—also confusing. Note that SPSS does not report total estimates for the repeated measures ANOVA. You will have to calculate these by hand if you want to generate a nice, clean table like the one presented in Figure 11.19.

FACTORIAL ANOVA ("UNIANOVA" COMMAND)

The *factorial ANOVA* is similar to the repeated-measures ANOVA in terms of SPSS specification (we have to do the GLM approach once again). However, because the example we're using has only *between-subjects* variables, our output is simplified. If one or both of our IVs were within-subjects, we would have to wade through the excessive output of the repeated measures analysis again. Instead, with between-subjects variables we get something that looks more similar to the simple one-way table. The syntax to retrieve the factorial ANOVA data file is shown in Figure 11.20.

Running this syntax gives us the data file shown in Figure 11.21.

Choosing Analyze>General Linear Model>Univariate from within my syntax diary gives me the Univariate dialog box shown in Figure 11.22.

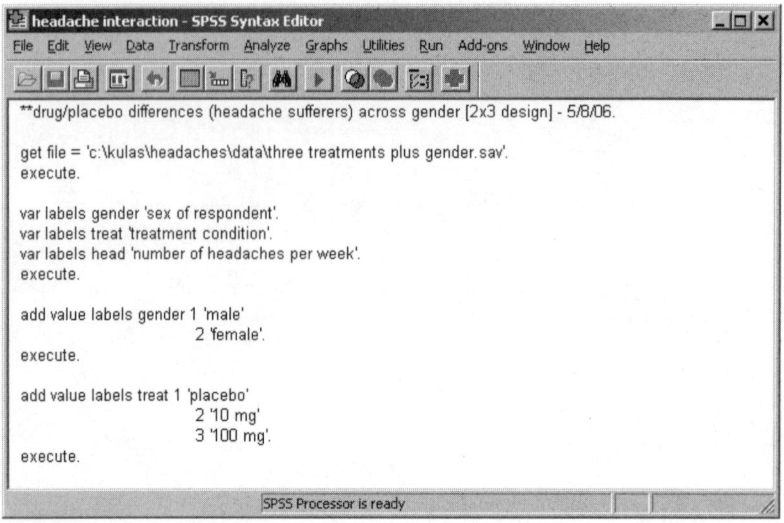

```
**drug/placebo differences (headache sufferers) across gender [2x3 design] - 5/8/06.

get file = 'c:\kulas\headaches\data\three treatments plus gender.sav'.
execute.

var labels gender 'sex of respondent'.
var labels treat 'treatment condition'.
var labels head 'number of headaches per week'.
execute.

add value labels gender 1 'male'
                        2 'female'.
execute.

add value labels treat 1 'placebo'
                       2 '10 mg'
                       3 '100 mg'.
execute.
```

FIGURE 11.20. *Retrieving Headache Data.*

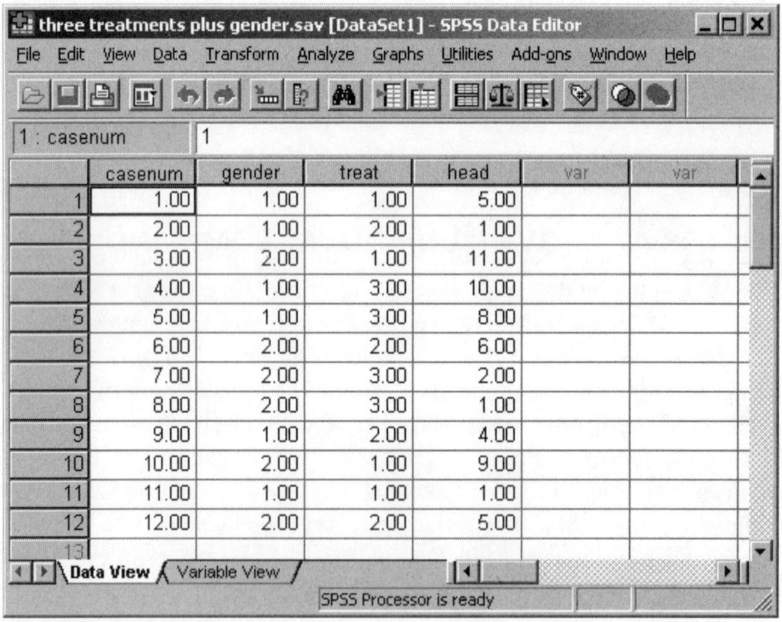

	casenum	gender	treat	head	var	var
1	1.00	1.00	1.00	5.00		
2	2.00	1.00	2.00	1.00		
3	3.00	2.00	1.00	11.00		
4	4.00	1.00	3.00	10.00		
5	5.00	1.00	3.00	8.00		
6	6.00	2.00	2.00	6.00		
7	7.00	2.00	3.00	2.00		
8	8.00	2.00	3.00	1.00		
9	9.00	1.00	2.00	4.00		
10	10.00	2.00	1.00	9.00		
11	11.00	1.00	1.00	1.00		
12	12.00	2.00	2.00	5.00		
13						

FIGURE 11.21. *Headache Data File (Containing Two IVs: Gender and Treatment).*

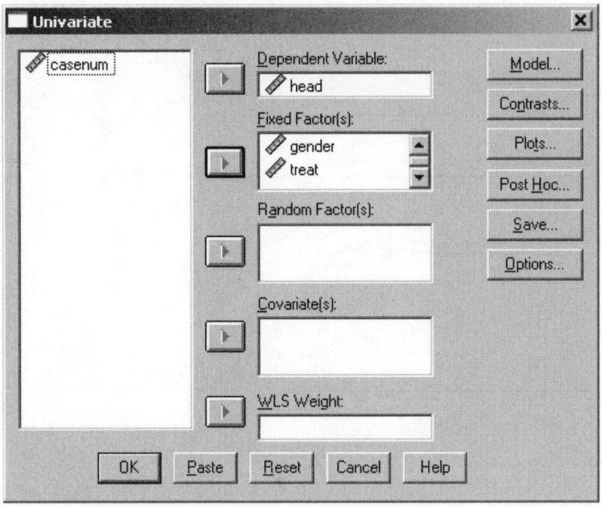

FIGURE 11.22. *Univariate Dialog Box.*

The IVs for this (and all) between-subjects situations can be specified as either fixed or random. Generally social sciences designs use fixed IVs—this means that the researcher or statistician intentionally *chooses* what levels are investigated; as shown in Figures 11.20 and 11.23, these are male, female and placebo, 10mg, and 100mg. If the researcher does not specify what specific levels he or she is interested in and stumbles across them randomly, the random factor option should be used. Note that this is just SPSS trying to be as flexible as possible once again. It's not *trying* to confuse you, but just being accommodating to all possible researchers. Use the Fixed Factor(s) option when you're running an ANOVA; you can also run a simple one-way ANOVA with the same Analyze>General Linear Mode> Univariate choice; this option gives the researcher more flexibility and options, whereas the "one-way" command is clean and simple.

Figure 11.23 shows the factorial ANOVA command pasted into my syntax diary.

Selecting Ctrl+A and running my entire analyses gives me the output shown in Figure 11.24.

This first table just summarizes how many individuals I have in each condition. There are six males and six females, and there are four people who received the placebo, four who received 10 mg of the drug, and four who received 100 mg of the drug: a total of twelve people. The table shown in Figure 11.25 is the only other piece of output reported.

```
execute.

add value labels gender 1 'male'
                        2 'female'.
execute.

add value labels treat 1 'placebo'
                       2 '10 mg'
                       3 '100 mg'.
execute.


UNIANOVA
  head  BY gender treat
  /METHOD = SSTYPE(3)
  /INTERCEPT = INCLUDE
  /CRITERIA = ALPHA(.05)
  /DESIGN = gender treat gender*treat .
```

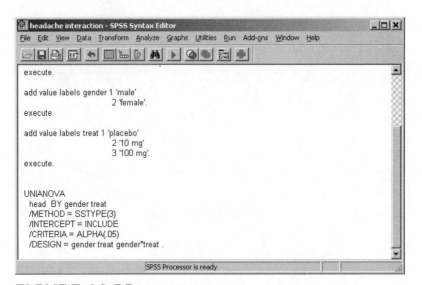

FIGURE 11.23. *Headache Interaction ANOVA Syntax.*

Univariate Analysis of Variance

Between-Subjects Factors

		Value Label	N
sex of respondent	1.00	male	6
	2.00	female	6
treatment condition	1.00	placebo	4
	2.00	10 mg	4
	3.00	100 mg	4

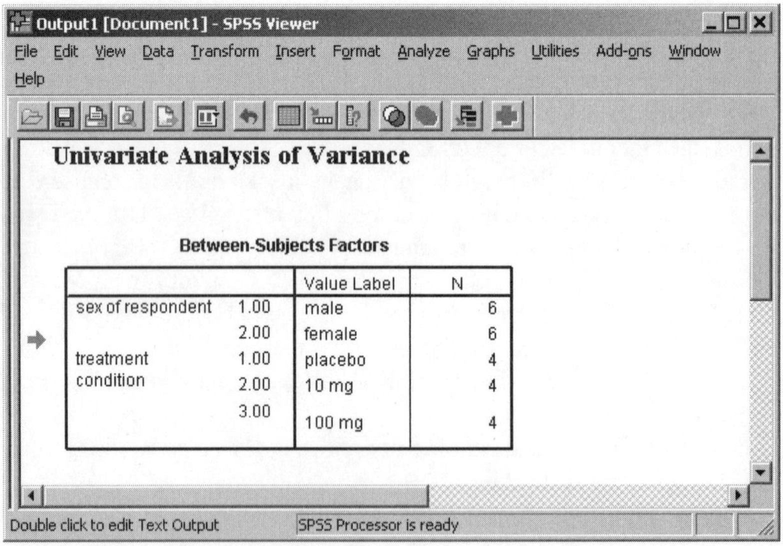

FIGURE 11.24. *Factorial ANOVA Table #1 (Numbers of Individuals in Each IV Condition).*

We have a significant interaction (drug effectiveness depends on gender; F = 19.23, $p < .05$) and no main effects. If I were to construct a simplified version of this table, it would be as shown in Figure 11.26.

Note that totals are reported in the SPSS table in Figure 11.25, but the row you actually want is labeled Corrected Total. The Corrected Model row presents the summated results of all three effects—it is used

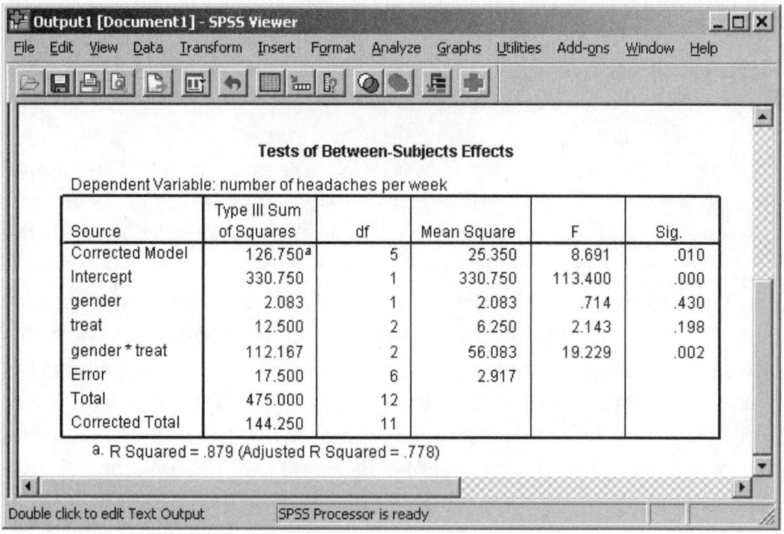

Tests of Between-Subjects Effects

Dependent Variable: number of headaches per week

Source	Type III Sum of Squares	df	Mean Square	F	Sig.
Corrected Model	126.750[a]	5	25.350	8.691	.010
Intercept	330.750	1	330.750	113.400	.000
gender	2.083	1	2.083	.714	.430
treat	12.500	2	6.250	2.143	.198
gender * treat	112.167	2	56.083	19.229	.002
Error	17.500	6	2.917		
Total	475.000	12			
Corrected Total	144.250	11			

a. R Squared = .879 (Adjusted R Squared = .778)

FIGURE 11.25. *Factorial ANOVA Table #2 (ANOVA Table).*

Headaches (DV)	SS	df	MS	F
Gender	2.08	1	2.083	.71
Drug	12.5	2	6.25	2.14
Gender x Drug	112.17	2	56.08	19.23
Error	17.5	6	2.92	
Total	144.25	11		

FIGURE 11.26. *Simplified Factorial ANOVA Table (Taken from Univariate Command Output).*

to estimate the R^2 at the bottom of the table, which is an estimate of the percent of total data variance that is associated with all of your IV effects. You do not typically report the Corrected Model F, although the R^2 may be of interest to you.

FOLLOW-UP CONTRASTS

We performed only omnibus ANOVAs. We did this because it greatly simplifies the output. When people first interact with the drop-down menu capabilities of SPSS (especially with inferential analyses), they have a tendency to check everything—by that I mean they are so nervous about what they are doing that they request all of the available options. With most of these ANOVAs you can request assumption checks, *follow-up contrasts*, descriptive statistics, different alphas, and so on. This makes a complete mess out of your output file. With the ANOVA, I recommend requesting and reporting only the omnibus F. If you want to make another run at the analysis and check assumptions, that's fine, but the first run-through should be "bare bones" so you know what you're dealing with in the output. As far as follow-up contrasts go, I generally recommend using t-tests. Once again, Tabachnick & Fidell (2007) is a good reference for finding and deciding on follow-up analyses. My recommendation is a general one, based on simplicity — their recommendations will be far more pointed and statistically appropriate.

The recommendations in this chapter for what output to report were mainly summarized from Tabachnick and Fidell (2007). If you need further guidance in conducting and reporting ANOVAs, this is the best ANOVA text I have encountered.

SUMMARY

There are three different commands to be specified with the three different types of ANOVAs. The simple one-way (to be used with one between-subjects variable) uses a "one-way" command. The repeated measures (to be used with one within-subjects variable) uses a "GLM" command. The factorial ANOVA (to be used with multiple independent variables) uses a "UNIANOVA" command. The output is fairly straightforward with the one-way and factorial ANOVAs—but with the repeated measures ANOVA, the output is complex and tough to navigate. Follow-up contrasts can be performed by doing targeted t-tests.

KEY TERMS

ANOVA General term used to classify a series of mean-difference testing procedures.

Corrected Model Combined impact of all estimated main and interaction effects.

Corrected total SPSS label for the total sums of squares and df estimates in a factorial ANOVA summary table.

Factor Term sometimes used for IVs, especially in ANOVA contexts.

Factorial ANOVA ANOVA model to be used when there are two or more IVs of interest.

Fixed IVs Researcher-determined levels.

Follow-up contrasts Targeted analyses to determine where differences may exist, given the occurrence of a significant omnibus F (for example, what levels differ from each other).

General linear model Encompassing theory from which most common analyses are derived.

"GLM" SPSS command for the general linear model; many different analyses can be specified through the GLM command.

Huynh-Feldt Recommended alternative to the "sphericity assumed" F if you have a violation of sphericity.

IV levels Specific values of an IV/factor (for example, male and female are two levels of the gender IV).

Omnibus ANOVA General, broad analysis assessing the ratio of column to row variance.

"One-way" SPSS command for a one-way ANOVA.

One-way ANOVA ANOVA model to be used in a between-subjects situation.

Quantitative IV Independent variable that differs in magnitude as well as category.

R^2 Percent of DV variance associated with all estimated IV effects.

Random IVs Randomly determined levels.

Repeated measures ANOVA ANOVA model to be used in a within-subjects situation.

Sphericity Lack of association among tested variables.

Sphericity assumed F ratio obtained on calculating a repeated-measures ANOVA by hand (type III SS).

Subjects effect Estimate of the amount of variance in a matrix of numbers that is attributable to differences across people.

"UNIANOVA" SPSS command for the factorial ANOVA (alternatively, "GLM" could also be specified).

Wilks' Lambda Multivariate statistic ranging from possible values of 0 to 1.

Within-subjects IV Independent variable, all levels of which are administered to all participating individuals.

DISCUSSION QUESTIONS

1. Why does SPSS use different terms than the terms that social science students learn?

2. Why is the repeated measures output so over-the-top?

3. Thirty chronic headache sufferers were assigned to one of three conditions: watch cartoons, go for a walk, or eat ice cubes. The researcher hopes that one of these treatments may help their suffering. Over the course of one month, the thirty people record the following number of reported headaches:

CARTOON WATCHERS	WALKERS	ICE-EATERS
5	20	5
2	16	6
13	25	20
8	8	25
20	6	6
25	9	30
15	11	11
11	15	5
6	5	15
8	6	8

Are any of these treatments more or less effective than the others?

4. Maybe the effectiveness of these treatments depends on the gender of the headache sufferer. Organizing the data a little bit differently,

we want to know if there is a difference in number of headaches across treatments for men and women.

	CARTOON WATCHERS	WALKERS	ICE-EATERS
Men	5	20	5
	2	16	6
	13	25	20
	8	8	25
	20	6	6
Women	25	9	30
	15	11	11
	11	15	5
	6	5	15
	8	6	8

5. Run the appropriate t-test as well as the appropriate ANOVA for the caffeine example from Chapter Ten. What's the relationship between your obtained F and t?

CHAPTER

INFERENTIAL ANALYSES (CORRELATION OR REGRESSION)

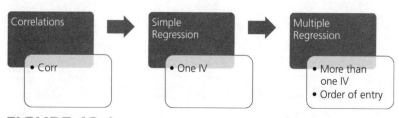

FIGURE 12.1. *Varieties of Analyses to Use with Continuous IVs.*

CHAPTER LEARNING OBJECTIVES

1. Select the appropriate analysis for your data
   - Correlation
   - Regression
2. Identify important and unimportant output
   - r
   - a
   - b
   - β
   - p

Welcome to the final chapter on data analyses. This chapter presents analyses that look a little different from ANOVAs and t-tests because the current analyses are used most commonly when you have *continuous* IVs (although they can also be used when you have categorical IVs). Just as ANOVAs are superordinate to t-tests, regression is superordinate to ANOVA (that is, anything you do with t-tests you can do with ANOVAs; anything you do with ANOVAs you can do with regression). The three chapters on inferential analyses therefore progress from the most specific analysis (t-test) to the most general analysis (regression). Although you can apply regression to all of the previous situations, I don't recommend doing that—instead, use the t-test and ANOVA when you have categorical IVs and use the regression or correlation when you have continuous IVs.

CORRELATION

Much as the t-test is a simplified ANOVA, the *correlation* is a simplified regression. The correlation is so simple that we aren't going to use drop-down menus. We're not even going to look at them. First, we call up a data file with multiple continuous variables, as shown in Figure 12.2.

This syntax, when activated, brings up the data file shown in Figure 12.3.

If I want to know the correlation between height and shoe size, the command is a simple "corr vars" as shown in Figure 12.4.

Selecting all (Ctrl+A) and running gives me the simple *correlation matrix* shown in Figure 12.5.

I generally recommend requesting one correlation at a time, although if you prefer, you can request a larger correlation matrix, as shown in Figure 12.6.

You do not need commas between your specified variables (I don't use commas with my correlation commands), but if you prefer to use commas, SPSS will still interpret and run the correlations. These 4 correlations are presented in Figure 12.7.

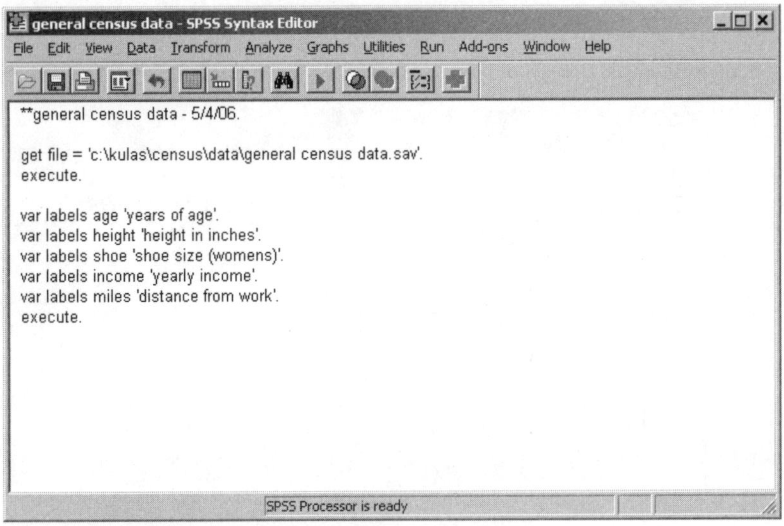

FIGURE 12.2. *Retrieving Census Data.*

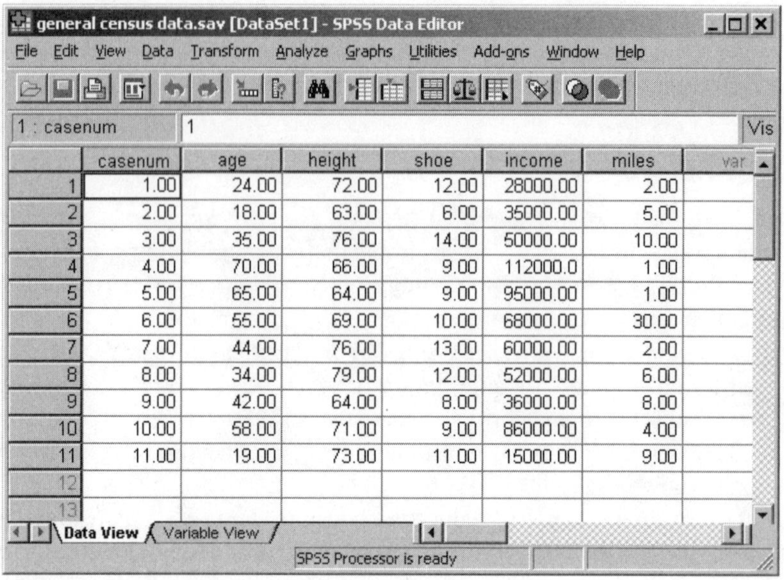

	casenum	age	height	shoe	income	miles	var
1	1.00	24.00	72.00	12.00	28000.00	2.00	
2	2.00	18.00	63.00	6.00	35000.00	5.00	
3	3.00	35.00	76.00	14.00	50000.00	10.00	
4	4.00	70.00	66.00	9.00	112000.0	1.00	
5	5.00	65.00	64.00	9.00	95000.00	1.00	
6	6.00	55.00	69.00	10.00	68000.00	30.00	
7	7.00	44.00	76.00	13.00	60000.00	2.00	
8	8.00	34.00	79.00	12.00	52000.00	6.00	
9	9.00	42.00	64.00	8.00	36000.00	8.00	
10	10.00	58.00	71.00	9.00	86000.00	4.00	
11	11.00	19.00	73.00	11.00	15000.00	9.00	
12							
13							

FIGURE 12.3. *General Census Data File.*

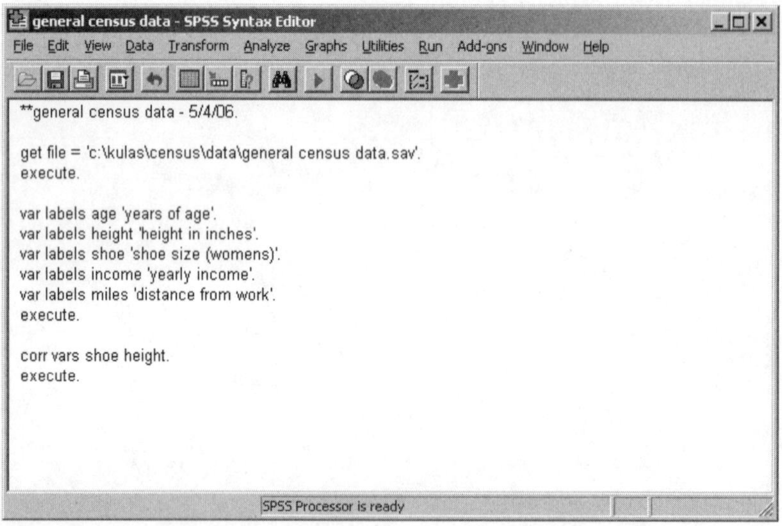


```
**general census data - 5/4/06.

get file = 'c:\kulas\census\data\general census data.sav'.
execute.

var labels age 'years of age'.
var labels height 'height in inches'.
var labels shoe 'shoe size (womens)'.
var labels income 'yearly income'.
var labels miles 'distance from work'.
execute.

corr vars shoe height.
execute.
```

FIGURE 12.4. *Requesting the Correlation Between Shoe Size and Height.*

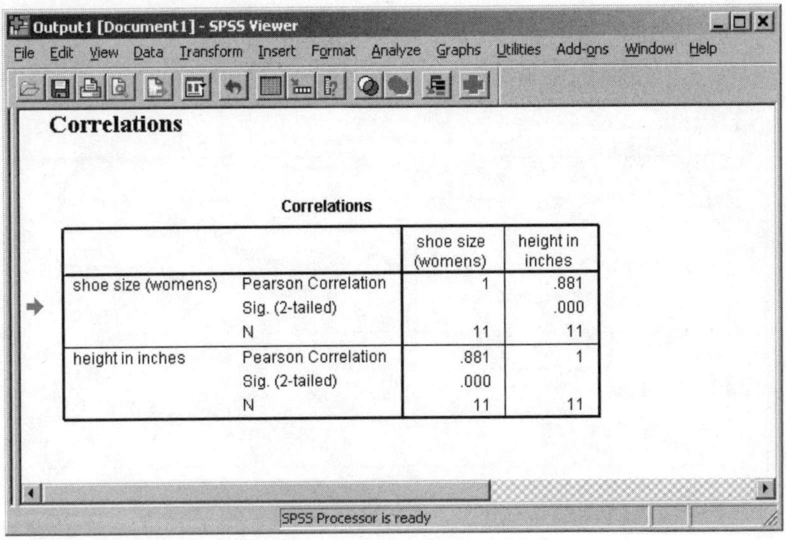

		shoe size (womens)	height in inches
shoe size (womens)	Pearson Correlation	1	.881
	Sig. (2-tailed)		.000
	N	11	11
height in inches	Pearson Correlation	.881	1
	Sig. (2-tailed)	.000	
	N	11	11

FIGURE 12.5. *Correlation Command Output.*

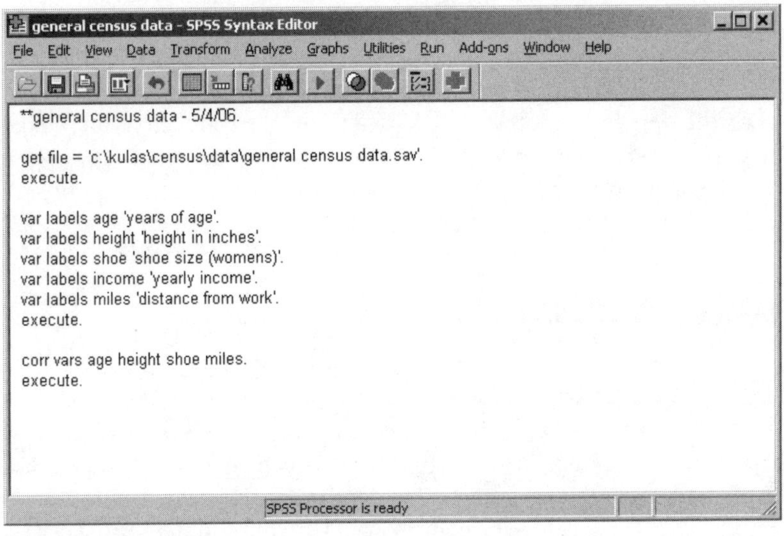


```
**general census data - 5/4/06.

get file = 'c:\kulas\census\data\general census data.sav'.
execute.

var labels age 'years of age'.
var labels height 'height in inches'.
var labels shoe 'shoe size (womens)'.
var labels income 'yearly income'.
var labels miles 'distance from work'.
execute.

corr vars age height shoe miles.
execute.
```

FIGURE 12.6. *Requesting Correlations Between Age, Height, Shoe Size, and Distance from Work.*

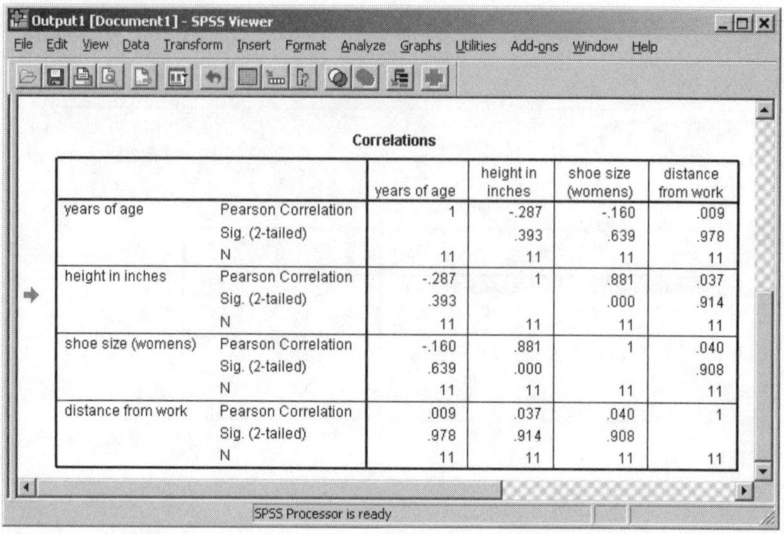

Correlations

		years of age	height in inches	shoe size (womens)	distance from work
years of age	Pearson Correlation	1	-.287	-.160	.009
	Sig. (2-tailed)		.393	.639	.978
	N	11	11	11	11
height in inches	Pearson Correlation	-.287	1	.881	.037
	Sig. (2-tailed)	.393		.000	.914
	N	11	11	11	11
shoe size (womens)	Pearson Correlation	-.160	.881	1	.040
	Sig. (2-tailed)	.639	.000		.908
	N	11	11	11	11
distance from work	Pearson Correlation	.009	.037	.040	1
	Sig. (2-tailed)	.978	.914	.908	
	N	11	11	11	11

FIGURE 12.7. *Correlation Matrix (4 Variables).*

Among the four variables I've specified, there is only one significant relationship (at $\alpha = .05$). The number in the Pearson Correlation row is your r ($r = .88$ for the significant shoe size [measured in the womens' shoe size metric] and height association). The number in the Sig. (2-tailed) row is your associated level of significance. Just like the t-test significance estimate, the significance level that is reported with the correlation can be considered *conservative*. If we had specified a directional hypothesis (as we likely would have with the shoe size–height relationship), the significance estimate would actually be smaller (closer to zero).

SIMPLE REGRESSION

Simple regression gives you the same information as correlation. Like the repeated-measures ANOVA, however, the regression also gives you information that you probably do not need or want. Using regression to replicate the relationship we estimated between shoe size and height, I need to specify which variable should be an X and which should be a Y. We also did this with the correlation—but with the correlation, the choice of assignment was completely arbitrary. With regression, the X and Y usually matter—the Y is the DV or criterion or outcome of interest, and the X is the IV or variable you hope will predict the DV. If I am a carnival barker interested in predicting a person's height once I find out his or her shoe size, I want height to be the Y variable. If I am a shoe salesperson and want to predict shoe size once a customer tells me his or her height, I want shoe size as the Y. We'll take the carnival barker route. From my syntax diary, choosing Analyze>Regression>Linear gives me the Linear Regression dialog box shown in Figure 12.8.

Pasting this information into my syntax diary gives me the syntax shown in Figure 12.9. Notice that I've placed asterisks in front of the correlation command from the previous run. Typically I'll use asterisks instead of deleting commands that I don't want to run—you don't want to clutter up your output file when you select all (Ctrl+A), but similarly you don't want to forget what you've done. Using asterisks is a good alternative.

Selecting the entire syntax file gives me the output shown in Figure 12.10.

The Variables Entered/Removed table is not relevant for your simple regression—if you do a multiple regression (as we do below) this table becomes more important. In the next output table shown in Figure 12.11, the R is "multiple R"—for the simple regression, it is also our Pearson's

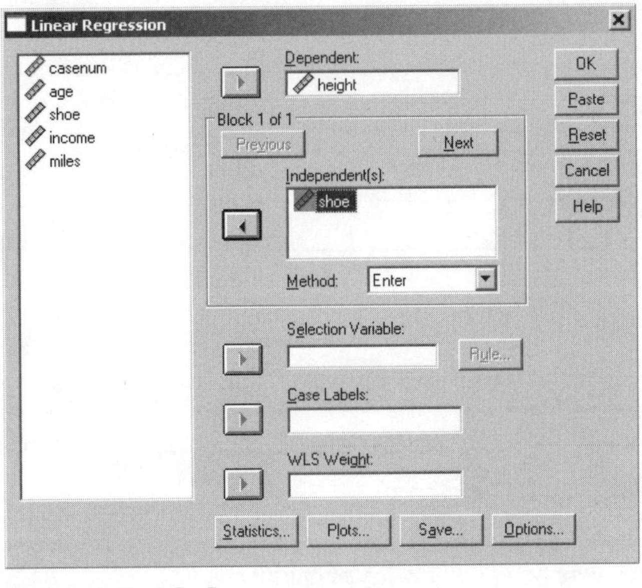

FIGURE 12.8. *Linear Regression Dialog Box.*

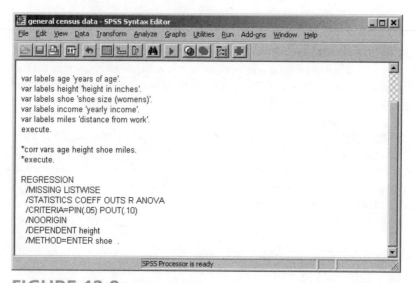

FIGURE 12.9. *Pasted Syntax Requesting a Simple Regression.*

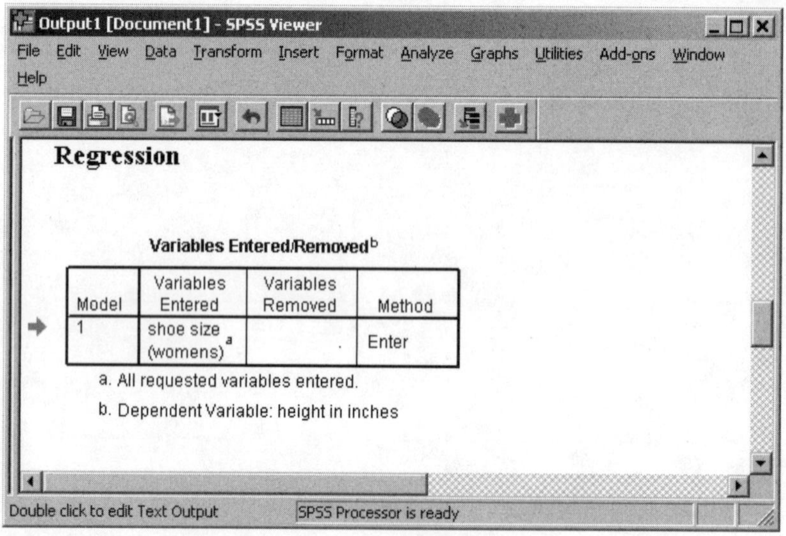

FIGURE 12.10. *Simple Regression Output Table #1 (Variables Entered/Removed).*

correlation. The *adjusted R^2* here reflects *shrinkage*. It is more useful in multiple regression; don't worry about it here.

The table in Figure 12.12 is an ANOVA table that has crashed our regression party. This table contains all of the "behind-the-scenes" numbers that were used to create the nice Model Summary table in Figure 12.11. The point is, the ANOVA table contains a lot of information, but all you *need* from it is the significance estimate. This tells us that the Multiple R/R^2 from the nice summary table is likely different from zero ($F = 31.24$, $p < .05$).

The table in Figure 12.13 is very important and presents information needed to create a regression equation. This table also (once again) presents

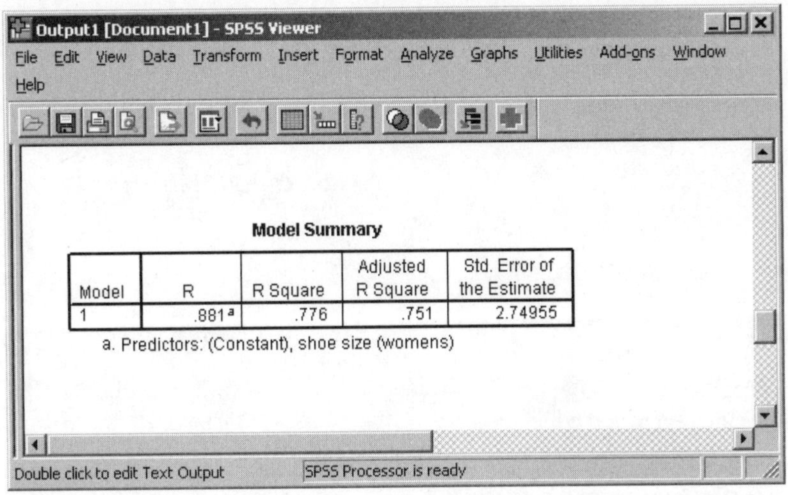

Model Summary

Model	R	R Square	Adjusted R Square	Std. Error of the Estimate
1	.881[a]	.776	.751	2.74955

a. Predictors: (Constant), shoe size (womens)

FIGURE 12.11. *Simple Regression Output Table #2 (R/R^2).*

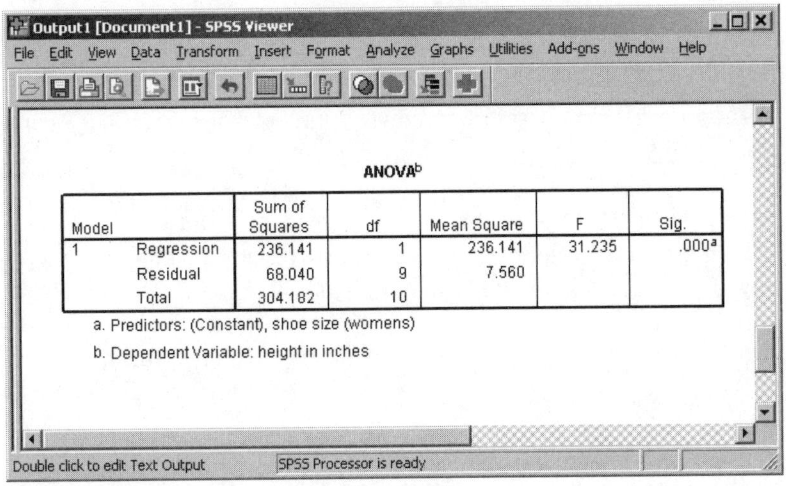

ANOVA[b]

Model		Sum of Squares	df	Mean Square	F	Sig.
1	Regression	236.141	1	236.141	31.235	.000[a]
	Residual	68.040	9	7.560		
	Total	304.182	10			

a. Predictors: (Constant), shoe size (womens)

b. Dependent Variable: height in inches

FIGURE 12.12. *Simple Regression Output Table #3 (R/R^2 Significance).*

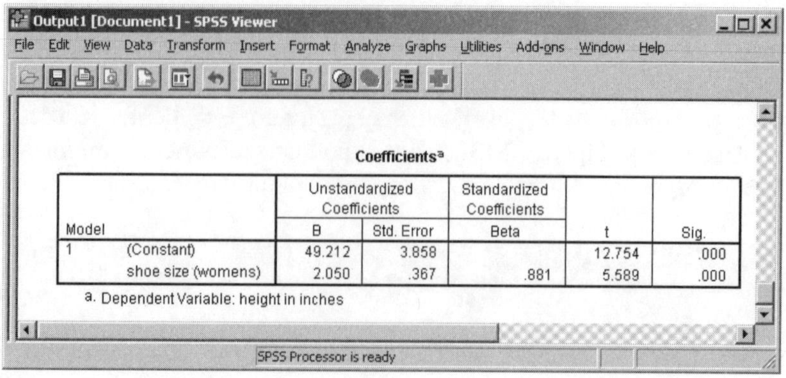

Coefficients[a]

Model		Unstandardized Coefficients		Standardized Coefficients	t	Sig.
		B	Std. Error	Beta		
1	(Constant)	49.212	3.858		12.754	.000
	shoe size (womens)	2.050	.367	.881	5.589	.000

a. Dependent Variable: height in inches

FIGURE 12.13. *Simple Regression Output Table #4 (Regression Coefficients).*

the Pearson's correlation in the form of a beta. From this table we can construct the following *regression equation*: predicted height = 49.212 + 2.05 (shoe size). This is generally written as Y′ = a + b(x). For our data, the specific regression equation is Y′ = 49.212 + 2.05(X).

MULTIPLE REGRESSION

To SPSS, multiple regression is the exact same thing as simple regression—the only difference is we are now considering more than one IV, so we can make decisions regarding IV priority. We are going to do two multiple regressions with the same dataset: one a bare-bones, no prioritization regression (straight regression), the other using variance partitioning or prioritization (hierarchical regression).

Straight Regression

One approach to multiple regression involves not placing priority on any of your IVs—I call this a straight regression to differentiate it from variance partitioning methods, although I am not sure if it has a specific name other than multiple regression. Activating the syntax diary, as shown in Figure 12.14, I see we're dealing with a geography/geology/biology example.

Activating this syntax file accesses the data file shown in Figure 12.15.

If I want to see if my variables can predict plant coverage, I can access the same drop-down menu that I did with the simple regression

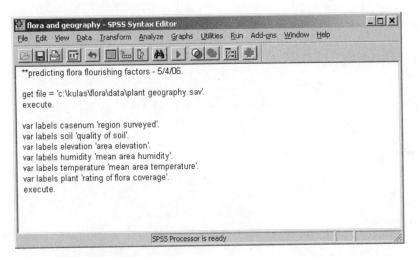

FIGURE 12.14. *Retrieving Plant Geography Data.*

	casenum	soil	elevation	humidity	temperature	plant	va
1	1.00	7.00	520.00	31.50	67.20	6.00	
2	2.00	6.00	610.00	31.65	64.00	11.00	
3	3.00	8.00	530.00	27.30	64.60	4.00	
4	4.00	9.00	540.00	32.60	65.60	8.00	
5	5.00	10.00	620.00	32.05	70.50	13.00	
6	6.00	6.00	520.00	30.10	70.00	3.00	
7	7.00	9.00	480.00	29.80	67.20	2.00	
8	8.00	10.00	530.00	30.40	61.20	10.00	
9	9.00	4.00	500.00	31.25	63.40	3.00	
10	10.00	4.00	590.00	32.06	68.40	11.00	
11	11.00	2.00	550.00	28.40	65.80	1.00	
12							
13							

FIGURE 12.15. *Plant Geography Data File.*

(Analyze>Regression>Linear). The only difference between the screenshot in Figure 12.16 and the simple regression example is the inclusion of multiple IVs in the current example.

Pasting to my syntax gives me the syntax shown in Figure 12.17.

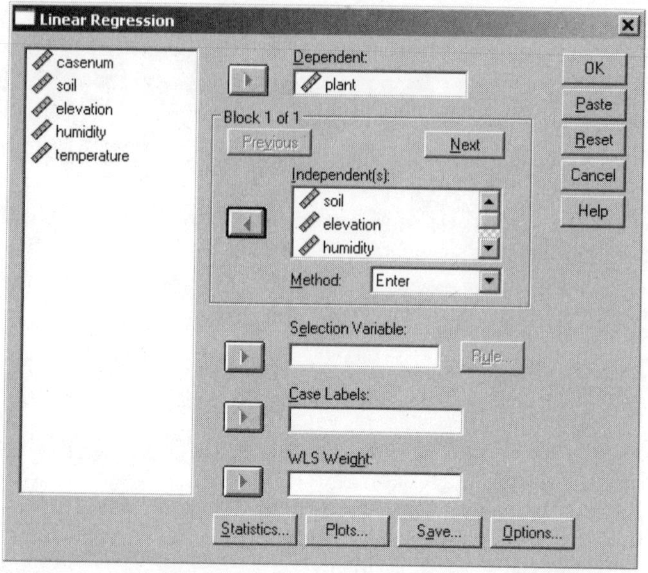

FIGURE 12.16. *Linear Regression Dialog Box.*

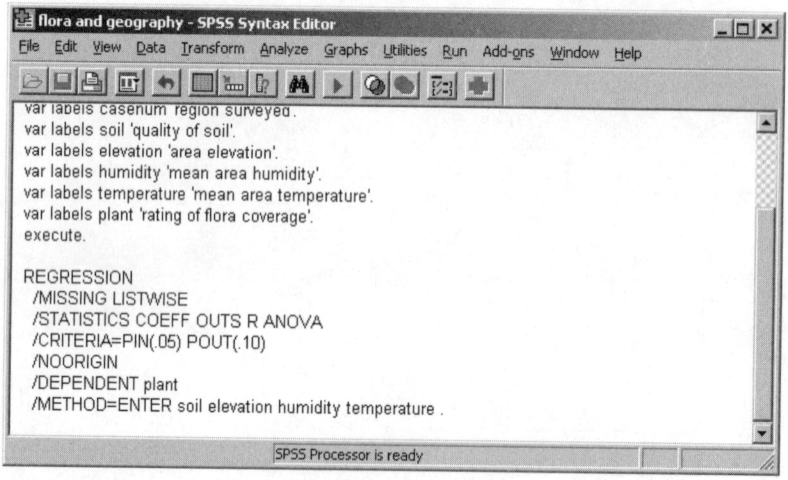

FIGURE 12.17. *Pasted Syntax for Straight Regression.*

Selecting all (Ctrl+A) and running this syntax brings up the output table shown in Figure 12.18. Like the simple regression, this table is not outrageously informative, although if you have extreme *multicollinearity* among your IVs, SPSS might "remove" one of them for you. Therefore, if you have any removed variables, you need to check your multicollinearity estimates. No problem identified here, however—all four IVs "made it."

Figure 12.19 presents, as in the simple regression, omnibus statistics for your entire regression model (four IVs and one DV). We are explaining a lot of the variability in plant ratings (92.7 percent) by consideration of our four predictors.

The table in Figure 12.20 tells us whether this 92.7 percent estimate can be considered to be significantly different from zero. Yes, the significance estimate is less than our α of .05, so we can consider the entire model to be useful.

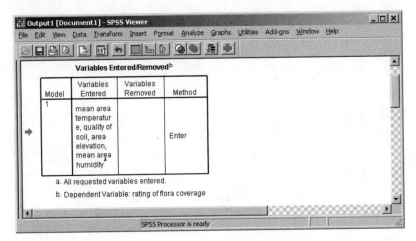

FIGURE 12.18. *Multiple Regression Output Table #1 (Variables Entered/Removed).*

Model Summary

Model	R	R Square	Adjusted R Square	Std. Error of the Estimate
1	.963[a]	.927	.879	1.47141

a. Predictors: (Constant), mean area temperature, quality of soil, area elevation, mean area humidity

FIGURE 12.19. *Multiple Regression Output Table #2 (R/R²).*

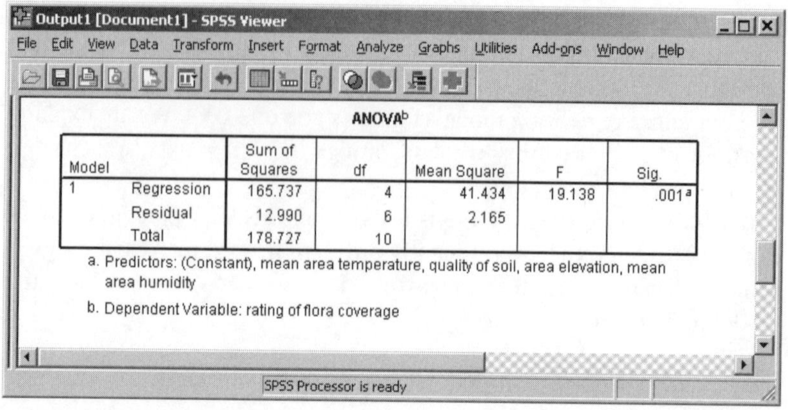

ANOVA[b]

Model		Sum of Squares	df	Mean Square	F	Sig.
1	Regression	165.737	4	41.434	19.138	.001[a]
	Residual	12.990	6	2.165		
	Total	178.727	10			

a. Predictors: (Constant), mean area temperature, quality of soil, area elevation, mean area humidity

b. Dependent Variable: rating of flora coverage

FIGURE 12.20. *Multiple Regression Output Table #3 (R/R^2 Significance).*

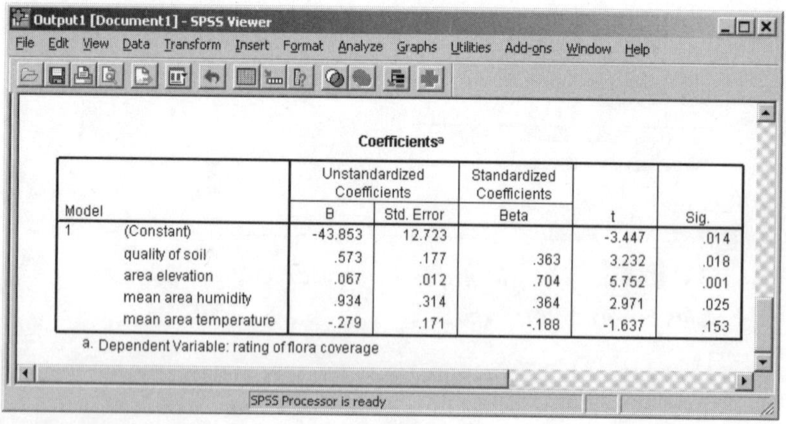

Coefficients[a]

Model		Unstandardized Coefficients		Standardized Coefficients	t	Sig.
		B	Std. Error	Beta		
1	(Constant)	-43.853	12.723		-3.447	.014
	quality of soil	.573	.177	.363	3.232	.018
	area elevation	.067	.012	.704	5.752	.001
	mean area humidity	.934	.314	.364	2.971	.025
	mean area temperature	-.279	.171	-.188	-1.637	.153

a. Dependent Variable: rating of flora coverage

FIGURE 12.21. *Multiple Regression Output Table #4 (Regression Coefficients).*

The last table, shown in Figure 12.21, lets me know which of my predictors are contributing to this very high multiple R.

Here I have three significant predictors. Note that even though the temperature variable is not significant, if I remove it and rerun the analysis, my multiple R/R^2 estimate will change (so will the regression coefficients for the three retained predictors).

Retaining all 4 predictors, the regression equation that results in a predicted/obtained DV correlation of .96 is

$$plant = -43.853 + .573(soil) + .067(elevation) + .934(humidity) - .279(temp)$$

Alternatively, this could be written as

$$Y' = -43.853 + .573(X1) + .067(X2) + .934(X3) - .279(X4).$$

Hierarchical Regression

An alternative approach to "throwing all IVs into the equation at once" is to successively enter IVs into the regression equation in different stages. There are two methods commonly used to do this: *hierarchical* and *stepwise*. With stepwise, the computer selects IV priorities based on correlations; with hierarchical, the researcher selects IV priorities based on theory, logic, or methodological considerations. As shown in Figure 12.22, we call up the same syntax diary, choosing Analyze>Regression>Linear again.

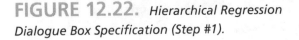

FIGURE 12.22. *Hierarchical Regression Dialogue Box Specification (Step #1).*

From my limited knowledge of geography, geology, and biology, I have an idea that elevation tends to be the best predictor of plant coverage in a region. So in my regression model I'm really interested in whether my other three predictors give me any additional information after I've already considered elevation. To test this model, I first enter the elevation predictor into the equation, then click Next to enter the remaining three predictors, as shown in Figure 12.23.

With any regression that you conduct in stages, you need one option from the statistics window shown in Figure 12.24: R^2 change (the other two checked boxes are defaults).

Now I can paste into my syntax diary, as shown in Figure 12.25.

Notice that I've asterisked out the previous regression and made a note to myself. The output for this hierarchical regression is shown in Figure 12.26.

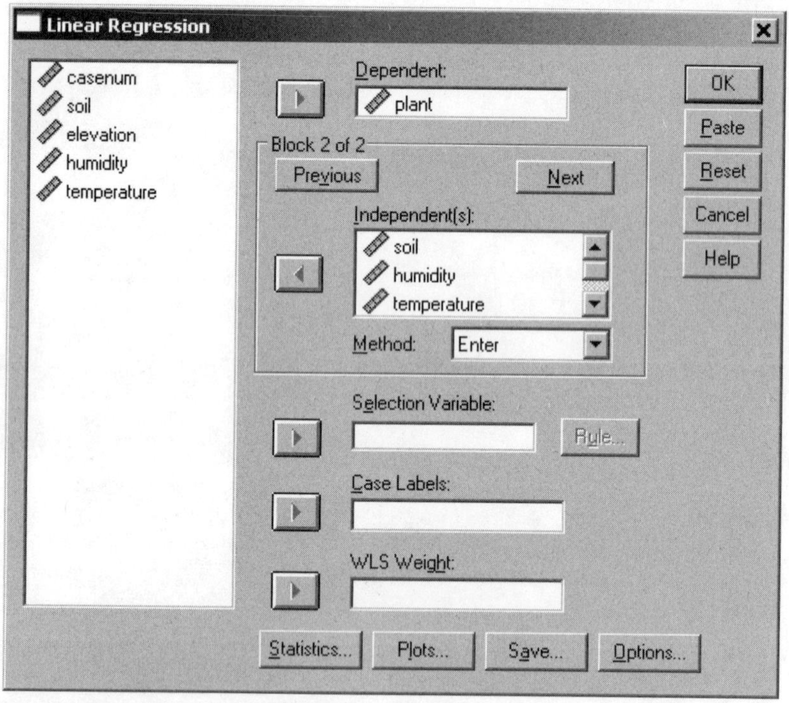

FIGURE 12.23. *Hierarchical Regression Dialogue Box Specification (Step #2).*

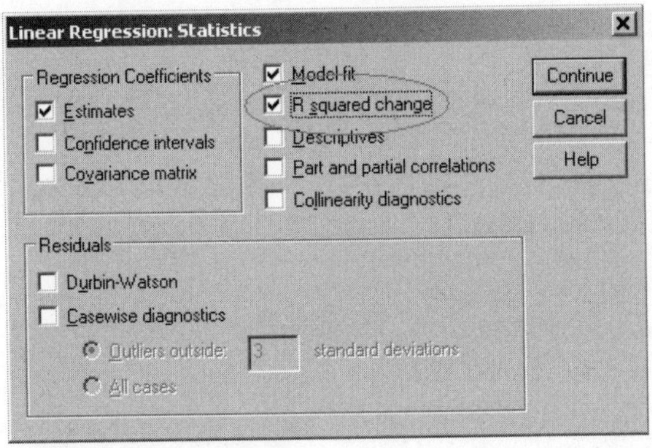

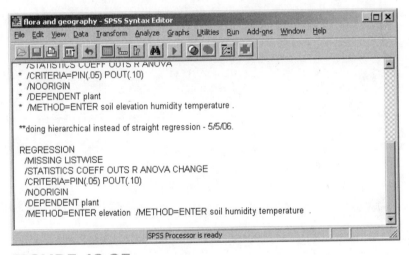

FIGURE 12.24. *Linear Regression: Statistics Dialogue Box.*

FIGURE 12.25. *Pasted Hierarchical Regression Syntax.*

You'll notice that this first table looks a little different—elevation is entered in the first stage, and the remaining three predictors are entered in the second stage.

In the table shown in Figure 12.27, because we selected R^2 change from the drop-down menu, we receive information about whether our additional three predictors are adding valued information, located in the second row. According to this table, they do ($\Delta F = 8.49$, p $<$ .05).

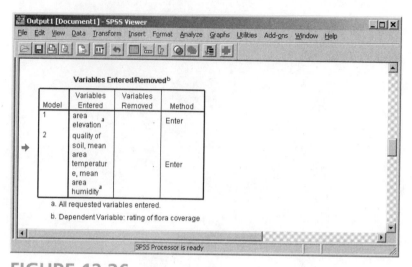

FIGURE 12.26. *Hierarchical Regression Output Table #1 (Variables Entered/Removed).*

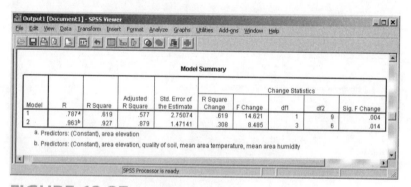

FIGURE 12.27. *Hierarchical Regression Output Table #3 (Significance of 1 and 4 Variable Models).*

If you don't select R^2 change when you're generating your syntax, the table shown in Figure 12.28 could mess you up. The first model is the information needed to compute the first row statistics in the 'Model Summary' table (Figure 12.27). The second model ANOVA statistics, however, are referring to all four IVs, not just the additional three that are included in the second step.

You'll note from the table in Figure 12.29 that the second model is actually the same information you would have received if you had run a

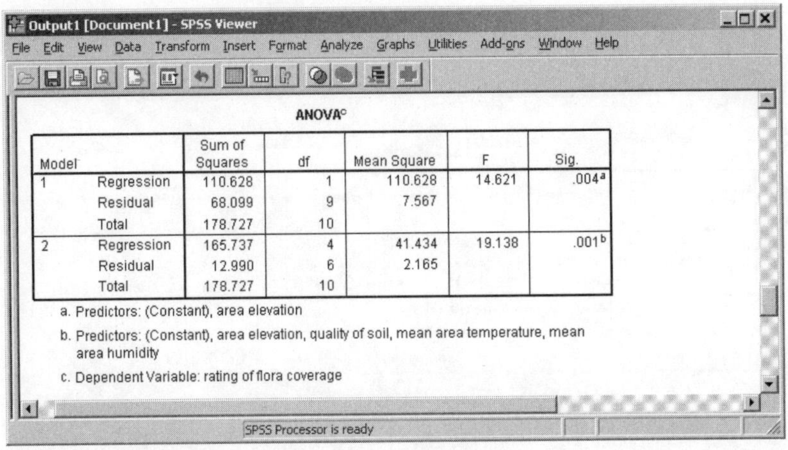

FIGURE 12.28 *Hierarchical Regression Output Table #4 (1 and 4 Variable Models).*

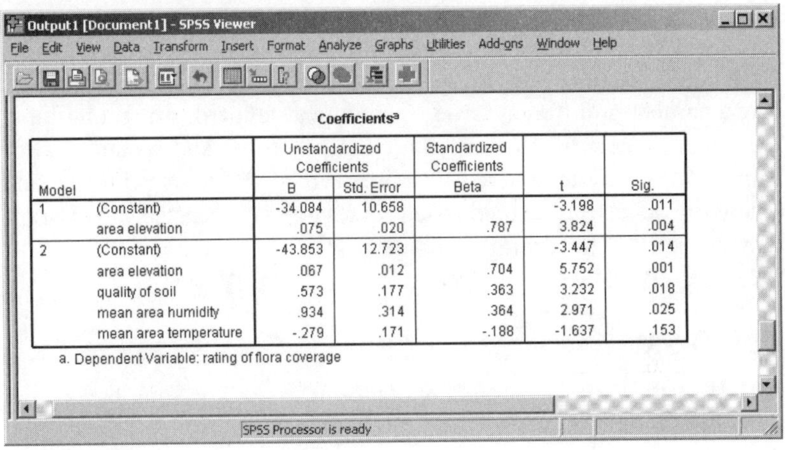

The ANOVA table shown in the figure:

ANOVA[c]

Model		Sum of Squares	df	Mean Square	F	Sig.
1	Regression	110.628	1	110.628	14.621	.004[a]
	Residual	68.099	9	7.567		
	Total	178.727	10			
2	Regression	165.737	4	41.434	19.138	.001[b]
	Residual	12.990	6	2.165		
	Total	178.727	10			

a. Predictors: (Constant), area elevation

b. Predictors: (Constant), area elevation, quality of soil, mean area temperature, mean area humidity

c. Dependent Variable: rating of flora coverage

FIGURE 12.29. *Hierarchical Regression Output Table #4 (Regression Coefficients).*

Coefficients[a]

Model		Unstandardized Coefficients		Standardized Coefficients	t	Sig.
		B	Std. Error	Beta		
1	(Constant)	-34.084	10.658		-3.198	.011
	area elevation	.075	.020	.787	3.824	.004
2	(Constant)	-43.853	12.723		-3.447	.014
	area elevation	.067	.012	.704	5.752	.001
	quality of soil	.573	.177	.363	3.232	.018
	mean area humidity	.934	.314	.364	2.971	.025
	mean area temperature	-.279	.171	-.188	-1.637	.153

a. Dependent Variable: rating of flora coverage

straight regression. The main thing you want to pay attention to in a hierarchical regression is that change in R^2 across stages.

There is one additional table that you receive with a hierarchical (or stepwise) regression, shown in Figure 12.30. This table is simply an acknowledgment that, in the first stage, these three IVs were not entered.

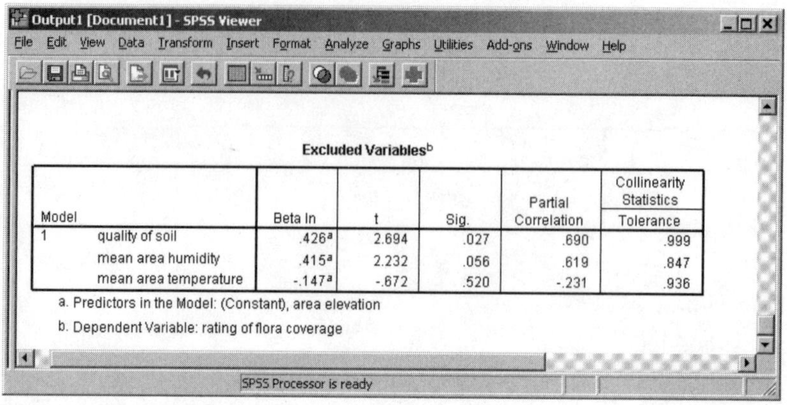

Excluded Variables[b]

Model		Beta In	t	Sig.	Partial Correlation	Collinearity Statistics Tolerance
1	quality of soil	.426[a]	2.694	.027	.690	.999
	mean area humidity	.415[a]	2.232	.056	.619	.847
	mean area temperature	-.147[a]	-.672	.520	-.231	.936

a. Predictors in the Model: (Constant), area elevation

b. Dependent Variable: rating of flora coverage

FIGURE 12.30. *Hierarchical Regression Output Table #5 (Excluded Variables at Each Step/Hierarchy).*

SUMMARY

Correlation is a very simple analysis in SPSS. Regression analyses can take a number of different forms, including a standard, straight multiple regression (where all IVs are entered at one time) and hierarchical or stepwise regression (where IVs are assigned different priorities and entered in stages). If a stage-based regression is requested, it is important to ask SPSS to report the change in R^2.

KEY TERMS

Adjusted R^2 Estimate of the population R^2, based on sample size and number of predictors.

Continuous IVs Predictor variables that are measured along a continuum (instead of by categories).

"Corr vars" SPSS command to request a bivariate (Pearson's) correlation.

Correlation Index of association between two variables.

Correlation matrix Square and symmetric matrix containing correlations from at least two variables.

Hierarchical regression Variance partitioning procedure in which the researcher specifies IV priority.

IV priority Relative importance of IVs, which can be specified through the use of variance partitioning regression models (such as stepwise or hierarchical).

Multicollinearity Excessive association among IVs.

Multiple R Correlation between your obtained and predicted DV scores.

Multiple regression Regression analysis with one DV and two or more IVs.

r Pearson's product moment correlation.

R^2 change Percentage of incremental DV variance explained by the contribution of additional IVs.

Regression equation Application of the regression analysis (an attempt to predict an unknown DV score based on known IV information).

Shrinkage Acknowledgment that the obtained multiple R tends to overestimate the population multiple R: a regression equation generated in one sample will exhibit a smaller predicted or observed correlation (multiple R) if applied to a different sample.

Sig. (2-tailed) Significance estimate based on a two-tailed hypothesis; this will always be more conservative than a significance estimate based on a one-tailed hypothesis.

Simple regression Regression analysis with one IV and one DV.

Stages Different blocks of IV specifications. The hierarchical and stepwise procedures are comprised of at least two stages.

Stepwise regression Variance partitioning procedure in which the computer specifies IV priority.

Straight regression Regression that does not assign IV priority.

X variable Regression term for IV or predictor.

Y variable Regression term for DV or outcome variable.

DISCUSSION QUESTIONS

1. Why is there an ANOVA table in my regression output?

2. Why doesn't SPSS include R^2 change as a default reported statistic?

3. Based on the following data, is there a relationship between shoe size and height? Friendliness and height? Shoe size and friendliness?

	SHOE SIZE	HEIGHT	FRIENDLINESS
Hector	12	68	2
Sue	7	66	10
Sally	17	75	9
Eugene	14	70	8
Valencia	8	64	7
Penelope	9.5	60	3
Fernando	5	63	2
Norbert	15	74	10

4. If I wanted to predict how tall someone might be, given their shoe size and friendliness rating, how would I go about doing that?

PART

3

ADVANCED MANIPULATIONS AND PROBLEM SOLVING

USING YOUR OUTPUT

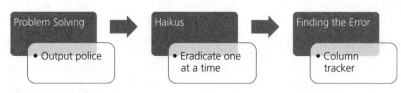

FIGURE 13.1. *Using Output to Problem-Solve.*

Contents

Maximizing Output Information

Summary

Key Terms

Discussion Questions

CHAPTER LEARNING OBJECTIVES

1. Problem solving with haikus
   - Offending word
   - Column location
2. Double-clicking in output files

Congratulations! You're now an SPSS pro—you possess enough knowledge to be truly dangerous. The current chapter further hones your ninja-like skills by teaching you how to maximize the utility of your output files.

PROBLEM SOLVING

Output files not only show up when you ask them to—sometimes they appear unexpectedly. This most commonly happens when you make an error with your syntax (say, you miss a period or put a comma where a space should be). When this happens, an output file pops up and reports the indiscretion. Here's what you do with these .spo intruders:

1. Take note of these elements:
   - The offending word
   - The column location of the error—when provided (SPSS does not always give you this information)
2. Close out of the .spo file—*don't* save it when you are prompted to do so.
3. Change your syntax based on the location and offending word.
4. Rerun your syntax and loop back to #1 if another error message pops up.

   Figure 13.2 provides a handy diagram of the cycle.

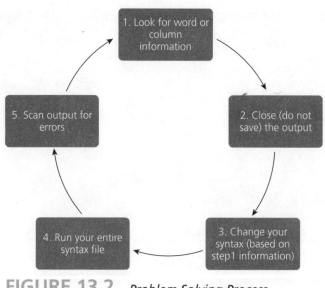

FIGURE 13.2. *Problem Solving Process (Using Output).*

Spaces in All the Wrong Places

As shown in Figure 13.3, I've introduced two common errors into the "add value labels" syntax from Chapter Five. Even with the give-away subhead of this section, you'll probably need to read over the commands four or five times before you catch the errors, which is why I included this chapter on problem solving. There's a better way to catch errors than visually scanning your syntax (although you should also generally do a visual check on your syntax before you run it).

When I run the syntax in Figure 13.3, I get the output file shown in Figure 13.4.

When output files (the SPSS police) show up, one of two things has happened. One possibility is that you requested some summary information (such as descriptives or frequencies) or some inferential information (such as t-test, ANOVA, correlation). Under these circumstances, you expect to see the police—you essentially called them and they're escorting your information to you. Alternatively, the police might be showing up unexpectedly to let you know about some suspicious activity that they've been noticing around the neighborhood.

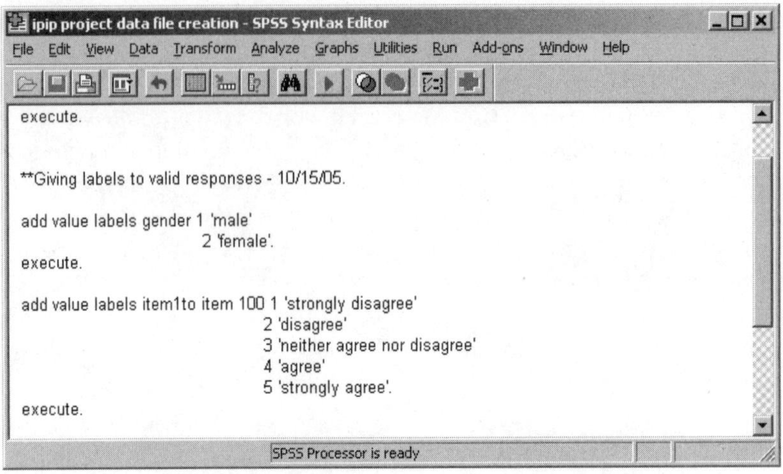

FIGURE 13.3. *Syntax Containing Errors.*

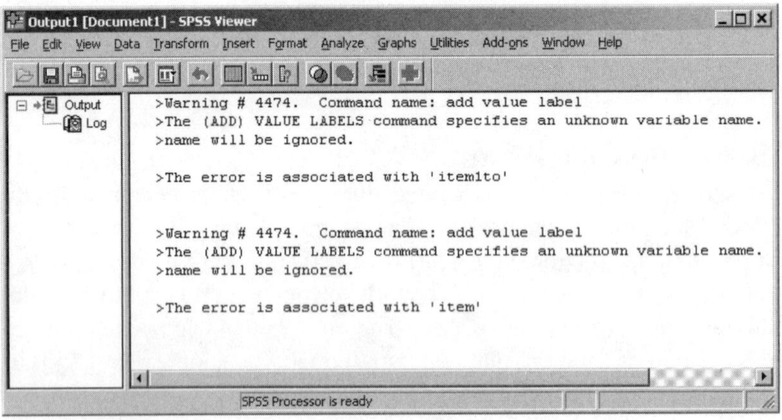

FIGURE 13.4. *Output Received When Your Syntax Contains Typos.*

This second reason for the police showing up (output file popping up) is actually quite helpful to the syntax writer. SPSS lets you know when this is the case (when you've made an error) by putting the $>$ character in the output file. When you see these $>$ characters, you know that something went terribly wrong with your syntax. Think of the $>$ as a big arrow pointing directly at *you*, assigning blame. Now you can fix the error and send the police on their way.

All errors are called out in three- to seven-line reports (typically three or four lines, one space, and one more line) that look to me somewhat like the haiku form of poetry—so I refer to them as haikus.

You should always try to remedy your errors *one at a time*, starting from the first reported error (the one closest to the top of the output file). I advise this because often one initial error will set off a chain of errors, but if you correct the first, it will be as if the other errors never existed.

In the output shown in Figure 13.4 there are two haikus or errors reported, but I'm focusing on just the first one. The first and last lines of the haiku are the most important. The first tells me what command SPSS thought I meant to invoke; the last line tells me what part of the command SPSS didn't like. I therefore know that there's a problem in my syntax associated with an "add value labels" command as well as the word "item1to". Now I need to scan my syntax file for an "item1to" associated with an "add value labels" command. Because your syntax files are often quite large, you may want to use the Find function in your syntax editor to locate the offending word (whatever is in quotes in the last line of your haiku), as shown in Figure 13.5.

Using the Find function, I've located a possible offender, as highlighted in Figure 13.6.

Sure enough, the offending word is associated with an "add value labels" command. This is good news for the SPSS user, because this is likely the cause of our error. We forgot to put a space between the words "item1" and "to" (see Figure 13.3). This is a very common error. Fixing the error, my revised syntax appears in Figure 13.7.

When I run this new syntax, in the new warning, shown in Figure 13.8, the police have less to report.

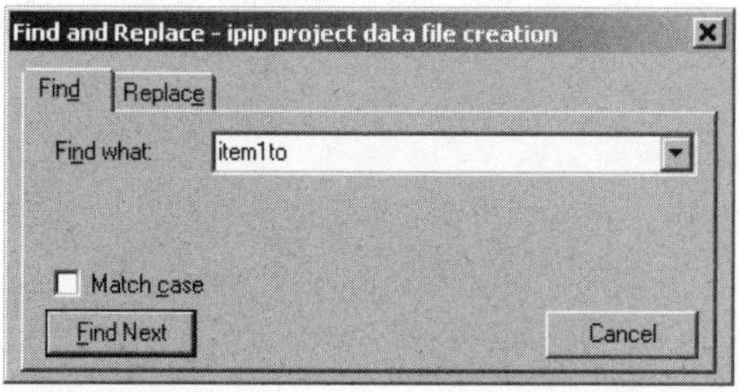

FIGURE 13.5. *Using the "Find" function of "Find and Replace" to Locate a Syntax Error.*

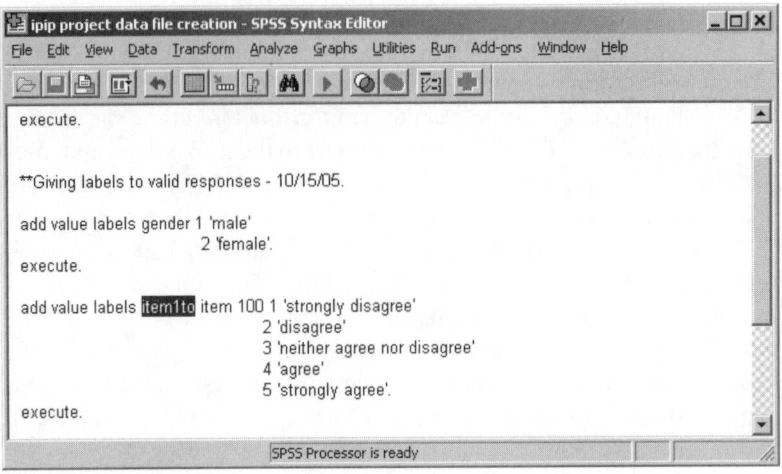

FIGURE 13.6. *Text Located by the "Find" function.*

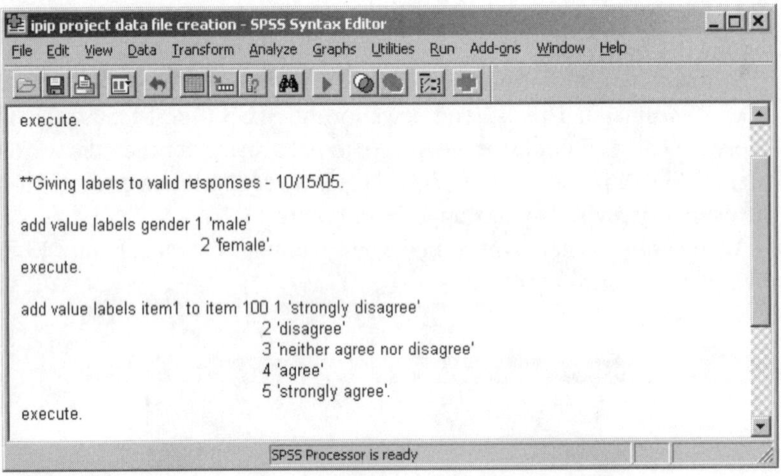

FIGURE 13.7. *Revised Syntax (item1 Corrected).*

We now have only one haiku; an improvement, but we still have work to do. As shown in Figure 13.9, we search for "__item" in our syntax.

But as shown in Figure 13.10, the find function is not as useful to us this time. The first possibly offending term that the Find function locates is not associated with an "add value label" command. The offending term

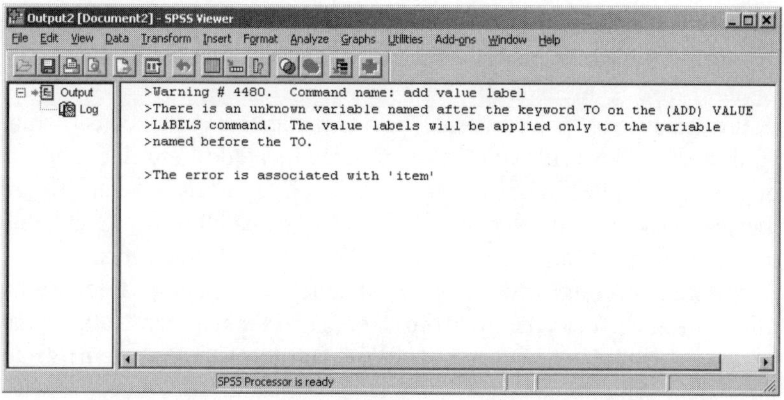

FIGURE 13.8. *Output File Identifying One Syntax Error.*

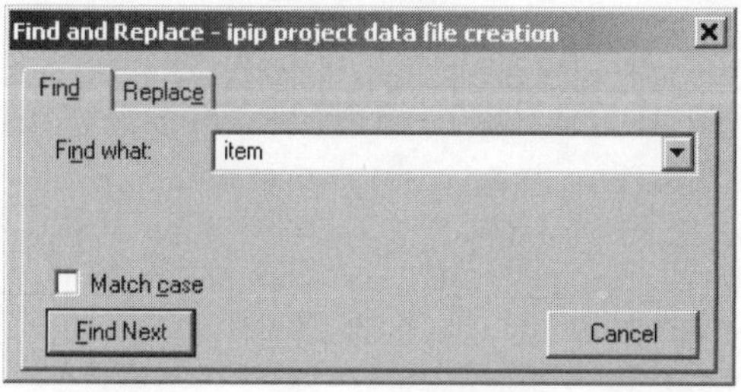

FIGURE 13.9. *Searching for "_item".*

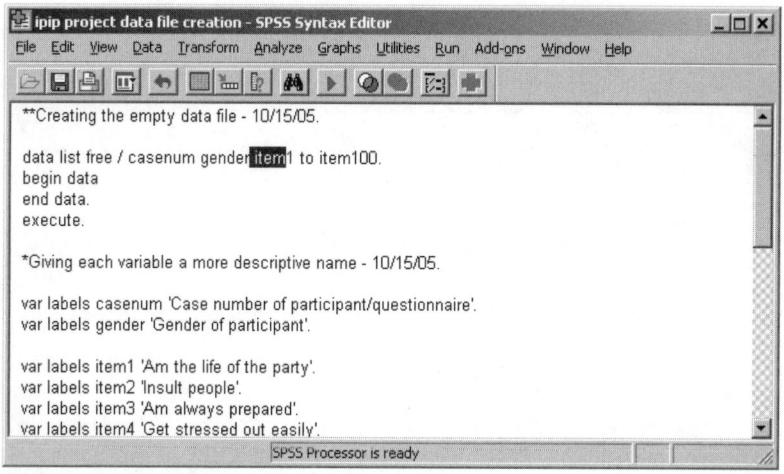

FIGURE 13.10. *Identified Syntax Element (Not the Offending Text).*

actually yields too many hits in this case for the Find function to provide any utility. I have to search visually through the syntax and locate the "_item" that is offensive.

It is because of such scenarios that you're best served by constructing your syntax files with similar commands located in similar sections of your syntax files—for example, all of my "var labels" commands are located consecutively. Notice in Figure 13.11 that all of my "add value labels" commands are located toward the bottom of my syntax.

Scanning through my "add value label" commands, I locate an offending space between the word "item" and the number "100". What I *intended* with the syntax was for all items (item1 through item100) to receive the same value labels. What I *did,* however, was wrongly specify a variable named "item 100". SPSS doesn't like spaces where they're not supposed to be—it believes that a space indicates that you've completed your previous thought and are moving on to the next thought.

If I now delete the space between "item" and "100" and run my syntax, I get no haikus. Spaces are frequently the cause of haikus—keep an eye out for them when you're problem solving.

Let's see what other kinds of haikus we can conjure with different errors. Figure 13.12 offers an example. Running this syntax (only slightly modified from the error-free syntax created in Chapter Six) results in the haiku shown in Figure 13.13.

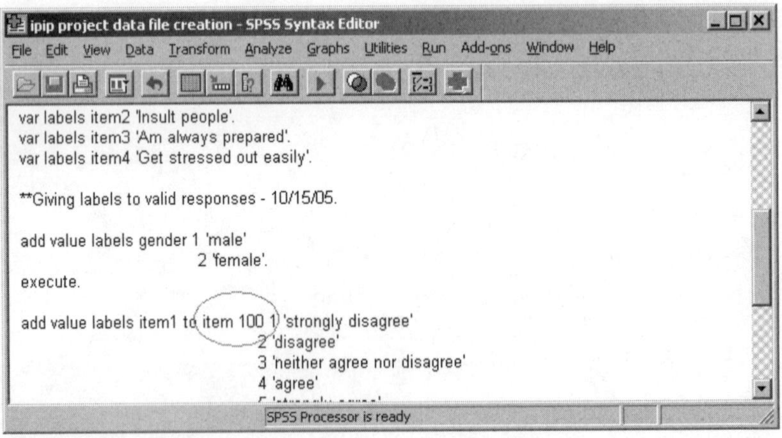

FIGURE 13.11. *Grouping of Similar Commands Within the Syntax File.*

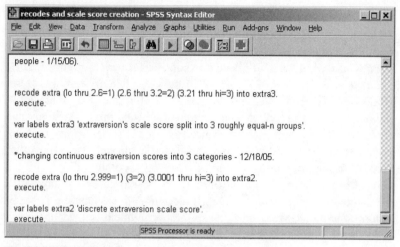

FIGURE 13.12. *Error-Filled Syntax.*

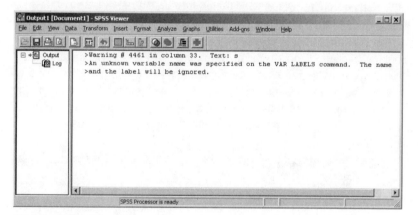

FIGURE 13.13. *Output File Reporting an Error.*

Notice the additional information located in the first line of this haiku: *where* SPSS has a problem (column 33). The column information, when provided, can be helpful, but it can also sometimes be misleading. The column where SPSS has a problem isn't necessarily the column where the error is, but generally it should be somewhere close. The information contained after the "Text:" is once again very important for our problem-solving efforts; in this case, we are looking for an offending "s".

Column Information

At the bottom right-hand corner of your syntax files is a *column tracker*. It will be hidden if your window is small, but if you increase the width of your syntax window, it will become visible (as shown in Figure 13.14).

The column tracker in Figure 13.14 indicates that my cursor is at line (row) 1 and column 1 in the syntax editor. To find the error indicated by the haiku, I need to look around column 33. To do this, I move my cursor until it's at column 33 (right after the word "scale" in my first-line comment; Figure 13.15), then I scroll down through the syntax file, looking for an offending "s" somewhere around column 33:

As I use the arrow key to scroll, my cursor will generally stay within the same column (when possible). If a command or statement is not 33 columns wide (for example, the execute commands), the cursor will place itself at the end of the command (closest to 33) and then correct itself at the next opportunity (when a command or statement does possess at least 33 characters). This makes it easier to visually scan the likely locations for your error. Eventually you'll find a likely culprit for the error, as shown in Figure 13.16.

It turns out that the problem isn't technically the "s" located at column 33, but the unwanted apostrophe in column 32. Along with orphaned spaces, these apostrophe hooligans are no strangers to the law, and you should always be on the lookout for them when you receive haikus. Deleting the offending apostrophe and rerunning the full syntax file yields no additional errors. We have successfully eradicated all haikus.

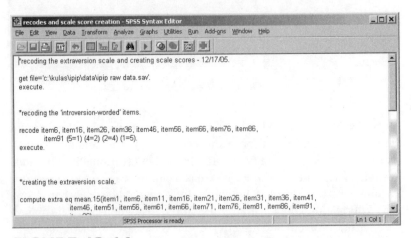

FIGURE 13.14. *Maximized Syntax Window with Column Tracker Visible (Lower Right-Hand Corner).*

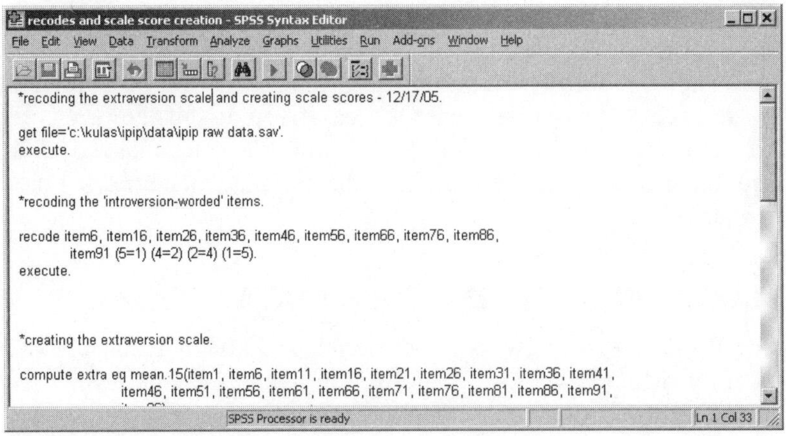

FIGURE 13.15. *Cursor Located in Line 1 (First Row) and Column 33.*

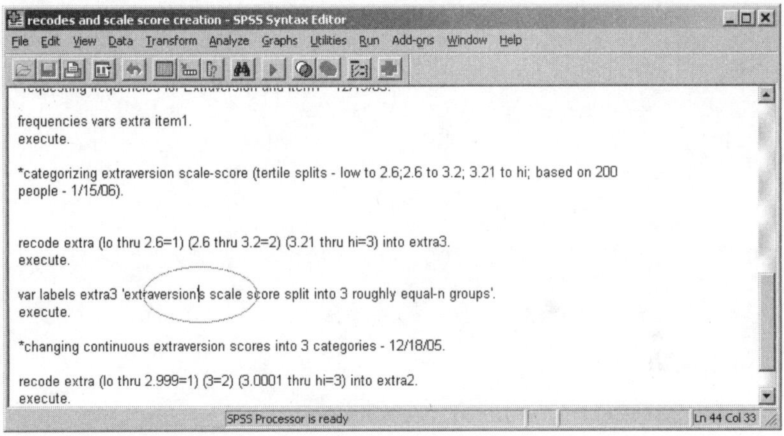

FIGURE 13.16. *Probable Error Located at Line 44 and Column 33.*

There Is One Little Thing . . .

A word of warning regarding the use of column information: although the column tracker gives you the location of your cursor, it technically does so by counting characters, not actual columns. This means that if you use the Tab key within your syntax file, as I do, the cursor will occasionally give you *bad* information. Keep in mind that the column number is accurate *as long as there are no tabs*. I really don't know why

SPSS works like this—it makes a mess out of problem solving—but I'm too attached to tabs not to use them, so I just complain. If you get into a really sticky problem-solving situation, you can always do a find and replace, replacing your tabs with spaces. If you do this, however, you need to rerun your syntax, as the column information contained in the error haiku may change as a result of the new column numbering used in your syntax file.

MAXIMIZING OUTPUT INFORMATION

Now to our second chapter objective, using the power of double-clicking within your output files. The information that is presented when you request output is actually shown in a truncated format. Sometimes you'll need a greater amount of accuracy or precision than what is reported. Fortunately, precise information is available—you just have to know how to ask for it. For instance, if I needed to know descriptive information to the millionths place, I would first run my "descriptives" command (introduced in Chapter Nine) as shown in Figure 13.17.

From this request I would get the output shown in Figure 13.18.

By double-clicking on the reported numbers, you can see the precise estimate (for the mean, for example) as shown in Figure 13.19.

The point is, even though SPSS reports information in a truncated, digestible format, there is a more precise estimate lurking in SPSS if you

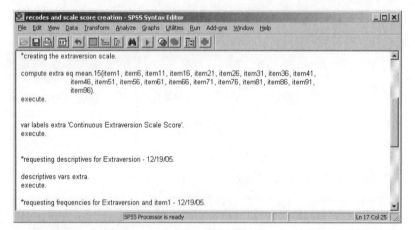

FIGURE 13.17. *Requesting Descriptive Statistics for the Extraversion Variable.*

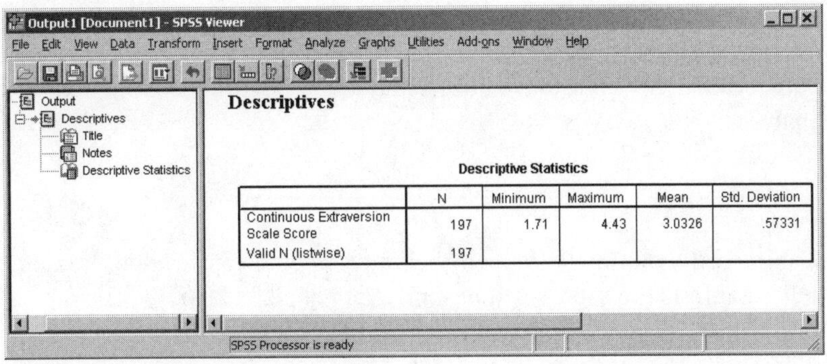

FIGURE 13.18. *Standard Descriptive Output Table (a Few Decimal Places Reported).*

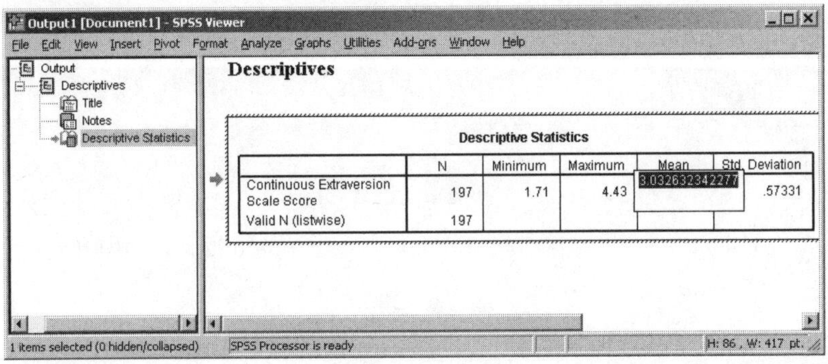

FIGURE 13.19. *More Specific Value of the Extraversion Scale Mean Score (Many Decimal Places Reported).*

go looking for it. SPSS uses these precise estimates for computations and analyses, but when it *reports* the numbers, it uses a convention (generally reporting to the nearest hundredth, thousandth, or ten thousandth).

SUMMARY

You will encounter haikus when you use SPSS. You should eradicate them one at a time, starting with the first reported haiku. If you use the column information to locate the error, remember that column actually refers to *characters*, including the tab character, so the information can be misleading.

Double-clicking in output files gives you more detailed information regarding SPSS estimates. Although truncated numbers are presented in output files, SPSS uses nontruncated numbers for calculations and analyses.

KEY TERMS

Column information Potentially helpful, potentially misleading problem-solving information (provided in some, but not all haikus).

Column tracker Number located in the lower right-hand corner of every syntax file, which identifies the location of the cursor (number of characters from the left).

Find function Useful with haiku information in problem-solving applications.

> Character that SPSS places before all lines in an output file, indicating that an error has occurred.

DISCUSSION QUESTIONS

1. Why do I have to start with the first haiku?

2. How can I make the most use out of the column tracker information?

CHAPTER

OTHER TRICKS OF THE TRADE

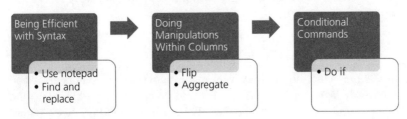

FIGURE 14.1. *Working Efficiently and Performing Advance Data Manipulations.*

Contents

CHAPTER LEARNING OBJECTIVES

1. Using Notepad

2. Doing manipulations across rows

3. Scanning for duplicate cases

4. Introducing conditional statements: "do if", "end if"

This chapter contains miscellany that didn't quite fit into the other chapters and continues your progress toward black-belt SPSS status. It basically contains commands and techniques that will make your syntax writing more efficient.

SALVAGING OLD SYNTAX

In Chapter One, an analogy was made between: (1) syntax files and Microsoft Word, and (2) data files and Microsoft Excel. Excel (and other spreadsheet) files can be directly imported into SPSS (see Chapter Four). Similarly, word processor information can be cut and pasted into syntax files (and vice versa).

The Importance of Notepad

Notepad is a stripped-down word processing program that is packaged with Microsoft Windows (you can find it at Start>Programs>Accessories). If you do not have Windows, any standard word processor will do. Notepad is particularly useful because it does not support formatting functions such as tables (syntax files do not support these formatting functions either). Notepad can be used to change variable names or analytical commands from one application to another (for example, salvaging old syntax); it is also useful for creating your variable labels (talked about in Chapter Five).

Using the Appendix A and B example, instead of individually typing variable labels for all one hundred items directly into my syntax file, I can use the information that's already stored in Microsoft Word (as a table). First I copy the first column of my table from Word, as shown in Figure 14.2.

Then I paste this information into Notepad, as shown in Figure 14.3.

Notice that the formatting information (table definitions such as lines/borders) did not transfer to Notepad; this is a good thing. Now I can get creative with the Find and Replace function of Notepad to get my text SPSS-ready. First I'll get rid of all apostrophes (notice the grammatically correct but SPSS-troublesome apostrophe for items #12 and #17). I do this by searching for an apostrophe and replacing it with nothing (you can do this), as shown in Figure 14.4.

Choosing Replace All gets rid of any apostrophes that were in my item prompts and results in the file as shown in Figure 14.5 (notice #12 and #17 again).

Now I need to get rid of the periods after my item numbers—I'm doing this by replacing "period, space, space" with "space, space, space, space, space". This will retain my periods at the *end* of the items while (1) getting rid of my periods after the numbers and (2) allowing me to use the "space, space, space, space, space" for a later Find and Replace. I use five spaces because there may be some accidental spaces at the end

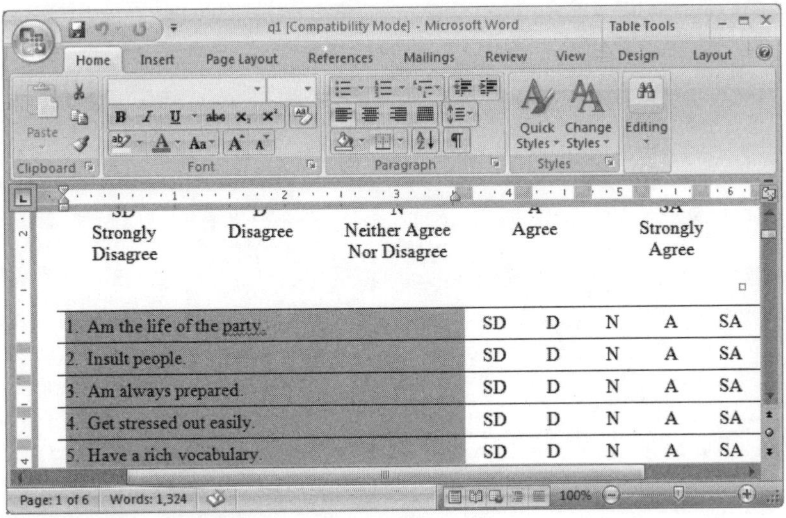

FIGURE 14.2. *Personality Questionnaire Variable Information (Word Format).*

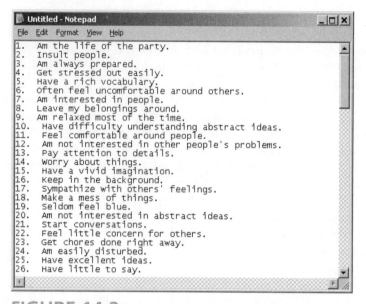

FIGURE 14.3. *Personality Questionnaire Variable Information (Notepad Format).*

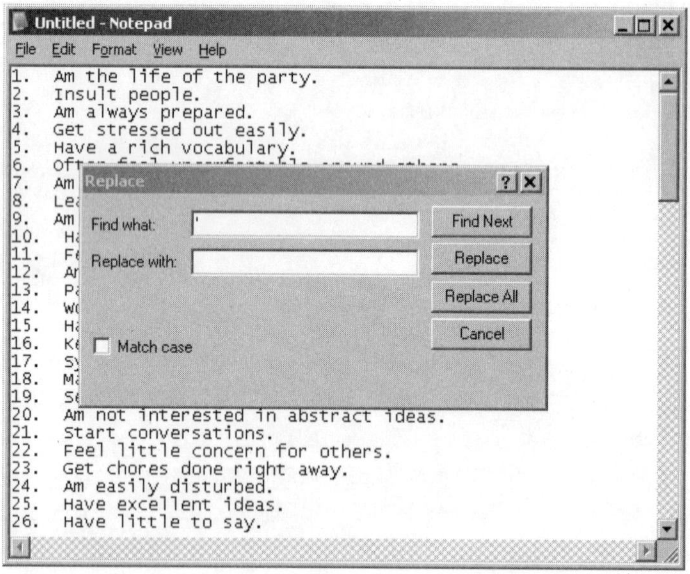

FIGURE 14.4. *Find and Replace (' with Nothing).*

```
Untitled - Notepad                                    _ □ ×
File  Edit  Format  View  Help
1.   Am the life of the party.
2.   Insult people.
3.   Am always prepared.
4.   Get stressed out easily.
5.   Have a rich vocabulary.
6.   Often feel uncomfortable around others.
7.   Am interested in people.
8.   Leave my belongings around.
9.   Am relaxed most of the time.
10.  Have difficulty understanding abstract ideas.
11.  Feel comfortable around people.
12.  Am not interested in other peoples problems.
13.  Pay attention to details.
14.  Worry about things.
15.  Have a vivid imagination.
16.  Keep in the background.
17.  Sympathize with others feelings.
18.  Make a mess of things.
19.  Seldom feel blue.
20.  Am not interested in abstract ideas.
21.  Start conversations.
22.  Feel little concern for others.
23.  Get chores done right away.
24.  Am easily disturbed.
25.  Have excellent ideas.
26.  Have little to say.
```

FIGURE 14.5. *Personality Questionnaire Variable Information Without Apostrophes.*

of some of my items (if you spaced over for some reason when originally typing the items, Notepad will store the "space" as a character— alternatively I could replace "period, space, space" with a unique character that's not otherwise in my file, such as a "$"). Figure 14.6 finds periods and replaces them with 5 space characters.

Now, as shown in Figure 14.7, I have a list of variables with five spaces between the item number and the item text.

Now I can replace five spaces with "space, apostrophe" to get an apostrophe at the beginning of my items, as shown in Figure 14.8.

Running that replace as well as a "period" for an "apostrophe, period" gives us the results shown in Figure 14.9.

Now you've made the most of the usefulness of Notepad and can copy "var labels item" and paste it repetitively down your one hundred rows. (There is one alternative: you can run eighteen separate find and replace cycles, first replacing "1" with "var labels item1", "2" with "var labels item2", and so on for numbers 1 through 9, then replacing "1var labels item1" with "1", "2var labels item2" with "2", and so on for the same numbers (1 through 9). You have to do this second step

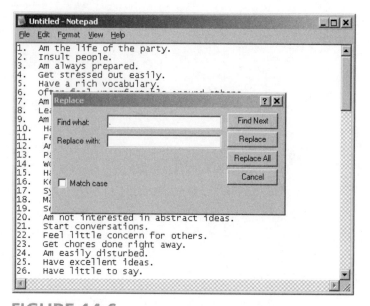

FIGURE 14.6. *Find and Replace (Period with 5 Spaces).*

FIGURE 14.7. *Personality Questionnaire Variable Information Without Periods after Numbers.*

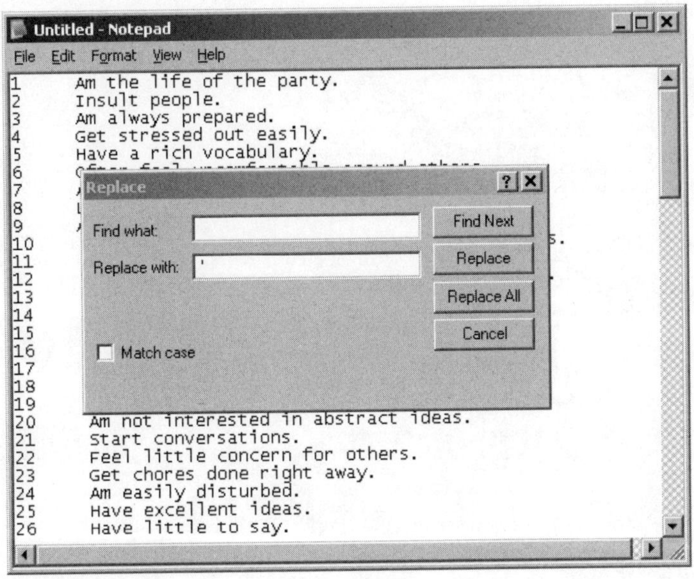

FIGURE 14.8. *Find & Replace (5 Spaces with Space & Apostrophe).*

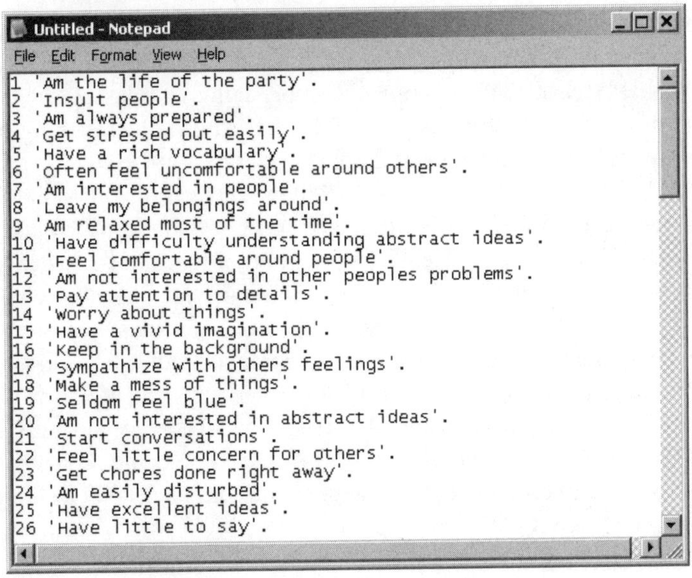

FIGURE 14.9. *Personality Questionnaire Variable Information Close to SPSS-Friendly Format.*

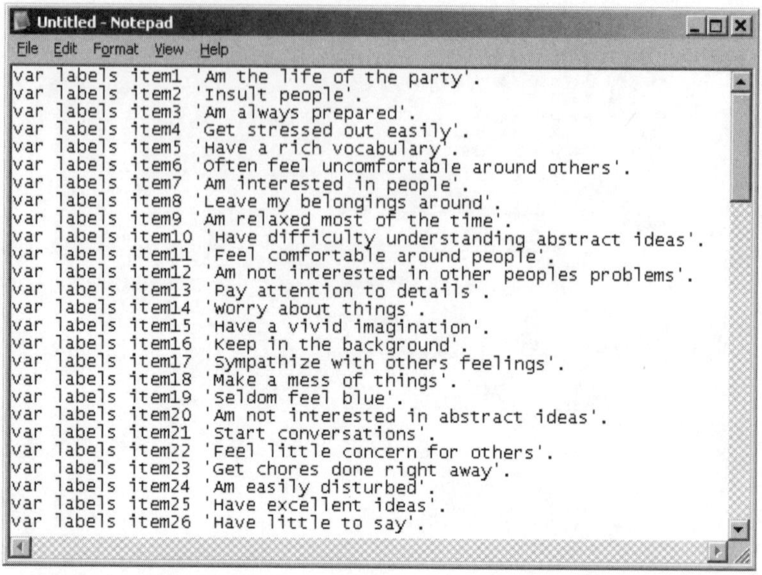


```
var labels item1 'Am the life of the party'.
var labels item2 'Insult people'.
var labels item3 'Am always prepared'.
var labels item4 'Get stressed out easily'.
var labels item5 'Have a rich vocabulary'.
var labels item6 'Often feel uncomfortable around others'.
var labels item7 'Am interested in people'.
var labels item8 'Leave my belongings around'.
var labels item9 'Am relaxed most of the time'.
var labels item10 'Have difficulty understanding abstract ideas'.
var labels item11 'Feel comfortable around people'.
var labels item12 'Am not interested in other peoples problems'.
var labels item13 'Pay attention to details'.
var labels item14 'Worry about things'.
var labels item15 'Have a vivid imagination'.
var labels item16 'Keep in the background'.
var labels item17 'Sympathize with others feelings'.
var labels item18 'Make a mess of things'.
var labels item19 'Seldom feel blue'.
var labels item20 'Am not interested in abstract ideas'.
var labels item21 'Start conversations'.
var labels item22 'Feel little concern for others'.
var labels item23 'Get chores done right away'.
var labels item24 'Am easily disturbed'.
var labels item25 'Have excellent ideas'.
var labels item26 'Have little to say'.
```

FIGURE 14.10. *Personality Questionnaire Variable Information SPSS-Ready.*

because the first step will insert "var labels item1", for example, in between the two "1"s of item11, the "2" and "1" of item21, and so forth. It's probably easier at this point to simply copy and paste "var labels item" in front of each number.) Figure 14.10 shows the resulting notepad information when either of these two methods are used.

Now you can copy and paste the whole shebang into your syntax file, stick one "execute." at the bottom, and you're good to go. Syntax files also contain the Find and Replace option, but it tends to be easier to do this within a separate file (that is, not your main syntax file). If you don't have Notepad, you actually *should* do this in a separate syntax file.

In the current example, the whole "apostrophe" problem could also be addressed through using double quotation marks instead of apostrophes. This is just one contrived example of how Notepad can generally help your syntax writing. People who frequently use SPSS could probably fill a whole book with different creative applications of this general technique.

TRICKING SPSS TO "THINK" ACROSS ROWS

Chapter Six focused on SPSS's tendency to think across columns for data manipulations. Occasionally you will want SPSS to think across rows for manipulations (say, to place a mean variable score in your data matrix instead of just having SPSS's output file report it). There are two main ways to do this: (1) you can transpose your data matrix (turn columns into rows, rows into columns), then do the data manipulation, or (2) you can aggregate the data file. Generally aggregating is more useful than a matrix transposition, but we will cover both options.

Transposing Your Matrix

If you've ever had a desire to turn your world (or at least your data) upside down, you can use the *matrix transposition* command. First, you specify "flip vars=", then you list all of the variables that you want to transpose, as shown in Figure 14.11. If you exclude some variables from your command, they will be lost from your transposed matrix.

Once again, here I can specify the "to" shortcut or list all variables separately. I could have actually specified "casenum to item100" and every variable would have been transposed—I don't recommend getting into that habit, however, because you may have to backtrack what you have done, and that is easier to do if you specify different variable groups (for example, I may forget that gender was included in the transposition).

If I now look at my data file, as shown in Figure 14.12, it will have as many columns as people, plus one—SPSS will create an additional variable called "CASE_LBL" that contains all of your variable names—this will be the first column in your newly transposed matrix.

The default is to label your "people" as var001>varXXX (the "X's represent the number of people in your original file). If I had one thousand people in my data file, SPSS would label the columns "var0001"→ "var1000". If I had a few hundred thousand, SPSS would label the columns

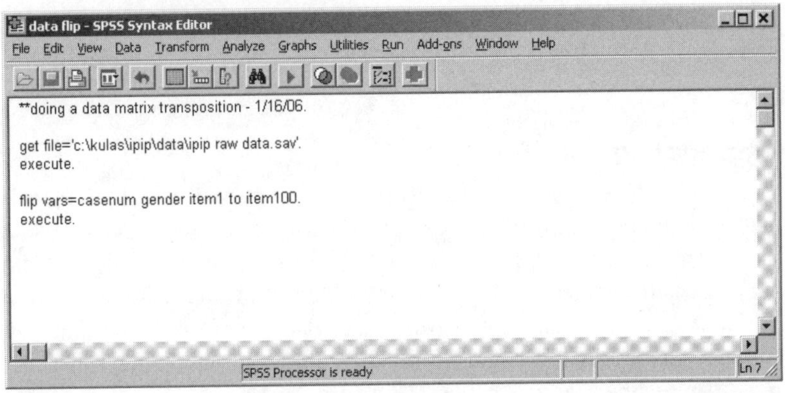

FIGURE 14.11. *Syntax Command for Matrix Transposition.*

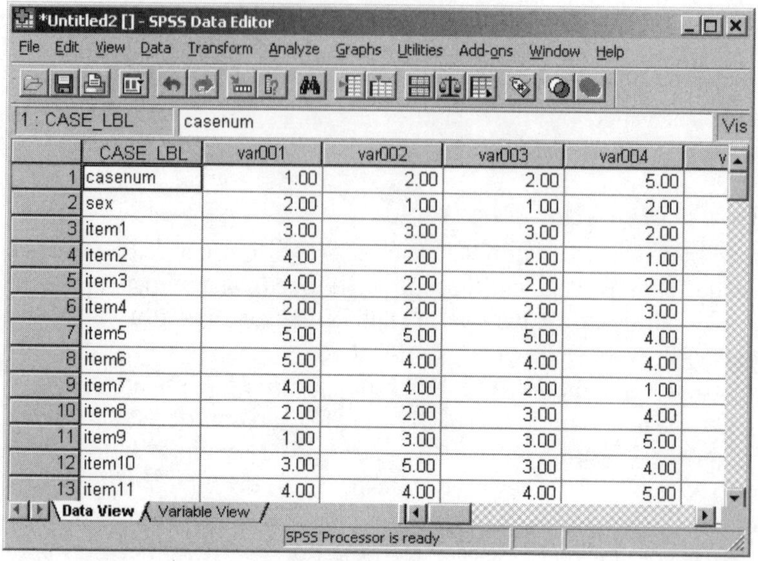

	CASE_LBL	var001	var002	var003	var004
1	casenum	1.00	2.00	2.00	5.00
2	sex	2.00	1.00	1.00	2.00
3	item1	3.00	3.00	3.00	2.00
4	item2	4.00	2.00	2.00	1.00
5	item3	4.00	2.00	2.00	2.00
6	item4	2.00	2.00	2.00	3.00
7	item5	5.00	5.00	5.00	4.00
8	item6	5.00	4.00	4.00	4.00
9	item7	4.00	4.00	2.00	1.00
10	item8	2.00	2.00	3.00	4.00
11	item9	1.00	3.00	3.00	5.00
12	item10	3.00	5.00	3.00	4.00
13	item11	4.00	4.00	4.00	5.00

FIGURE 14.12. *Transposed Data.*

"var000001">"varXXXXXX". Now if I want to create a mean score for each item (that will be retained in my data file), I simply write a compute statement, as shown in Figure 14.13 (there are two hundred people in my original data file, so my compute statement will include var001 through var200).

Now if I want to get my data file back to its original state, I can do a second transposition, but now my last *row* (row #201) will contain item averages. Figure 14.14 documents the general procedure for the full 2-flip loop, and Figure 14.15 presents the syntax to accomplish this with our personality data.

Aggregating Your Files

There actually are more occasions on which you will find the "aggregate" command useful than occasions on which you will want to use a matrix transposition—more so than then "flip" command, I think. One such occasion is the identification and deletion of duplicate cases. It is not unusual when dealing with very large data sets to discover that you have duplicate rows of data (you'd likely find this out through inspecting a "frequencies" output table). There are numerous reasons why these things happen—one common cause of data duplication is related to the

```
data flip - SPSS Syntax Editor                                    _ □ ×
File  Edit  View  Data  Transform  Analyze  Graphs  Utilities  Run  Add-ons  Window  Help

**doing a data matrix transposition - 1/16/06.

get file='c:\kulas\ipip\data\ipip raw data.sav'.
execute.

flip vars=casenum to item100.
execute.

*now computing mean scores for each item - 1/16/06.

compute item_avg eq mean.150(var001 to var200).
execute.

                        SPSS Processor is ready                      Ln 1
```

FIGURE 14.13. *Computing Item Averages That Will Be Placed in the Data File (Rather than Reported in an Output File).*

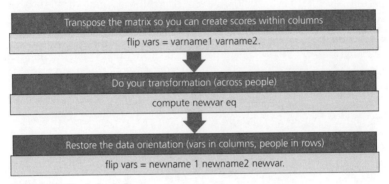

Transpose the matrix so you can create scores within columns

flip vars = varname1 varname2.

Do your transformation (across people)

compute newvar eq

Restore the data orientation (vars in columns, people in rows)

flip vars = newname 1 newname2 newvar.

FIGURE 14.14. *Matrix Transposition Process.*

```
data flip - SPSS Syntax Editor                                    _ □ ×
File  Edit  View  Data  Transform  Analyze  Graphs  Utilities  Run  Add-ons  Window  Help

execute.

flip vars=casenum to item100.
execute.

*now computing mean scores for each item - 1/16/06.

compute item_avg eq mean.150(var001 to var200).
execute.

*transposing back so items are in columns.

flip vars=case_lbl to item_avg.
execute.

                        SPSS Processor is ready                      Ln 1
```

FIGURE 14.15. *Syntax for Transposing, Computing Item Menus, then Restoring the Data to Its Original Configuration.*

data storage and retrieval process used by many organizations. It's not unusual to ask for a "data dump" (retrieving stored data) for a particular range of dates. If you later request a second "data dump" and accidentally overlap the date range, you'll likely end up with duplicate information in your data files. It doesn't really matter how it happens if you're staring at a 250,000-person data file and asked to delete duplicate cases. The point is, you need a tool to help identify and delete duplicates.

Figure 14.16 shows an example of a situation in which we have duplicate information in our personality questionnaire data file. This could happen if two people accidentally entered the same questionnaire into the file, for example.

Typically you do *not* want to visually scroll through your data file and manually delete duplicate cases—first of all, that's a process that is just begging for mistakes to be made, and second, you'll burn your retinas out—don't do it. Instead, you can control everything through syntax by using the "aggregate" command, as Figure 14.17 describes; Figure 14.18 shows the syntax.

The command "first" tells the aggregate function to take the first nonmissing value it finds for each individual "casenum" (the break variable).

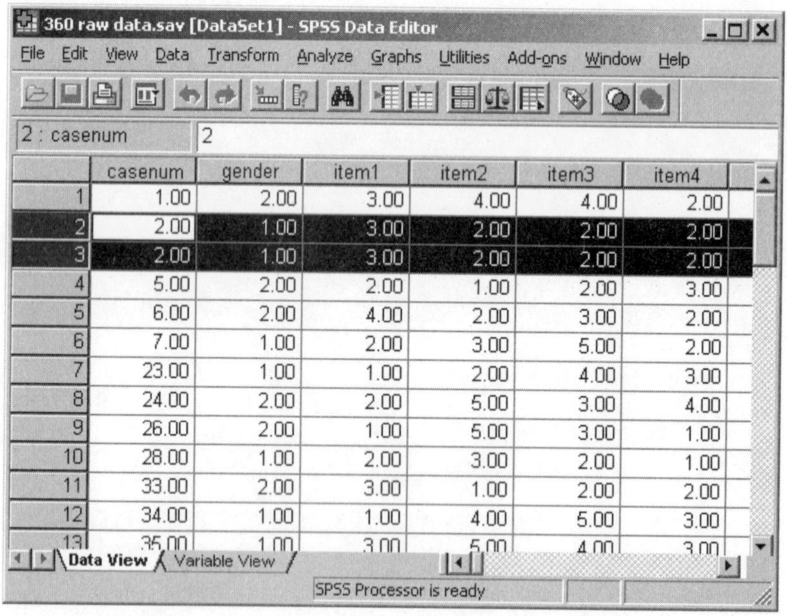

	casenum	gender	item1	item2	item3	item4
1	1.00	2.00	3.00	4.00	4.00	2.00
2	2.00	1.00	3.00	2.00	2.00	2.00
3	2.00	1.00	3.00	2.00	2.00	2.00
4	5.00	2.00	2.00	1.00	2.00	3.00
5	6.00	2.00	4.00	2.00	3.00	2.00
6	7.00	1.00	2.00	3.00	5.00	2.00
7	23.00	1.00	1.00	2.00	4.00	3.00
8	24.00	2.00	2.00	5.00	3.00	4.00
9	26.00	2.00	1.00	5.00	3.00	1.00
10	28.00	1.00	2.00	3.00	2.00	1.00
11	33.00	2.00	3.00	1.00	2.00	2.00
12	34.00	1.00	1.00	4.00	5.00	3.00
13	35.00	1.00	3.00	5.00	4.00	3.00

FIGURE 14.16. *Data File with Duplicate Cases.*

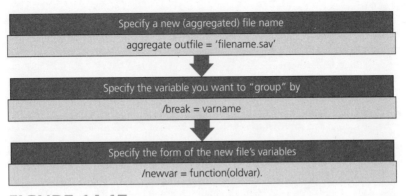

FIGURE 14.17. *Important Aggregate Commands.*

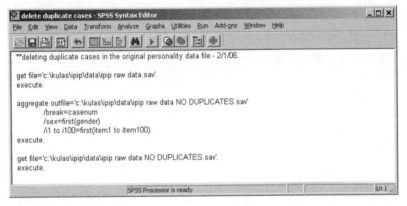

FIGURE 14.18. *Creating a New Data File That Contains No Duplicate Casenums.*

SPSS will delete the extra rows that contain the same casenum and save the new file wherever you tell the program to put it. The only real drawback to this approach is you'll lose all of your variable and value label information, because you renamed all of your variables in the new data file, so gender is now "sex", item1 is now "i1", and so on). Figure 14.19 shows the data file created by running the Figure 14.18 syntax.

This really isn't a big deal if you know how to use the "rename" command, as shown in Figure 14.20.

Now you're back to your original file format. You can now paste your previously created "var labels" and "add value labels" commands to the end of this syntax (but make sure to place it before the "save outfile"

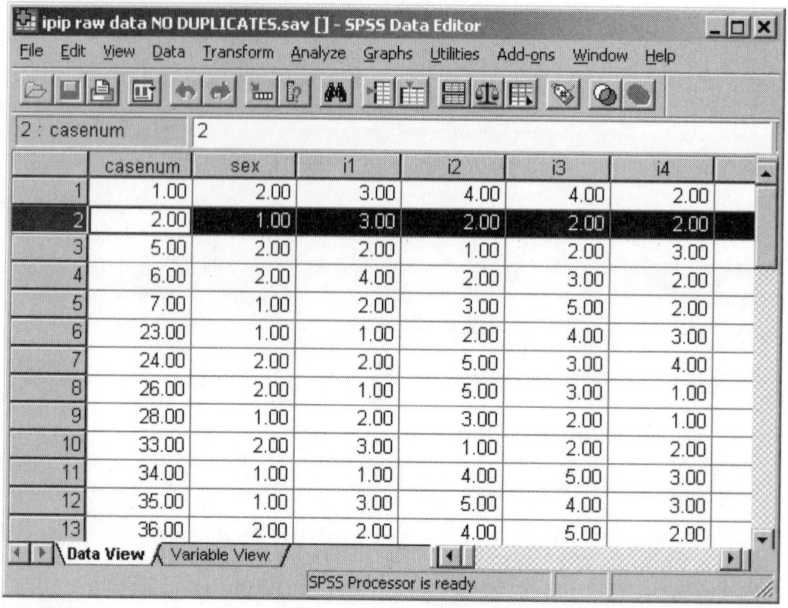

FIGURE 14.19. *Data File with Duplicate Cases Deleted.*

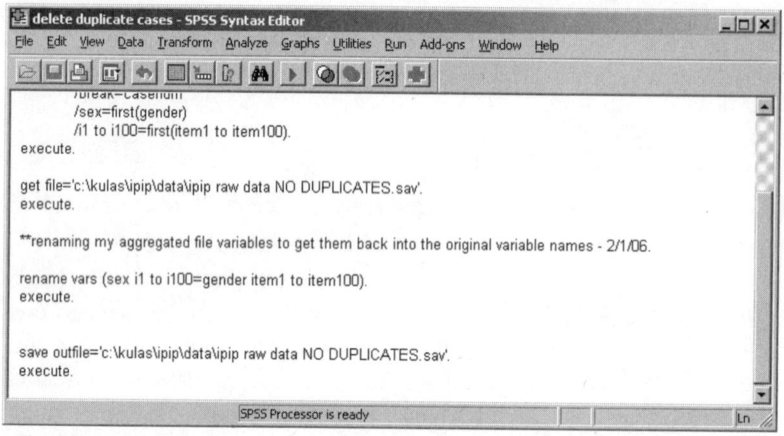

FIGURE 14.20. *Renaming Variables to Their Original Specification.*

command). You'll notice in the preceding syntax that this is one of the few times I'll actually save an "outfile" using the same file name as the "get file" name. Generally you should avoid doing this, but similarly you do not want to create *too many* data files that are essentially similar to each other.

"DO IF" AND "END IF"

One of the most *useful* sets of commands you will use is a set of logical statements: "do if", "else if", and "end if". These statements allow you to set up logical parameters around data manipulations. You may find yourself having a choice of doing either "recode . . . into" or "do if", "end if" statements. They can often be used for the same purpose. For example, in Chapter Six, questionnaire respondents were classified as either introverted, extraverted, or on the fence. To make this classification with the recode statement, we had to pick maximum (2.999) and minimum (3.0001) values for the introverted and extraverted classifications.

The "do if", "end if" command allows you to classify without specifying maximums and minimums. You use the "do if", "end if" commands to enclose a transformation command (usually "compute'), as described in Figure 14.21; Figure 14.22 shows the syntax. Trichotomizing extraversion with these commands is pretty easy.

It is best to learn the "do if", "end if" commands this way, through using separate four-line commands for each possible "if". Notice that I used the "lt" and "gt" commands—any score less than 3 (i.e., 2.9999 or 2.99999999999) is covered. Just like "split file," the "do if" statement is a light-switch command. You need to remember to turn off the conditional statement by specifying the "end if".

When you get a little more familiar with the "do if", "end if"s, you can throw a few "else if" commands in there, as shown in Figure 14.23 (this makes your syntax a bit more efficient, but is not necessary).

Appendix D contains an example syntax file that incorporates multiple commands—I've annotated the file so you should be able to follow

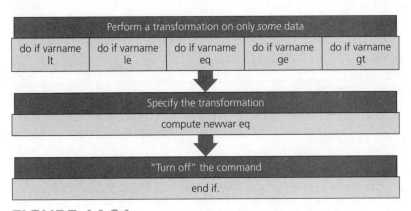

FIGURE 14.21. *Using the "do if," "end if" Function.*

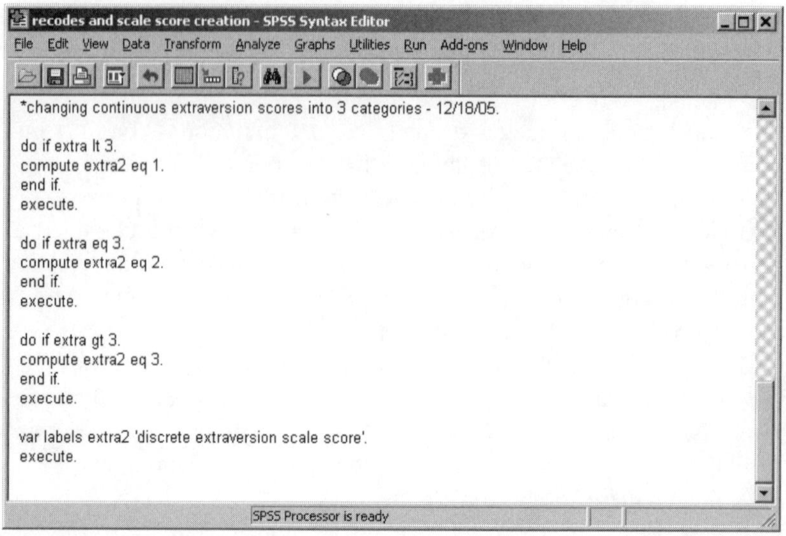
recodes and scale score creation - SPSS Syntax Editor
File Edit View Data Transform Analyze Graphs Utilities Run Add-ons Window Help
*changing continuous extraversion scores into 3 categories - 12/18/05.
do if extra lt 3.
compute extra2 eq 1.
end if.
execute.
do if extra eq 3.
compute extra2 eq 2.
end if.
execute.
do if extra gt 3.
compute extra2 eq 3.
end if.
execute.
var labels extra2 'discrete extraversion scale score'.
execute.
SPSS Processor is ready

FIGURE 14.22. *Trichotomizing Extraversion.*

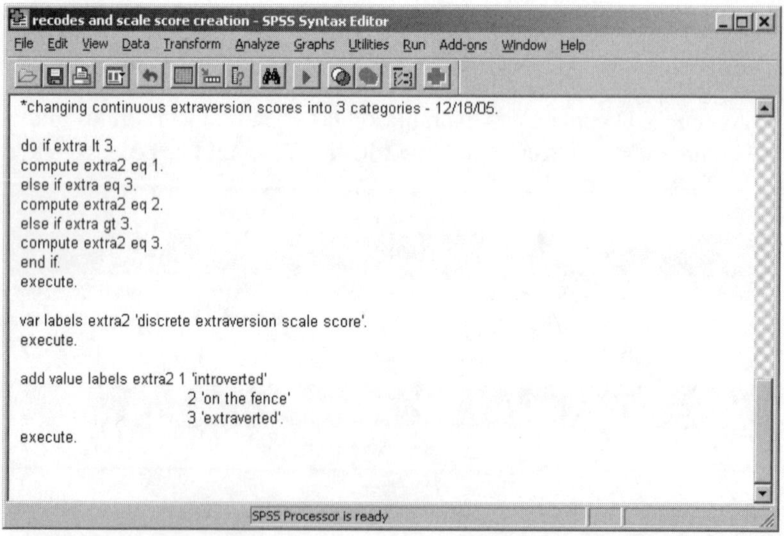
recodes and scale score creation - SPSS Syntax Editor
File Edit View Data Transform Analyze Graphs Utilities Run Add-ons Window Help
*changing continuous extraversion scores into 3 categories - 12/18/05.
do if extra lt 3.
compute extra2 eq 1.
else if extra eq 3.
compute extra2 eq 2.
else if extra gt 3.
compute extra2 eq 3.
end if.
execute.
var labels extra2 'discrete extraversion scale score'.
execute.
add value labels extra2 1 'introverted'
2 'on the fence'
3 'extraverted'.
execute.
SPSS Processor is ready

FIGURE 14.23. *Trichotomizing Extraversion Through Using the "else if" Command.*

along with the procedures. There are many other useful commands that haven't been covered in this book, but if this type of book gets too long, it somewhat defeats the purpose. I've included some of these commands along with the commands actually used in the book in Appendix E. It's my hope that at this point you have enough exposure to feel comfortable using SPSS through keeping syntax diaries.

Remember, the main point of this book is to get you used to operating SPSS through the specification of syntax files—never use the Data Editor when doing data manipulations or analyses. The first file you should access *every time* you use SPSS is a syntax file.

Use syntax.
End if.
Execute.

SUMMARY

You can use Notepad to make your monotonous syntax writing a lot more efficient. Develop skill with Notepad and you will benefit within SPSS. If you want to do operations or manipulations across rows, you can either transpose or aggregate the data file. One practical application of aggregating is to "get rid" of duplicate cases. One useful manipulation command that can be used in many different applications is "do if". Using all of the manipulation commands listed in this book, there should be no data management problem beyond your capability.

KEY TERMS

Aggregate SPSS command to collapse across rows; if you use aggregate, you must specify a new outfile name.

CASE_LBL SPSS creates this variable when you transpose your matrix; old variable names are kept in this SPSS-generated string variable.

"Do if" Command that tells SPSS there are conditions to be met prior to any transformation or analysis; must be accompanied by an "end if".

"Else if" Optional command to use in a "do if", "end if" sequence.

"End if" Command that notifies SPSS that your conditional statement has been completed; each "do if" must be followed (eventually) by an "end if".

First Subcommand to the aggregate function. Many more subcommands can be specified; "first" is useful for deleting duplicate cases.

"Flip" SPSS command to perform a matrix transposition.

Matrix transposition Turning columns into rows and rows into columns; flipping a matrix along its diagonal.

Notepad Standard, simplified PC word processor, very useful for monotonous or repetitive syntax commands.

To Shortcut word to be used in various syntax commands; you can specify a range of variables by using the "to" command (instead of specifying each individual variable).

DISCUSSION QUESTIONS

1. Why can't I do the Notepad Find and Replace function in my syntax file?

2. When would I use the "aggregate" function?

BIBLIOGRAPHY

Goldberg, L. R. (1999). A broad-bandwidth, public-domain, personality inventory measuring the lower-level facets of several five-factor models. In I. Mervielde, I. Deary, F. De Fruyt, & F. Ostendorf (Eds.), *Personality psychology in Europe, Vol. 7* (pp. 7–28). Tilburg, The Netherlands: Tilburg University Press.

Johnson, J. A. (2005). Ascertaining the validity of individual protocols from Web-based personality inventories. *Journal of Research in Personality*, *39*, 103–129.

Stevens, S. S. (1946). On the theory of scales of measurement. *Science, 103*, 677–680.

Tabachnick, B. G., & Fidell, L. S. (2007). *Experimental Designs Using ANOVA*. Belmont, CA: Duxbury Press.

OTHER USEFUL REFERENCES

SPSS BASE SYSTEM SYNTAX REFERENCE GUIDE

This is the "bible" of using SPSS. The *Syntax Reference Guide* is updated with each issued version of SPSS. The reference contains command language and is necessary if your job or school responsibilities involve much use of SPSS.

RAYNALD'S SPSS TOOLS

Raynald Levesque is an actuary who is apparently in love with SPSS. He has designed (and frequently updates) a website devoted to SPSS. The site contains syntax "shells" for lots of different purposes—if you're stuck on a problem, this is a great site to check out (and if he doesn't already have a developed answer to your problem, he's often willing to develop an answer for you and add it to his library). www.spsstools.net

SPSS LISTSERV

The University of Georgia hosts a listserv (a mailing list that you can join whose members ask and respond to questions about SPSS). I have not joined this listserv, so I can't speak to its usefulness, but these sorts of virtual discussion groups generally tend to be *very* helpful. The current listserv address is SPSSX-L@listserv.uga.edu.

APPENDIX

COMPLETED QUESTIONNAIRE FORM EXAMPLE

34

Please indicate your gender: Male   Female

On the following pages, there are phrases describing people's behaviors. Please use the rating scale below to describe how accurately each statement describes *you*. Describe yourself as you generally are now, not as you wish to be in the future. Describe yourself as you honestly see yourself, in relation to other people you know of the same sex as you are, and roughly your same age. So that you can describe yourself in an honest manner, your responses will be kept in absolute confidence. Please read each statement carefully, and then indicate to what extent you agree or disagree with each of the statements using the following scale:

SD	D	N	A	SA
Strongly Disagree	Disagree	Neither Agree Nor Disagree	Agree	Strongly Agree

	SD	D	N	A	SA
1. Am the life of the party.	SD	D	N	A	SA
2. Insult people.	SD	D	N	A	SA
3. Am always prepared.	SD	D	N	A	SA
4. Get stressed out easily.	SD	D	N	A	SA
5. Have a rich vocabulary.	SD	D	N	A	SA
6. Often feel uncomfortable around others.	SD	D	N	A	SA
7. Am interested in people.	SD	D	N	A	SA
8. Leave my belongings around.	SD	D	N	A	SA
9. Am relaxed most of the time.	SD	D	N	A	SA
10. Have difficulty understanding abstract ideas.	SD	D	N	A	SA
11. Feel comfortable around people.	SD	D	N	A	SA
12. Am not interested in other people's problems.	SD	D	N	A	SA
13. Pay attention to details.	SD	D	N	A	SA
14. Worry about things.	SD	D	N	A	SA
15. Have a vivid imagination.	SD	D	N	A	SA
16. Keep in the background.	SD	D	N	A	SA
17. Sympathize with others' feelings.	SD	D	N	A	SA
18. Make a mess of things.	SD	D	N	A	SA
19. Seldom feel blue.	SD	D	N	A	SA
20. Am not interested in abstract ideas.	SD	D	N	A	SA
21. Start conversations.	SD	D	N	A	SA

22. Feel little concern for others.	SD	D	N	A	**(SA)**
23. Get chores done right away.	SD	D	**(N)**	A	SA
24. Am easily disturbed.	SD	**(D)**	N	A	SA
25. Have excellent ideas.	SD	D	N	**(A)**	SA
26. Have little to say.	SD	D	**(N)**	A	SA
27. Have a soft heart.	SD	D	**(N)**	A	SA
28. Often forget to put things back in their proper place.	SD	D	N	**(A)**	SA
29. Am not easily bothered by things.	SD	D	N	**(A)**	SA
30. Do not have a good imagination.	SD	D	N	**(A)**	SA
31. Talk to a lot of different people at parties.	SD	**(D)**	N	A	SA
32. Am not really interested in others.	SD	**(D)**	N	A	SA
33. Like order.	SD	D	**(N)**	A	SA
34. Get upset easily.	SD	D	N	A	**(SA)**
35. Am quick to understand things.	**(SD)**	D	N	A	SA
36. Don't like to draw attention to myself.	**(SD)**	D	N	A	SA
37. Take time out for others.	SD	D	N	**(A)**	SA
38. Shirk my duties.	SD	D	**(N)**	A	SA
39. Rarely get irritated.	SD	**(D)**	N	A	SA
40. Try to avoid complex people.	SD	**(D)**	N	A	SA
41. Don't mind being the center of attention.	SD	**(D)**	N	A	SA
42. Am hard to get to know.	SD	D	**(N)**	A	SA
43. Follow a schedule.	SD	D	N	**(A)**	SA
44. Change my mood a lot.	SD	D	**(N)**	A	SA
45. Use difficult words.	SD	D	**(N)**	A	SA
46. Am quiet around strangers.	SD	D	N	**(A)**	SA
47. Feel others' emotions.	SD	D	N	**(A)**	SA
48. Neglect my duties.	SD	D	N	**(A)**	SA
49. Seldom get mad.	SD	D	**(N)**	A	SA
50. Have difficulty imagining things.	SD	**(D)**	N	A	SA
51. Make friends easily.	**(SD)**	D	N	A	SA
52. Am indifferent to the feelings of others.	**(SD)**	D	N	A	SA

	SD	D	N	A	SA
53. Am exacting in my work.	(SD)	D	N	A	SA
54. Have frequent mood swings.	SD	D	(N)	A	SA
55. Spend time reflecting on things.	SD	D	(N)	A	SA
56. Find it difficult to approach others.	SD	(D)	N	A	SA
57. Make people feel at ease.	SD	(D)	N	A	SA
58. Waste my time.	SD	D	N	(A)	SA
59. Get irritated easily.	SD	D	N	(A)	SA
60. Avoid difficult reading material.	SD	D	(N)	A	SA
61. Take charge.	SD	D	(N)	A	SA
62. Inquire about others' well-being.	(SD)	D	N	A	SA
63. Do things according to a plan.	(SD)	D	N	A	SA
64. Often feel blue.	SD	D	(N)	A	SA
65. Am full of ideas.	SD	D	N	(A)	SA
66. Don't talk a lot.	SD	D	N	(A)	SA
67. Know how to comfort others.	SD	D	N	A	(SA)
68. Do things in a half-way manner.	SD	D	N	(A)	SA
69. Get angry easily.	SD	D	(N)	A	SA
70. Will not probe deeply into a subject.	SD	(D)	N	A	SA
71. Know how to captivate people.	SD	D	(N)	A	SA
72. Love children.	SD	(D)	N	A	SA
73. Continue until everything is perfect.	(SD)	D	N	A	SA
74. Panic easily.	(SD)	D	N	A	SA
75. Carry the conversation to a higher level.	SD	(D)	N	A	SA
76. Bottle up my feelings.	SD	(D)	N	A	SA
77. Am on good terms with nearly everyone.	SD	D	N	(A)	SA
78. Find it difficult to get down to work.	SD	D	N	(A)	SA
79. Feel threatened easily.	SD	D	N	A	(SA)
80. Catch on to things quickly.	SD	D	N	(A)	SA
81. Feel at ease with people.	SD	D	N	(A)	SA
82. Have a good word for everyone.	SD	D	(N)	A	SA
83. Make plans and stick to them.	SD	(D)	N	A	SA

84. Get overwhelmed by emotions.	(SD)	D	N	A	SA
85. Can handle a lot of information.	(SD)	D	N	A	SA
86. Am a very private person.	SD	D	(N)	A	SA
87. Show my gratitude.	SD	(D)	N	A	SA
88. Leave a mess in my room.	SD	(D)	N	A	SA
89. Take offense easily.	SD	D	(N)	A	SA
90. Am good at many things.	SD	D	(N)	A	SA
91. Wait for others to lead the way.	SD	D	N	(A)	SA
92. Think of others first.	SD	D	N	A	(SA)
93. Love order and regularity.	SD	D	(N)	A	SA
94. Get caught up in my problems.	SD	(D)	N	A	SA
95. Love to read challenging material.	SD	(D)	N	A	SA
96. Am skilled in handling social situations.	SD	D	(N)	A	SA
97. Love to help others.	SD	D	N	(A)	SA
98. Like to tidy up.	(SD)	D	N	A	SA
99. Grumble about things.	SD	D	N	A	(SA)
100. Love to think up new ways of doing things.	SD	D	N	(A)	SA

APPENDIX B

EXAMPLE CODE SHEET FOR QUESTIONNAIRE

Casenum

gender

Please indicate your gender: 1 Male 2 Female

On the following pages, there are phrases describing people's behaviors. Please use the rating scale below to describe how accurately each statement describes ***you***. Describe yourself as you generally are now, not as you wish to be in the future. Describe yourself as you honestly see yourself, in relation to other people you know of the same sex as you are, and roughly your same age. So that you can describe yourself in an honest manner, your responses will be kept in absolute confidence. Please read each statement carefully, and then indicate to what extent you agree or disagree with each of the statements using the following scale:

SD	D	N	A	SA
Strongly Disagree	Disagree	Neither Agree Nor Disagree	Agree	Strongly Agree

	1	2	3	4	5
item1 1. Am the life of the party.	SD	D	N	A	SA
2. Insult people.	SD	D	N	A	SA
3. Am always prepared.	SD	D	N	A	SA
4. Get stressed out easily.	SD	D	N	A	SA
5. Have a rich vocabulary.	SD	D	N	A	SA
6. Often feel uncomfortable around others.	SD	D	N	A	SA
7. Am interested in people.	SD	D	N	A	SA
8. Leave my belongings around.	SD	D	N	A	SA
9. Am relaxed most of the time.	SD	D	N	A	SA
10. Have difficulty understanding abstract ideas.	SD	D	N	A	SA
11. Feel comfortable around people.	SD	D	N	A	SA
12. Am not interested in other people's problems.	SD	D	N	A	SA
13. Pay attention to details.	SD	D	N	A	SA
14. Worry about things.	SD	D	N	A	SA
15. Have a vivid imagination.	SD	D	N	A	SA
16. Keep in the background.	SD	D	N	A	SA
17. Sympathize with others' feelings.	SD	D	N	A	SA
18. Make a mess of things.	SD	D	N	A	SA
19. Seldom feel blue.	SD	D	N	A	SA
20. Am not interested in abstract ideas.	SD	D	N	A	SA
item21 21. Start conversations.	SD	D	N	A	SA

item22

item52

	1	2	3	4	8
22. Feel little concern for others.	SD	D	N	A	SA
23. Get chores done right away.	SD	D	N	A	SA
24. Am easily disturbed.	SD	D	N	A	SA
25. Have excellent ideas.	SD	D	N	A	SA
26. Have little to say.	SD	D	N	A	SA
27. Have a soft heart.	SD	D	N	A	SA
28. Often forget to put things back in their proper place.	SD	D	N	A	SA
29. Am not easily bothered by things.	SD	D	N	A	SA
30. Do not have a good imagination.	SD	D	N	A	SA
31. Talk to a lot of different people at parties.	SD	D	N	A	SA
32. Am not really interested in others.	SD	D	N	A	SA
33. Like order.	SD	D	N	A	SA
34. Get upset easily.	SD	D	N	A	SA
35. Am quick to understand things.	SD	D	N	A	SA
36. Don't like to draw attention to myself.	SD	D	N	A	SA
37. Take time out for others.	SD	D	N	A	SA
38. Shirk my duties.	SD	D	N	A	SA
39. Rarely get irritated.	SD	D	N	A	SA
40. Try to avoid complex people.	SD	D	N	A	SA
41. Don't mind being the center of attention.	SD	D	N	A	SA
42. Am hard to get to know.	SD	D	N	A	SA
43. Follow a schedule.	SD	D	N	A	SA
44. Change my mood a lot.	SD	D	N	A	SA
45. Use difficult words.	SD	D	N	A	SA
46. Am quiet around strangers.	SD	D	N	A	SA
47. Feel others' emotions.	SD	D	N	A	SA
48. Neglect my duties.	SD	D	N	A	SA
49. Seldom get mad.	SD	D	N	A	SA
50. Have difficulty imagining things.	SD	D	N	A	SA
51. Make friends easily.	SD	D	N	A	SA
52. Am indifferent to the feelings of others.	SD	D	N	A	SA

item53

item83

		1	2	3	4	5
53.	Am exacting in my work.	SD	D	N	A	SA
54.	Have frequent mood swings.	SD	D	N	A	SA
55.	Spend time reflecting on things.	SD	D	N	A	SA
56.	Find it difficult to approach others.	SD	D	N	A	SA
57.	Make people feel at ease.	SD	D	N	A	SA
58.	Waste my time.	SD	D	N	A	SA
59.	Get irritated easily.	SD	D	N	A	SA
60.	Avoid difficult reading material.	SD	D	N	A	SA
61.	Take charge.	SD	D	N	A	SA
62.	Inquire about others' well-being.	SD	D	N	A	SA
63.	Do things according to a plan.	SD	D	N	A	SA
64.	Often feel blue.	SD	D	N	A	SA
65.	Am full of ideas.	SD	D	N	A	SA
66.	Don't talk a lot.	SD	D	N	A	SA
67.	Know how to comfort others.	SD	D	N	A	SA
68.	Do things in a half-way manner.	SD	D	N	A	SA
69.	Get angry easily.	SD	D	N	A	SA
70.	Will not probe deeply into a subject.	SD	D	N	A	SA
71.	Know how to captivate people.	SD	D	N	A	SA
72.	Love children.	SD	D	N	A	SA
73.	Continue until everything is perfect.	SD	D	N	A	SA
74.	Panic easily.	SD	D	N	A	SA
75.	Carry the conversation to a higher level.	SD	D	N	A	SA
76.	Bottle up my feelings.	SD	D	N	A	SA
77.	Am on good terms with nearly everyone.	SD	D	N	A	SA
78.	Find it difficult to get down to work.	SD	D	N	A	SA
79.	Feel threatened easily.	SD	D	N	A	SA
80.	Catch on to things quickly.	SD	D	N	A	SA
81.	Feel at ease with people.	SD	D	N	A	SA
82.	Have a good word for everyone.	SD	D	N	A	SA
83.	Make plans and stick to them.	SD	D	N	A	SA

item 84

	1	2	3	4	5
84. Get overwhelmed by emotions.	SD	D	N	A	SA
85. Can handle a lot of information.	SD	D	N	A	SA
86. Am a very private person.	SD	D	N	A	SA
87. Show my gratitude.	SD	D	N	A.	SA
88. Leave a mess in my room.	SD	D	N	A	SA
89. Take offense easily.	SD	D	N	A	SA
90. Am good at many things.	SD	D	N	A	SA
91. Wait for others to lead the way.	SD	D	N	A	SA
92. Think of others first.	SD	D	N	A	SA
93. Love order and regularity.	SD	D	N	A	SA
94. Get caught up in my problems.	SD	D	N	A	SA
95. Love to read challenging material.	SD	D	N	A	SA
96. Am skilled in handling social situations.	SD	D	N	A	SA
97. Love to help others.	SD	D	N	A	SA
98. Like to tidy up.	SD	D	N	A	SA
99. Grumble about things.	SD	D	N	A	SA
100. Love to think up new ways of doing things.	SD	D	N	A	SA

item 100

APPENDIX

SUMMARY OF CREATING AND DEFINING A DATA FILE

1. Determine what information should be stored as words (usually not much) and what information should be stored as numbers (the majority of your information).

2. Develop a "code sheet" identifying how your information will look in SPSS.

3. Activate SPSS and immediately open a "new syntax file" as shown in Figure C.1.

4. Specify your code-sheet variables in your new syntax file (these will create your empty [but defined] data file) as shown in Figure C.2.

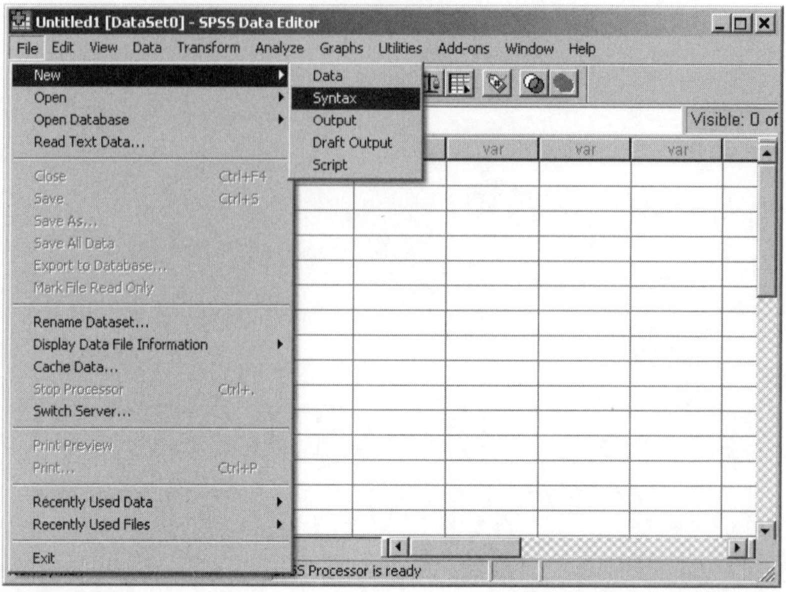

FIGURE C.1. *Open a New Syntax (Rather than a Data) File.*

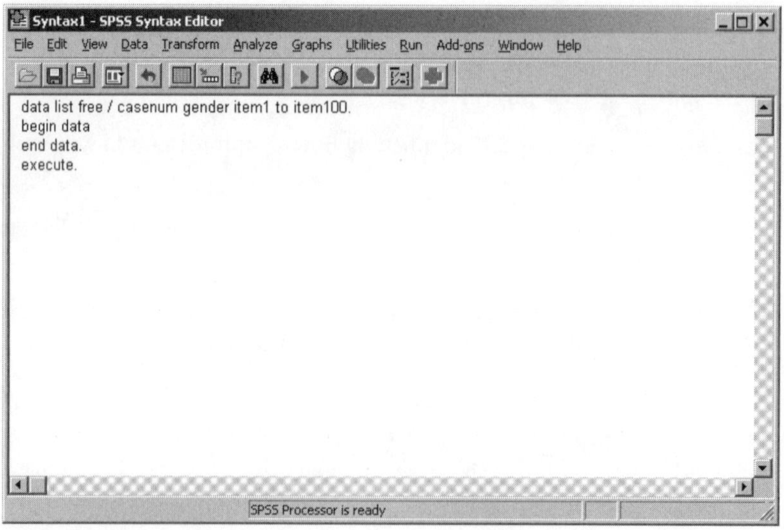

FIGURE C.2. *Specify Your Variable Names (to the Right of the "/").*

5. Save your syntax file within your organized file system as shown in Figure C.3.

6. Add your variable and value labels as shown in Figures C.4 and C.5.

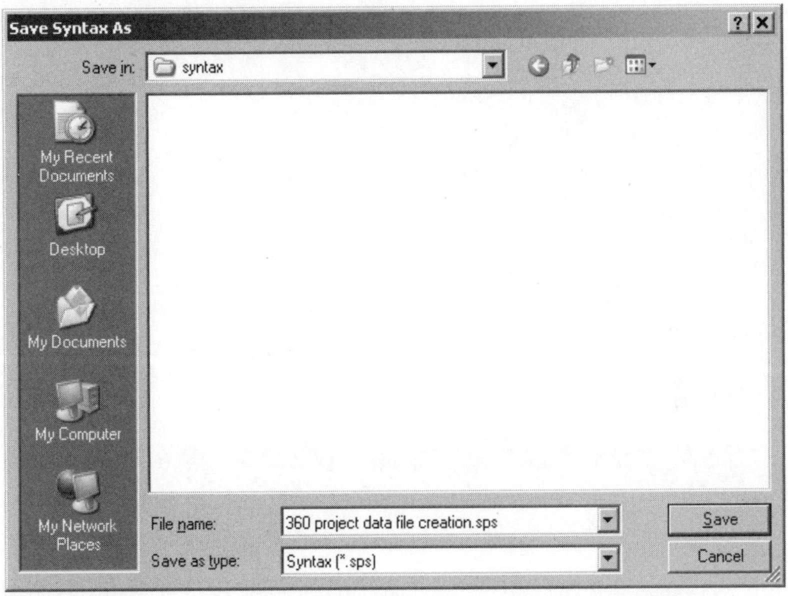

FIGURE C.3. *Save the Data File Specification Syntax.*

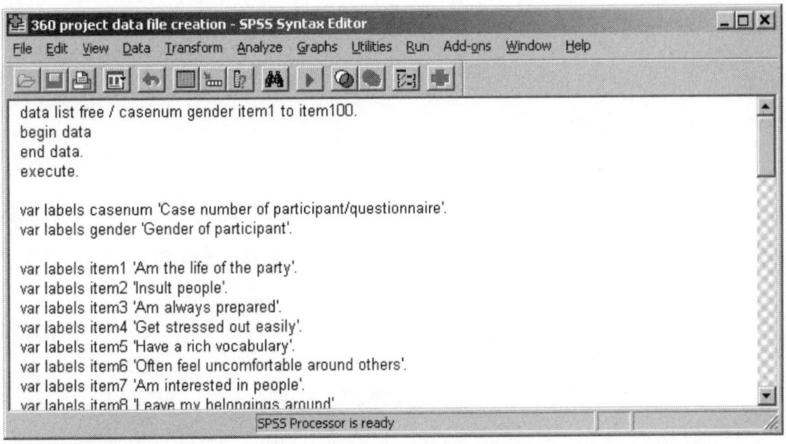

FIGURE C.4. *Add Labels (Descriptions) to Your Variable Names.*

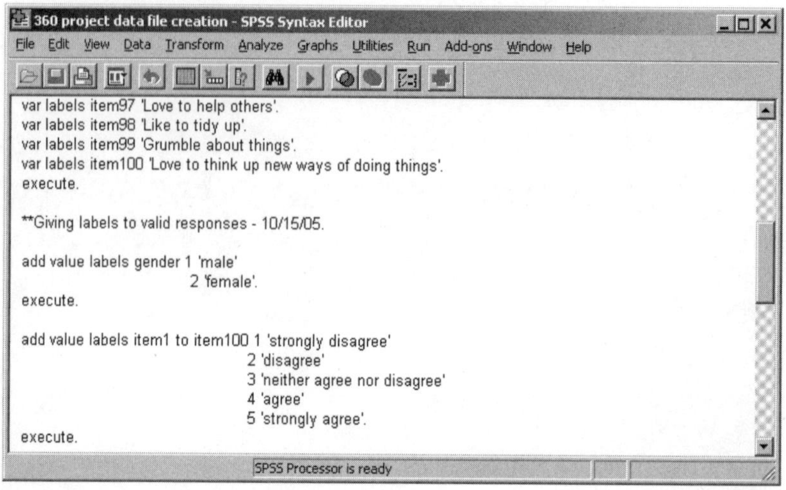

FIGURE C.5. *Add Labels to Possible Values for Appropriate Variables.*

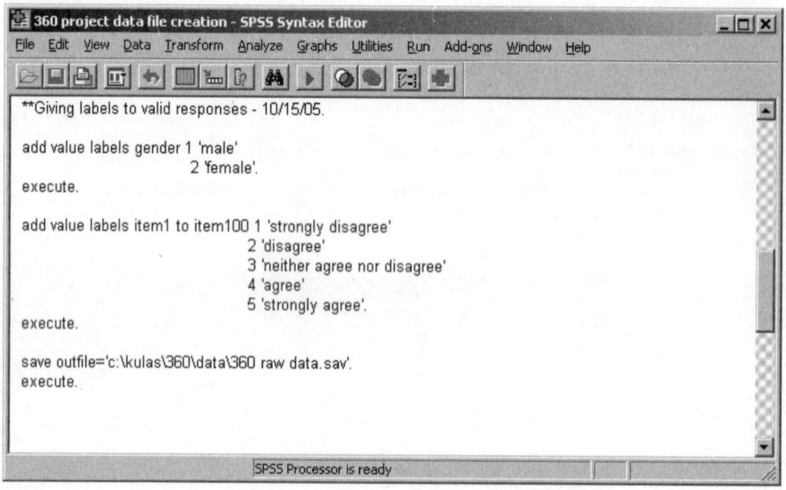

FIGURE C.6. *Save the Data Shell (Save Outfile Command).*

7. Save your empty data file within your organized file system as shown in Figure C.6.

8. Select all (Ctrl+A) as shown in Figure C.7 and run (with the Play button) your syntax to create an empty (but defined) data file.

9. Enter data into your empty but defined data shell as shown in Figure C.8.

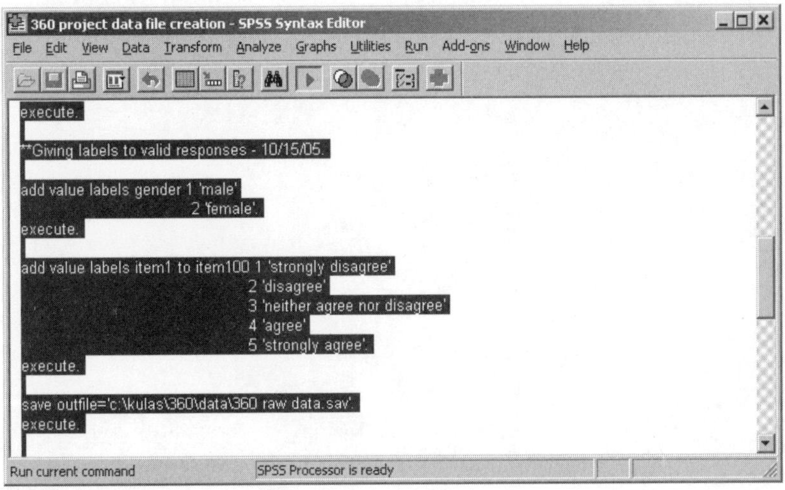

FIGURE C.7. *Select & Run (Play Button) Your Data File Specification Syntax.*

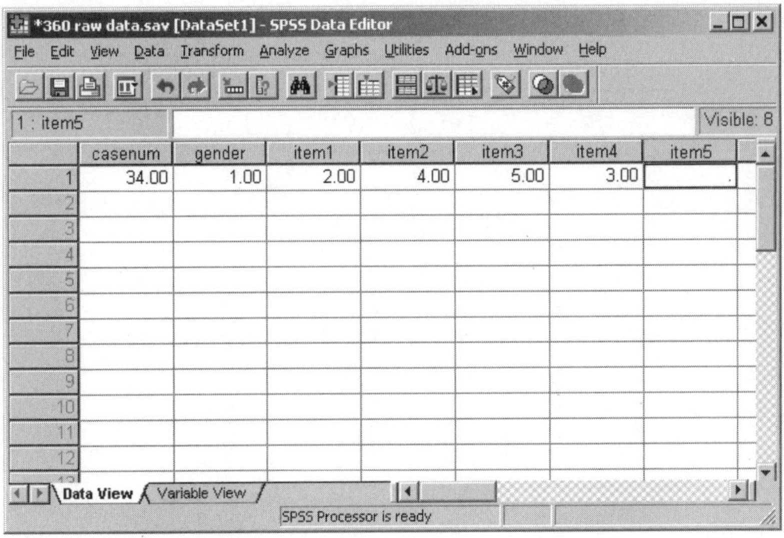

FIGURE C.8. *Manual Data Entry.*

10. Go ahead and save your data file after you've entered data into the empty cells (*this is the only time you'll save a data file without doing it within a syntax file—when you have physically entered data*).

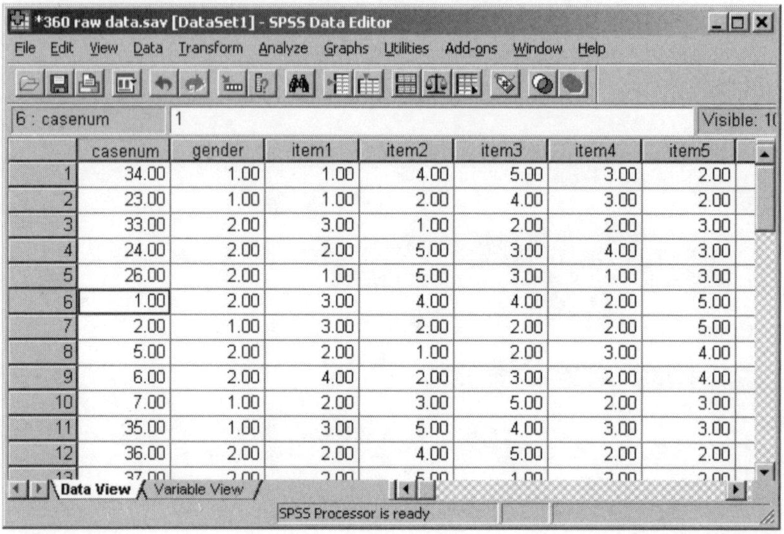

	casenum	gender	item1	item2	item3	item4	item5
1	34.00	1.00	1.00	4.00	5.00	3.00	2.00
2	23.00	1.00	1.00	2.00	4.00	3.00	2.00
3	33.00	2.00	3.00	1.00	2.00	2.00	3.00
4	24.00	2.00	2.00	5.00	3.00	4.00	3.00
5	26.00	2.00	1.00	5.00	3.00	1.00	3.00
6	1.00	2.00	3.00	4.00	4.00	2.00	5.00
7	2.00	1.00	3.00	2.00	2.00	2.00	5.00
8	5.00	2.00	2.00	1.00	2.00	3.00	4.00
9	6.00	2.00	4.00	2.00	3.00	2.00	4.00
10	7.00	1.00	2.00	3.00	5.00	2.00	3.00
11	35.00	1.00	3.00	5.00	4.00	3.00	3.00
12	36.00	2.00	2.00	4.00	5.00	2.00	2.00
13	37.00	2.00	2.00	5.00	1.00	2.00	2.00

FIGURE C.9. *Press the "Save" Button in Your Data File or Alternatively Select & Run Only Your Save Outfile Command at the End of Your Data File Specification Syntax.*

APPENDIX

EXAMPLE SYNTAX FILE INTEGRATING MULTIPLE COMMANDS (FULFILLING MULTIPLE PURPOSES)

The following example demonstrates how to combine two initially separate (and quite different) datasets. One dataset contains employee personality information; the other contains performance ratings from employees' supervisors, subordinates, and peers. In the personality dataset, each row represents one rated employee. The performance rating file contains several rows per rated employee (the different rows reflect supervisor, subordinate, or peer ratings of the rated employee). Additionally, these performance rating files typically contain different numbers of raters per rated individual. The goal of the syntax is to create a new data file in which one row contains (1) employee personality information, (2) one supervisor rating, (3) one peer rating, and (4) one subordinate rating. To start this example, I bring up the employee personality information, as shown in Figure D.1.

This brings up the original data file (personality.sav) and saves it as an ordered and sorted file (sorted personality.sav), as shown in Figure D.2.

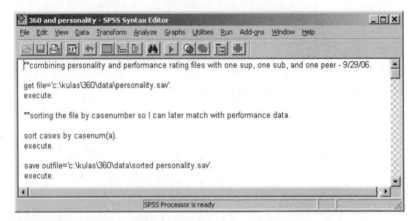

FIGURE D.1. *Retrieve, Sort, & Save the Personality Data.*

	casenum	open	cons	extra	agree	neuro	var
1	1234.00	2.54	2.65	2.11	4.84	2.54	
2	1235.00	1.55	1.54	2.11	3.55	2.65	
3	1253.00	4.52	3.55	3.12	2.10	2.11	
4	1645.00	1.64	4.55	4.52	1.22	3.42	
5	2135.00	3.42	3.42	1.22	3.42	1.54	
6	2153.00	3.55	2.11	1.44	3.42	3.84	
7	2164.00	3.12	2.00	3.55	4.22	1.22	
8	2213.00	1.22	4.54	3.42	3.22	1.33	
9	3151.00	2.52	3.55	2.65	4.52	3.42	
10	4651.00	2.65	2.54	3.12	4.54	1.44	
11	6512.00	2.11	2.65	1.55	3.12	3.55	
12	6554.00	4.03	2.01	2.65	2.54	2.55	
13	6845.00	4.65	4.52	3.55	2.11	1.55	

FIGURE D.2. *Personality Data File.*

Next I grab the performance file and do the same sort procedure, as shown in Figure D.3.

The performance rating file has three performance rating items, as well as rater and ratee (that is, casenum) information. Figure D.4 shows the result.

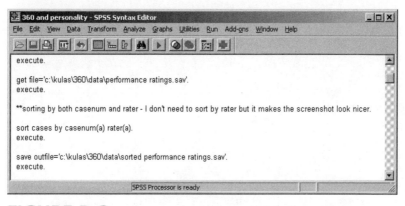

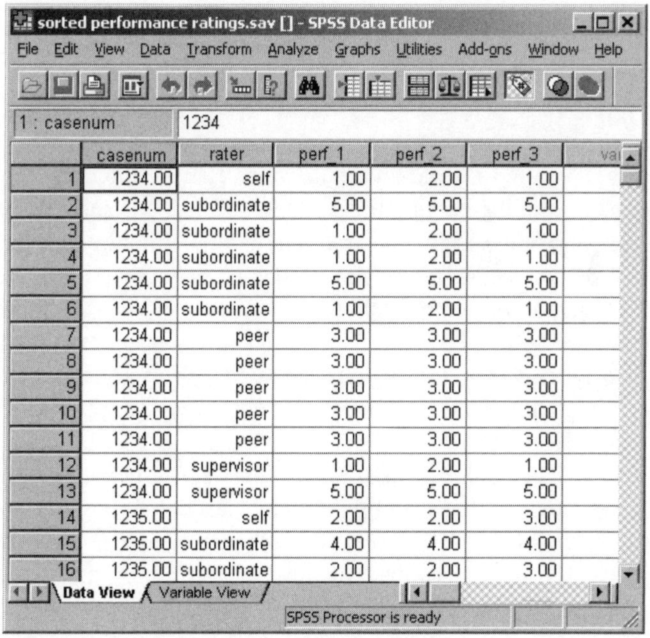

FIGURE D.3. *Retrieve, Sort, & Save the Performance Rating Data.*

	casenum	rater	perf_1	perf_2	perf_3
1	1234.00	self	1.00	2.00	1.00
2	1234.00	subordinate	5.00	5.00	5.00
3	1234.00	subordinate	1.00	2.00	1.00
4	1234.00	subordinate	1.00	2.00	1.00
5	1234.00	subordinate	5.00	5.00	5.00
6	1234.00	subordinate	1.00	2.00	1.00
7	1234.00	peer	3.00	3.00	3.00
8	1234.00	peer	3.00	3.00	3.00
9	1234.00	peer	3.00	3.00	3.00
10	1234.00	peer	3.00	3.00	3.00
11	1234.00	peer	3.00	3.00	3.00
12	1234.00	supervisor	1.00	2.00	1.00
13	1234.00	supervisor	5.00	5.00	5.00
14	1235.00	self	2.00	2.00	3.00
15	1235.00	subordinate	4.00	4.00	4.00
16	1235.00	subordinate	2.00	2.00	3.00

FIGURE D.4. *Performance Rating Data File (Value Labels Shown).*

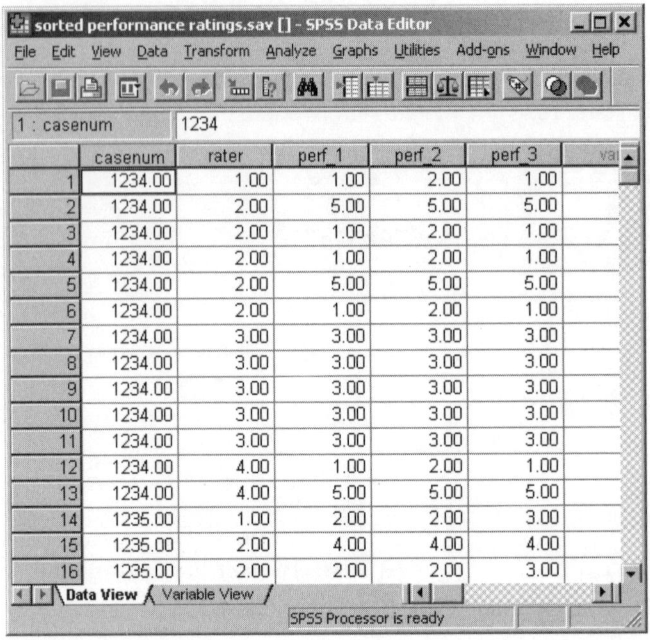

	casenum	rater	perf_1	perf_2	perf_3
1	1234.00	1.00	1.00	2.00	1.00
2	1234.00	2.00	5.00	5.00	5.00
3	1234.00	2.00	1.00	2.00	1.00
4	1234.00	2.00	1.00	2.00	1.00
5	1234.00	2.00	5.00	5.00	5.00
6	1234.00	2.00	1.00	2.00	1.00
7	1234.00	3.00	3.00	3.00	3.00
8	1234.00	3.00	3.00	3.00	3.00
9	1234.00	3.00	3.00	3.00	3.00
10	1234.00	3.00	3.00	3.00	3.00
11	1234.00	3.00	3.00	3.00	3.00
12	1234.00	4.00	1.00	2.00	1.00
13	1234.00	4.00	5.00	5.00	5.00
14	1235.00	1.00	2.00	2.00	3.00
15	1235.00	2.00	4.00	4.00	4.00
16	1235.00	2.00	2.00	2.00	3.00

FIGURE D.5. *Performance Rating Data File (Value Labels Hidden).*

Figure D.5 shows the data with the Value Labels function off.

Prior to combining the two files, I need to select one subordinate, one supervisor, and one peer for each rated individual. First I create data files with only subordinates, supervisors, and peers, as shown in Figure D.6.

Within each of these three data files (sorted subordinates, sorted peers, and sorted supervisors) I now need to "count" the number of raters per rated individual (number the raters within each rated employee; Figure D.7).

This command creates a new column within my supervisor data file, as shown in Figure D.8.

Now I can save each supervisor, subordinate, and peer file with either one or two raters per rated individual. To later combine the files, however, I'll need to rename the variables (other than casenum—I'm going to use casenum to match files, so this variable needs the same name across files), as shown in Figure D.9.

The new data file has one supervisor rating per rated individual; I dropped the "rater" variable because I identified who is doing the rating in

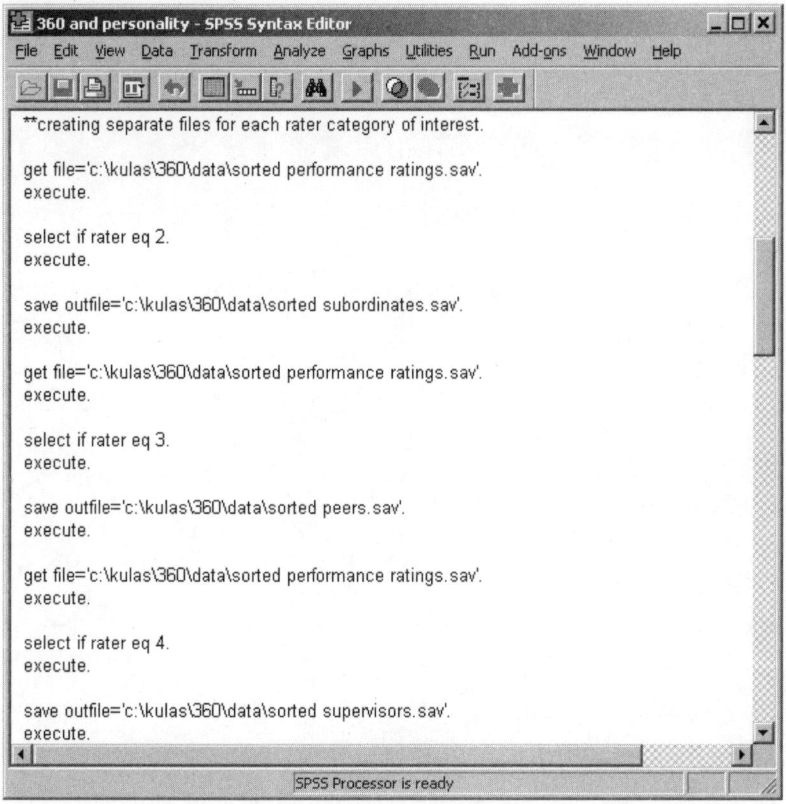

FIGURE D.6. *Creating Performance-Rating Data Files Each Containing Only Subordinates, Supervisors, or Peers.*

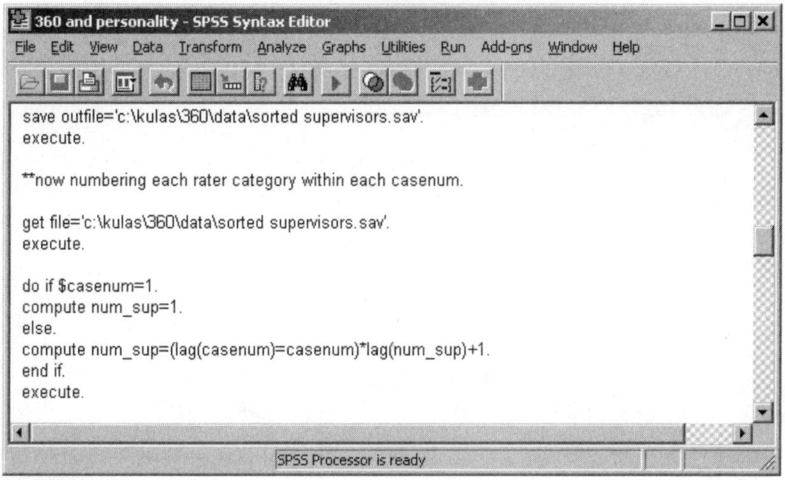

FIGURE D.7. *Asking SPSS to Number Each Supervisor Within Rated Individuals (Casenums).*

	casenum	rater	perf_1	perf_2	perf_3	num_sup
1	1234.00	4.00	1.00	2.00	1.00	1.00
2	1234.00	4.00	5.00	5.00	5.00	2.00
3	1235.00	4.00	2.00	2.00	3.00	1.00
4	1235.00	4.00	4.00	4.00	4.00	2.00
5	1253.00	4.00	4.00	4.00	5.00	1.00
6	1253.00	4.00	1.00	2.00	2.00	2.00
7	1645.00	4.00	5.00	5.00	5.00	1.00
8	2135.00	4.00	5.00	5.00	5.00	1.00
9	2135.00	4.00	1.00	2.00	3.00	2.00
10	2135.00	4.00	5.00	5.00	5.00	3.00
11	2135.00	4.00	5.00	5.00	5.00	4.00
12	2135.00	4.00	5.00	5.00	5.00	5.00
13	2153.00	4.00	4.00	4.00	4.00	1.00
14	2153.00	4.00	3.00	3.00	3.00	2.00
15	2153.00	4.00	4.00	4.00	4.00	3.00

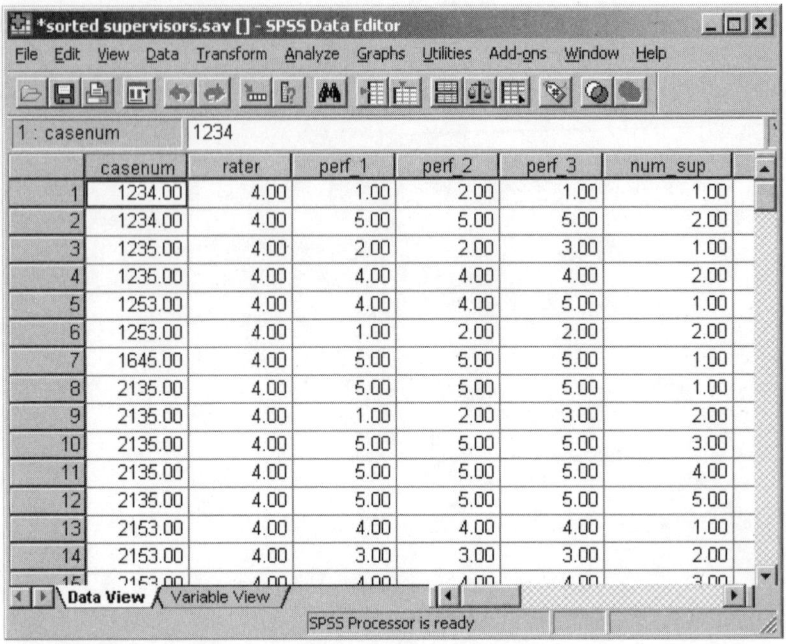

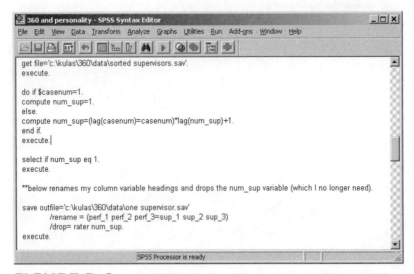

FIGURE D.8. *Supervisor Performance Ratings with Different Supervisors Identified.*

```
get file='c:\kulas\360\data\sorted supervisors.sav'.
execute.

do if $casenum=1.
compute num_sup=1.
else.
compute num_sup=(lag(casenum)=casenum)*lag(num_sup)+1.
end if.
execute.

select if num_sup eq 1.
execute.

**below renames my column variable headings and drops the num_sup variable (which I no longer need).

save outfile='c:\kulas\360\data\one supervisor.sav'
        /rename = (perf_1 perf_2 perf_3=sup_1 sup_2 sup_3)
        /drop= rater num_sup.
execute.
```

FIGURE D.9. *Selecting the First Supervisor and Renaming the Performance Rating Variables.*

the new performance rating names (sup_1, sup_2, and sup_3), as shown in Figure D.10.

The syntax to repeat this with the subordinate and peer files is shown in Figures D.11 and D.12.

	casenum	sup_1	sup_2	sup_3	var
1	1234.00	1.00	2.00	1.00	
2	1235.00	2.00	2.00	3.00	
3	1253.00	4.00	4.00	5.00	
4	1645.00	5.00	5.00	5.00	
5	2135.00	5.00	5.00	5.00	
6	2153.00	4.00	4.00	4.00	
7	2164.00	1.00	2.00	2.00	
8	2213.00	3.00	3.00	3.00	
9	3151.00	1.00	2.00	1.00	
10	4651.00	2.00	2.00	3.00	
11	6512.00	5.00	5.00	5.00	
12	6554.00	4.00	4.00	4.00	

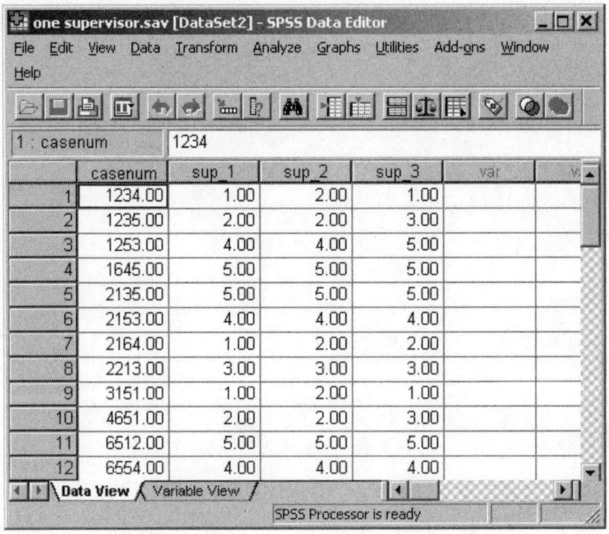

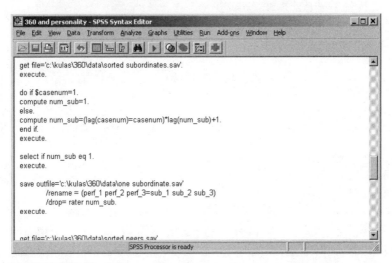

FIGURE D.10. *Supervisor Performance Rating File with Only One Supervisor Retained for Each Rated Individual.*

```
get file='c:\kulas\360\data\sorted subordinates.sav'.
execute.

do if $casenum=1.
compute num_sub=1.
else.
compute num_sub=(lag(casenum)=casenum)*lag(num_sub)+1.
end if.
execute.

select if num_sub eq 1.
execute.

save outfile='c:\kulas\360\data\one subordinate.sav'
        /rename = (perf_1 perf_2 perf_3=sub_1 sub_2 sub_3)
        /drop= rater num_sub.
execute.


get file='c:\kulas\360\data\sorted peers.sav'.
```

FIGURE D.11. *Numbering, Selecting, Renaming, and Saving One Subordinate Rating per Rated Individual.*

Now I have four files ready to be combined. First, as shown in Figure D.13, I call up my original personality file and then add each "other" rating file separately.

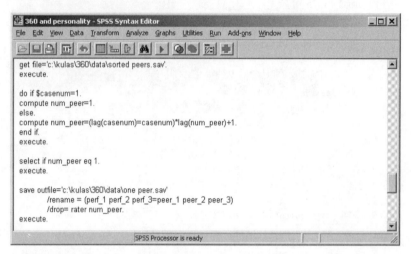

FIGURE D.12. *Numbering, Selecting, Renaming, and Saving One Rating per Rated Individual.*

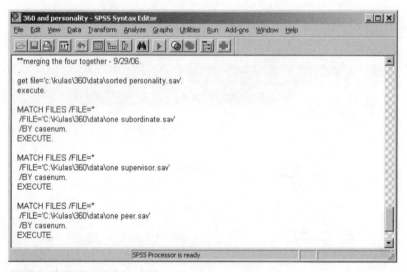

FIGURE D.13. *Retrieving the Rated Individual Data File and Adding 1 Subordinate, 1 Supervisor, and 1 peer Rating to Each Rated Individual.*

Now I save the new file and take a look. Figures D.14 and D.15 show the results.

Figure D.16 shows the view after scrolling to the right.

```
MATCH FILES /FILE=*
 /FILE='C:\Kulas\360\data\one subordinate.sav'
 /BY casenum.
EXECUTE.

MATCH FILES /FILE=*
 /FILE='C:\Kulas\360\data\one supervisor.sav'
 /BY casenum.
EXECUTE.

MATCH FILES /FILE=*
 /FILE='C:\Kulas\360\data\one peer.sav'
 /BY casenum.
EXECUTE.

save outfile='c:\kulas\360\data\personality and performance combined.sav'.
execute.

get file='c:\kulas\360\data\personality and performance combined.sav'.
execute.
```

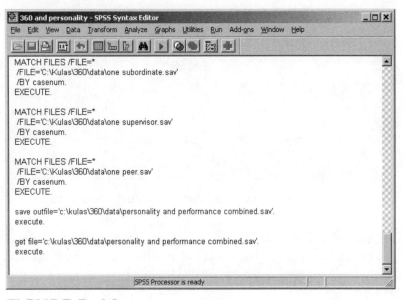

FIGURE D.14. *Saving and Retrieving the Combined Personality and Performance Rating Data File.*

	casenum	open	cons	extra	agree	neuro	sub_1	sub_2
1	1234.00	2.54	2.65	2.11	4.84	2.54	5.00	5.00
2	1235.00	1.55	1.54	2.11	3.55	2.65	4.00	4.00
3	1253.00	4.52	3.55	3.12	2.10	2.11	1.00	2.00
4	1645.00	1.64	4.55	4.52	1.22	3.42	3.00	3.00
5	2135.00	3.42	3.42	1.22	3.42	1.54	1.00	2.00
6	2153.00	3.55	2.11	1.44	3.42	3.84	2.00	2.00
7	2164.00	3.12	2.00	3.55	4.22	1.22	5.00	5.00
8	2213.00	1.22	4.54	3.42	3.22	1.33	4.00	4.00
9	3151.00	2.52	3.55	2.65	4.52	3.42	1.00	2.00
10	4651.00	2.65	2.54	3.12	4.54	1.44	3.00	3.00
11	6512.00	2.11	2.65	1.55	3.12	3.55	1.00	2.00
12	6554.00	4.03	2.01	2.65	2.54	2.55	1.00	2.00

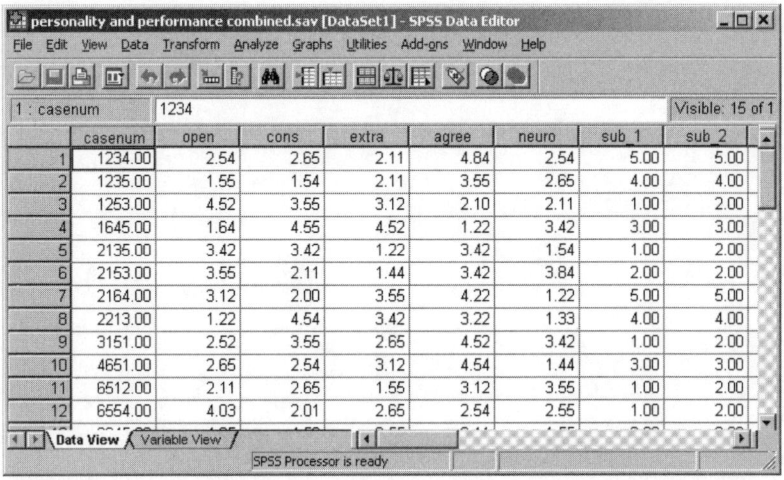

FIGURE D.15. *Combined Data File (First Few Variables Shown).*

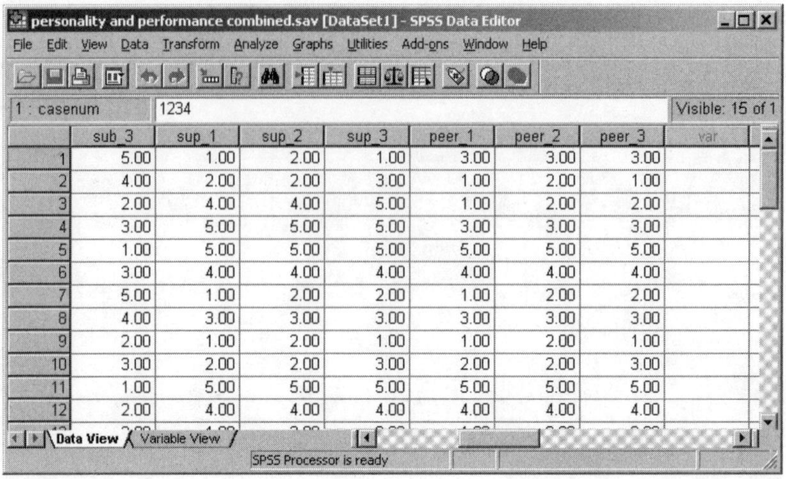

	sub_3	sup_1	sup_2	sup_3	peer_1	peer_2	peer_3	var
1	5.00	1.00	2.00	1.00	3.00	3.00	3.00	
2	4.00	2.00	2.00	3.00	1.00	2.00	1.00	
3	2.00	4.00	4.00	5.00	1.00	2.00	2.00	
4	3.00	5.00	5.00	5.00	3.00	3.00	3.00	
5	1.00	5.00	5.00	5.00	5.00	5.00	5.00	
6	3.00	4.00	4.00	4.00	4.00	4.00	4.00	
7	5.00	1.00	2.00	2.00	1.00	2.00	2.00	
8	4.00	3.00	3.00	3.00	3.00	3.00	3.00	
9	2.00	1.00	2.00	1.00	1.00	2.00	1.00	
10	3.00	2.00	2.00	3.00	2.00	2.00	3.00	
11	1.00	5.00	5.00	5.00	5.00	5.00	5.00	
12	2.00	4.00	4.00	4.00	4.00	4.00	4.00	

FIGURE D.16. *Combined Data File (More Variables Shown).*

There are alternatives to this method, but if you can get in the habit of compulsively using "get file" and "save outfile" commands, you can pretty much apply this general procedure to any major manipulation you wish to accomplish.

APPENDIX

COMMANDS TO KNOW, ORGANIZED BY IMPORTANCE

The following essential SPSS syntax terms (ones you should know how to use) are organized by their importance.

COMMAND	IMPORTANCE	PAGES (OR EXPLANATION)
get file	Very, Very Important	36–40
save outfile		36–40
compute		57–59
eq, gt, lt, ge, le		58; 86; 199–201
recode		55–57
descriptives		96–98
frequencies		98–101
var labels		47–48
add value labels		48–51
match files		75–77

add files		77–80
sort cases		74–75
split file		85–90
do if, else if, end if		199–201
formats		Changes the format of variables (for example, f8.2→f1.0)
write outfile		Changes your data to ASCII format (no grids/cells)
casenum		Numbers cases in your data file (number of nonempty rows); use this with compute
select if		83–85
aggregate		194–198
flip	Very Important	193–194

ANSWERS TO CHAPTER DISCUSSION QUESTIONS

CHAPTER 1

Questions

1. Why is SPSS superior to Excel?

2. What are some advantages and disadvantages associated with SPSS's evolution toward an Excel-Word hybrid?

Answers

1. You can keep a record of what you've done and what you're going to do. Formulas don't "run automatically"—they run only when you tell them to run.

2. The data file interface is nice for data entry and organization, but there is too much capability in the data file. Ideally you should not be able to run analyses straight from your data file.

CHAPTER 2

Questions

1. I have a friend who doesn't use syntax, and she's never made a mistake. Why couldn't I expect to do the same?

2. How common is the mistake that Kulas made?

Answers

1. It's only a matter of time before everyone who uses SPSS makes a mistake that they're unable to "undo" if they do not use syntax. There are plenty of people who haven't made mistakes yet, but they're living a charmed SPSS life.

2. I talk about SPSS with people at cocktail parties—everyone has made similar mistakes.

CHAPTER 3

Questions

1. What numbers can be used to code the following values?
   a. Gender
   b. Military rank
   c. Height
2. Why would anyone include covariates in a data file?

Answers

1. Gender doesn't matter (nominal value), military rank needs to follow a sequence (ordinal value), and height needs *real* numbers (ratio value).
   a. Many possibilities
      - Male (1) Female (2)
      - Male (100) Female (−1)
      - Male (.24) Female (.6)
   b. Fewer possibilities
      - Private (1) Corporal (2) Sergeant (3)
      - Private (−1) Corporal (0) Sergeant (1)
      - Private (10) Corporal (8) Sergeant (6)
   c. Very few possibilities (you have no options other than the metric [inches, mm, cm] with ratio-level variables)
      - 1 inch = 1, 1 and 1/2 inches = 1.5

2. You include covariates when you do not have an experimental design (these situations are either classified as quasi-experimental or nonexperimental). They allow for control to be exerted analytically instead of methodologically (as is the case with experimental designs).

CHAPTER 4

Questions

1. What is the importance of the case number?

2. Why are the "get file" and "save outfile" commands so important?

Answers

1. If you find a mistake in your electronic data file (for example, an out-of-range value), it's helpful to know what person or data is associated with that mistake. Instead of looking through many hardcopies for a possible match, you can go directly to the associated hardcopy.

2. Especially with newer versions of SPSS, in which multiple data files can be open at the same time, it's *critical* that the user specifies which data file he or she is dealing with. You can *avoid* having more than one data file open at a time by religiously using the "get file" and "save outfile" commands.

CHAPTER 5

Questions

1. If my variable names are self-explanatory, do I still need to give them labels?

2. Does the coding scheme make a difference if I add value labels?

Answers

1. Yes, output will report labels, so even if your label is the same as your variable name (that is, gender), go ahead and get in the habit of giving every variable a label.

2. The coding scheme could potentially make a difference depending on the measurement of your variables (see the Chapter Three discussion questions). If you have a nominal variable, the coding scheme does not matter. If you have an ordinal variable, the coding scheme should match the variable sequence.

CHAPTER 6

Questions

1. Is it ever advisable to not run the entire syntax at once?

2. If I'm going to use drop-down menus, why don't I just skip the "paste" part?

Answers

1. If you are testing out a command (for example, to see if it works), you can highlight and run a small part of your syntax file. Even in this situation, however, after you have determined that your syntax works, you need to close any open output file and run the entire syntax file at once prior to interpreting your results.

2. One of the primary reasons you are using syntax is to keep a record of everything that you have done to your data. You paste so you have such a record.

CHAPTER 7

Question

1. Why do I need to save a new data file instead of just merging or adding separate files each time I work on a project?

Answer

1. You never want to save over your original data file, remember? Always keep the original pristine; if you want to work with something different from the original, create a new data file.

CHAPTER 8

Questions

1. "Select if" and "split file" do essentially the same thing; why do I need to learn both?

2. What happens if I forget to turn the "split file" command off?

Answers

1. "Select if" creates a smaller data file; "split file" keeps all of your data but organizes analyses, manipulations, and output. They have similar effects, but they actually do different things.

2. All of your manipulations, analyses, and output will be done separately for your split. This can really screw up manipulation and transformation requests that you write.

CHAPTER 9

Questions

1. What are some applications of the descriptives information?

2. What are some applications of the frequencies information?

Answers

1. Some possible uses
   - Computing z-scores
   - Reporting means and standard deviations
2. Some possible uses
   - Determining tertile, median, quartile, and so on split locations
   - Scanning for out-of-range values—these are usually data entry errors

CHAPTER 10

Questions and Problems

1. What would happen to my obtained t if I ran a paired-samples t-test situation as an independent-samples t-test?

2. How practical is the one-sample t-test?

3. Your parents claim college students sleep too much. They claim the average amount of sleep "normal" people get is eight hours. You survey seven of your classmates, who sleep nine, eleven, seven, eight, thirteen, twelve, and ten hours per night. Do college students sleep more than what your parents claim is "average"?

4. You believe men at your college have bigger feet than the men at the neighboring rival college. You spend one half hour at each campus, guessing the shoe size of the men who walk by. Your school: 10, 9, 10, 7, 5, 6, 8, 9, 10, 10. Neighbor U: 4, 6, 2, 7, 8, 3, 10, 6, 8, 4, 8. Do the guys at your school have bigger feet (on average)?

5. You want to know the effect of caffeine on reaction time. You recruit your friends on two different occasions. Once you have them drink five cups of coffee before you throw foam-tipped darts at them; on the second occasion you have them drink five cups of water before trying to hit them with darts. You record the following number of hits (out of twenty throws):

	CAFFEINE	WATER
Bob	5	10
Sally	15	16
Persephone	12	15
June	4	6
Eunice	8	12

Does caffeine affect reaction time?

Answers

1. I would obtain a "lower" t-value (closer to zero) with the independent-samples t-test—try it.

2. Not very—it's not usual to be given a value to compare a sample against.

3. One-sample t-test situation: $t = 2.45$, $p < .05$ (one-tailed). Yes, college students sleep more than average.

4. Two independent-samples situation: $t = 2.50$, $p < .05$. Yes, your school's men have bigger feet.

5. Two paired-samples situation: $t = 4.24$, $p < .05$ (two-tailed). Caffeine does help reaction time.

CHAPTER 11

Questions

1. Why does SPSS use different terms than the terms that social science students learn?

2. Why is the repeated measures output so over-the-top?

3. Thirty chronic headache sufferers were assigned to one of three conditions: watch cartoons, go for a walk, or eat ice cubes. The researcher hopes that one of these treatments may help their suffering. Over the course of one month, the thirty people record the following number of reported headaches:

CARTOON WATCHERS	WALKERS	ICE-EATERS
5	20	5
2	16	6
13	25	20
8	8	25
20	6	6
25	9	30
15	11	11
11	15	5
6	5	15
8	6	8

Are any of these treatments more or less effective than the others?

4. Maybe the effectiveness of these treatments depends on the gender of the headache sufferer. Organizing the data a little bit differently we want to know if there is a difference in number of headaches across treatments for men and women. Is there?

	CARTOON WATCHERS	WALKERS	ICE-EATERS
Men	5	20	5
	2	16	6
	13	25	20
	8	8	25
	20	6	6
Women	25	9	30
	15	11	11
	11	15	5
	6	5	15
	8	6	8

5. Run the appropriate t-test as well as the appropriate ANOVA for the caffeine example from Chapter 10. What's the relationship between your obtained F and t?

Answers

1. Social science fields use statistics, but statistics does not serve only the social sciences. Some of the terms used by statisticians make more sense to physicists and astronomers than they do to psychologists, geographers, or economists.

2. Because it is such a flexible analysis—you can run this procedure or command for many reasons other than doing a repeated-measures ANOVA.

3. No, there is no difference among treatments: $F = .14$, $p > .05$.

4. It still doesn't matter; the interaction effect is nonsignificant ($F = .95$, $p > .05$).

5. Two (paired samples) t (t = 4.24, p < .05) and repeated measures ANOVA (F = 18, p < .05). Your t is the square-root of your F (alternatively, your F is your t squared). This is true for any t situation (between or within subjects) for which you specify an ANOVA rather than the simpler t.

CHAPTER 12

Questions

1. Why is there an ANOVA table in my regression output?

2. Why doesn't SPSS include R^2 change as a default reported statistic?

3. Based on the following data, is there a relationship between shoe size and height? Friendliness and height? Shoe size and friendliness?

	SHOE SIZE	HEIGHT	FRIENDLINESS
Hector	12	68	2
Sue	7	66	10
Sally	17	75	9
Eugene	14	70	8
Valencia	8	64	7
Penelope	9.5	60	3
Fernando	5	63	2
Norbert	15	74	10

4. If I wanted to predict how tall someone might be, given their shoe size and friendliness rating, how would I go about doing that?

Answers

1. This is the statistic (F) used to report the significance of your overall regression equation (Multiple R/R^2), so you need it.

2. Probably because a straight regression (in which you have only one step) is so common. Putting an R^2 change column in the default output table would be confusing in this situation. It is informative only in a hierarchical or stepwise regression (these are less common regression procedures than the straight regression).

3. Correlation is appropriate here. Shoe size and height are related ($r = .85$, $p < .05$), but shoe size and friendliness ($r = .44$, $p > .05$) and height and friendliness ($r = .64$, $p > .05$) are unrelated. Note that we have pretty high correlations (.44 and .64) that are nonsignificant—this means that there is a relationship in our sample, but it's not strong enough (and our sample's too small) for us to say that these sample relationships reflect meaningful associations in the larger population.

4. Regression: height $= 54.66 + .89*$height $+ .49*$friendliness. This could also be written generally as: $Y' = 54.66 + .89(X1) + .49(X2)$.

CHAPTER 13

Questions

1. Why do I have to start with the first haiku?

2. How can I make the most use out of the column tracker information?

Answers

1. Later errors may actually be consequences of the first error. Once you correct the first one, the others may be resolved.

2. If you're going to rely heavily on the column tracker, don't use tabs in your syntax file. If you do use tabs, remember that the column tracker reflects characters, not actual columns.

CHAPTER 14

Questions

1. Why can't I do the Notepad Find and Replace function in my syntax file?

2. When would I use the "aggregate" function?

Answers

1. You *can* do this within a syntax file; it's just important that you don't do it within the same syntax file that you're going to use the

information in. If you do this within the syntax file that you want to eventually use, the Find and Replace is too broad; it will find and replace stuff that you don't want to replace.

2. In addition to deleting duplicate cases, anytime you want to collapse across rows to create a new data file, you need to use this command; it's actually very flexible and you'll use it for reasons that I haven't yet thought of.

GLOSSARY

* Indicator that information after the asterisk is an internal comment "for your eyes only"; SPSS won't read this information.

> Character that SPSS places before all lines in an output file, indicating that an error has occurred.

"Add files" SPSS command for combining files containing the same variables but different individuals.

"Add value labels" SPSS command that describes your coding scheme for possible values on categorical variables (for example, does "1" represent male and "2" represent female or vice versa?).

Adjusted R^2 Estimate of the population R^2, based on sample size and number of predictors.

Aggregate SPSS command to collapse across rows; if you use aggregate, you must specify a new outfile name.

Alpha criterion Percentage of the time you're willing to incorrectly state that an effect exists when in fact it does not. This is set by the researcher, but the common social sciences convention is to set alpha at 5 percent.

ANOVA General term used to classify a series of mean-difference testing procedures.

"Begin data" SPSS subcommand used with the "data list free" command.

CASE_LBL SPSS creates this variable when you transpose your matrix; old variable names are kept in this SPSS-generated string variable.

Case number Confidential person or case identifier.

Code sheet Hardcopy that specifies SPSS variable names and value codes.

Column information Potentially helpful, potentially misleading problem-solving information (provided in some, but not all haikus).

Column tracker Number located in the lower right-hand corner of every syntax file, which identifies the location of the cursor (number of characters from the left).

Command Wording that tells SPSS what to do.

"Compute" SPSS command used to create a new variable.

Continuous IVs Predictor variables that are measured along a continuum (instead of by categories).

Continuous Variables Variables that can assume a large number of possible values.

Corrected Model Combined impact of all estimated main and interaction effects.

Corrected total SPSS label for the total sums of squares and df estimates in a factorial ANOVA summary table.

Correlation Index of association between two variables.

Correlation matrix Square and symmetric matrix containing correlations from at least two variables.

"Corr vars" SPSS command to request a bivariate (Pearson's) correlation.

Covariate Variable not of primary interest, but thought to be related to a DV.

Critical value Tabled value of a test statistic (for example, t, F, r) associated with a particular α and df; the threshold that the obtained statistic has to breech to be considered significant.

Ctrl+A Keystroke combination to "select all."

Data Anything informative.

Data list free SPSS command used to create a new data file.

Data (.sav) files Where data is stored in SPSS.

Data "shell" Empty data file, in which variables have been defined but numbers have not been entered.

Data View Traditional view in data (.sav) files—data is stored here.

Date SPSS specification of a calendar date.

Degrees of freedom (df) A mutual consideration of the number of statistical parameters estimated and the number of numbers used to estimate the parameters.

Dependent Variable (DV) Outcome or criterion variable.

"Descriptives" SPSS command requesting summary sample characteristics (such as mean, standard deviation).

Descriptive statistics Information summarizing a set of numbers.

Discrete Variables Variables that have only a limited number of possible values.

"Do if" Command that tells SPSS there are conditions to be met prior to any transformation or analysis; must be accompanied by an "end if".

"Drop" Subcommand used with "save outfile," specifying which variables are to be excluded in the newly saved data file.

"Else if" Optional command to use in a "do if", "end if" sequence.

"End data" SPSS subcommand to be used with the "data list free" file creation command, along with "begin data."

"End if" Command that notifies SPSS that your conditional statement has been completed; each "do if" must be followed (eventually) by an "end if".

Eq SPSS shorthand for "equals."

Excel Computer spreadsheet application.

"Execute" SPSS command that tells the SPSS processor to start working.

F Ratio of treatment to error variance.

F8.2 The default format of SPSS variables.

Factor Term sometimes used for IVs, especially in ANOVA contexts.

Factorial ANOVA ANOVA model to be used when there are two or more IVs of interest.

File space System of folder organization within your computer.

Find function Useful with haiku information in problem-solving applications.

First Subcommand to the aggregate function. Many more subcommands can be specified; "first" is useful for deleting duplicate cases.

Fixed IVs Researcher-determined levels.

"Flip" SPSS command to perform a matrix transposition.

Follow-up contrasts Targeted analyses to determine where differences may exist, given the occurrence of a significant omnibus F (for example, what levels differ from each other).

Ge SPSS shorthand for "greater than or equal to."

General linear model Encompassing theory from which most common analyses are derived.

"Get file" SPSS command used to retrieve a specified data file.

"GLM" SPSS command for the general linear model; many different analyses can be specified through the GLM command.

Groups SPSS label for "levels" of an IV within the t-test analysis.

Gt SPSS shorthand for "greater than."

Hardcopy Paper version.

Hierarchical regression Variance partitioning procedure in which the researcher specifies IV priority.

Huynh-Feldt Recommended alternative to the "sphericity assumed" F if you have a violation of sphericity.

Independent-samples t-test The two-sample t-test to be used with between-subjects situations.

Independent Variable (IV) Predictor or manipulated variable.

Inferential statistics Procedures estimating the probability that a given sample effect would occur if there were no effect present in the population.

Inferential statistics Probability-based information relating sample to population characteristics.

"In" variables Variables created by SPSS to identify which original file is associated with each combined file case/row.

IV levels Specific values of an IV/factor (for example, male and female are two levels of the gender IV).

IV priority Relative importance of IVs, which can be specified through the use of variance partitioning regression models (such as stepwise or hierarchical).

"Keep" Subcommand used with "save outfile," specifying which variables are to be kept in the newly saved data file.

Known mean A value that is given instead of being computed.

Le SPSS shorthand for "less than or equal to."

Levene's test Estimate of the t-test assumption of equal group variances.

Light-switch command Command that must be turned off after it's activated.

Lt SPSS shorthand for "less than."

Match files SPSS command for combining files containing the same individuals but different variables.

"Matching" variables Organizing/identifying variables that exist in more than one data file.

Matrix A grid formation of two or more rows and columns.

Matrix transposition Turning columns into rows and rows into columns; flipping a matrix along its diagonal.

Mean Statistical average.

Multicollinearity Excessive association among IVs.

Multiple R Correlation between your obtained and predicted DV scores.

Multiple regression Regression analysis with one DV and two or more IVs.

Notepad Standard, simplified PC word processor, very useful for monotonous or repetitive syntax commands.

Numeric SPSS specification of a number.

Obtained value The computed value of a test statistic (such as t, F, r). To be compared against a tabled or critical value.

Omnibus ANOVA General, broad analysis assessing the ratio of column to row variance.

One-sample t-test Difference between a sample mean and a given mean.

One-tailed hypothesis Prediction that specifies the direction of an effect.

"One-way" SPSS command for a one-way ANOVA.

One-way ANOVA ANOVA model to be used in a between-subjects situation.

Output (.spo) files Where results are reported in SPSS.

Paired-samples t-test Two two-sample t-tests to be used with within-subjects situations.

Paste Option that allows you to activate the operation from syntax when using drop-down menus.

Play button SPSS button, located in syntax files, that activates selected syntax.

Population The larger group of interest from which the sample was drawn.

Quantitative IV Independent variable that differs in magnitude as well as category.

r Pearson's product moment correlation.

R^2 Percent of DV variance associated with all estimated IV effects.

R^2 change Percentage of incremental DV variance explained by the contribution of additional IVs.

Raw data file Electronic storage of variable and person information (a data shell with information in it).

Random IVs Randomly determined levels.

"Readnames=on" Subcommand to be used when retrieving Excel data if the Excel file contains variable names.

"Recode" SPSS command used to change the entered values of variables.

Regression equation Application of the regression analysis (an attempt to predict an unknown DV score based on known IV information).

Repeated measures ANOVA ANOVA model to be used in a within-subjects situation.

"Save outfile" SPSS command used to save the currently open data file.

Scale scores New variables that are defined by two or more existing variables.

"Select if" SPSS command used to identify and retain only certain rows (people) within your data file.

Shrinkage Acknowledgment that the obtained multiple R tends to overestimate the population multiple R: a regression equation generated in one sample will exhibit a smaller predicted or observed correlation (multiple R) if applied to a different sample.

Sig. (2-tailed) Significance estimate based on a two-tailed hypothesis; this will always be more conservative than a significance estimate based on a one-tailed hypothesis.

Significance estimate Alternative to comparing obtained and tabled or critical test statistics—SPSS reports specific probabilities associated with each estimated obtained test statistic.

Simple regression Regression analysis with one IV and one DV.

"Sort cases by" SPSS command for reorganizing data sequentially.

Sphericity Lack of association among tested variables.

Sphericity assumed F ratio obtained on calculating a repeated-measures ANOVA by hand (type III SS).

"Split file" SPSS command to perform analyses and manipulations separately (within groups).

"Split file off" The "other half" of the "split file" command, it tells SPSS to "stop organizing what you do by group and consider all my data at once."

SPSS Computer program used to do data manipulations and analyses.

SPSS code Language used by SPSS.

Stages Different blocks of IV specifications. The hierarchical and stepwise procedures are comprised of at least two stages.

Standard deviation Average distance from mean within a set of numbers.

Standard error Standard deviation of a sampling distribution, commonly the denominator in inferential analyses.

Stepwise regression Variance partitioning procedure in which the computer specifies IV priority.

Straight regression Regression that does not assign IV priority.

String SPSS specification of a word.

Subjects effect Estimate of the amount of variance in a matrix of numbers that is attributable to differences across people.

Syntax (.sps) files Where operations are specified in SPSS.

To Shortcut word to be used in various syntax commands; you can specify a range of variables by using the "to" command (instead of specifying each individual variable).

T-test Analysis used to determine whether or not sample mean differences indicate population differences.

Two-sample t-test Difference between two estimated sample means.

Two-tailed hypothesis Prediction that does not specify the direction of an effect.

"UNIANOVA" SPSS command for the factorial ANOVA (alternatively, "GLM" could also be specified).

Valence "Sign" (+/–) of a statistic value

Value Labels button SPSS function allowing you to view category labels within the data file itself.

Variable Anything that can possess different values or quantities.

Variable names Names, of eight characters or fewer, used in the SPSS data file.

Variables tool Allows you to peek into your data file without directly accessing it.

Variable View Capability, in newer versions of SPSS, that allows you to define variables from within the data (.sav) file.

"Var labels" SPSS command used to give your variables more descriptive definitions (more descriptive than the eight-character variable name).

Wilks' Lambda Multivariate statistic ranging from possible values of 0 to 1.

Within-subjects IV Independent variable, all levels of which are administered to all participating individuals.

X variable Regression term for IV or predictor.

.xx Specification to be made when computing a new variable; this defines how many original values must be present to create a new summary variable.

Y variable Regression term for DV or outcome variable.

INDEX

* (asterisk) character, 34, 42, 46
\> (arrow) character, 174, 184
. (period) character, 30, 40, 46
/ (slash) character, 40

A

"Add files" command, 78–79, 80
"Add value labels" command, 49–51, 84, 100
Adjusted R^2, 154, 166
"Aggregate" command, 194, 196–198, 201
Alpha criterion, 112, 122
Analysis commands, 102–103
Analysis of variance. *See* ANOVA
Annotation, 46–47
ANOVA (analysis of variance), 125–145;
  definition of, 143; factorial, 137–142;
  follow-up contrasts and, 142; general
  overview of, 126; one-way, 126–129;
  repeated-measures, 129–137
Arrow (>) character, 174, 184
Asterisk (*) character, 34, 42, 46

B

"Begin data" subcommand, 30
Between-Subjects dialog box, 131
Between-subjects variables, 137
Bibliography, 203

C

CASE_LBL variable, 193, 201
Case numbers, 27–28
Categorical IVs, 148
Categorization, 101, 104
Code sheets, 27
Column information, 180–182, 184
Column tracker, 180, 184
Columns: errors located by, 180–182; infor-
  mation in rows vs., 54–55; transposing
  rows and, 193–194, 195
Combining data files, 72–80, 225–234;
  with different people, same information,
  77–80; with same people, different
  information, 72–77

Commands, 28; analysis, 102–103; errors
  in, 175; generated by SPSS, 59–61, 102;
  integrating multiple, 225–234; list of
  essential, 235–236; manipulation, 102;
  one-at-a-time use of, 63–67; transforma-
  tion, 199. *See also specific commands*
Comments, 34, 42
"Compute" command, 55
Confidence interval, 111–112
Continuous IVs, 148, 166
Continuous variables, 19, 23
"Corr vars" command, 149, 166
Corrected Model, 141–142, 143
Corrected total, 141, 143
Correlated samples t-test, 117–122
Correlation, 149–152, 166
Correlation matrix, 149, 166
Covariates, 19, 23
Covariates dialog box, 131
Critical value, 111, 122
Ctrl+A key combination, 31, 42, 63
Cumulative percent column, 100–101, 104

D

Data, 10, 18–19; hardcopies of, 26; importing,
  40–42; isolating, 82–90; matrix of, 19–20;
  recoding, 55–57, 59–63; types of, 21–22
Data (.sav) files, 6–7, 10; combining, 72–80,
  225–234; creating new, 82–85, 219–224;
  guidelines for working with, 34–40;
  information contained in, 20–21;
  introduced into SPSS, 12; nonsyntax way
  of creating, 28–29; numeric vs. string
  variables in, 33–34; saving, 224; splitting,
  85–90; syntax way of creating, 30–32
Data dump, 196
Data Editor, 7, 13, 201; rows and columns,
  20; Value Labels button, 50–51; view
  options, 28, 29
"Data list free" command, 30
Data "shell," 28, 30
Data View, 28, 29